The 6 Disciplines of

CUSTOMER EXPERIENCE

The 6 Disciplines of CUSTOMER EXPERIENCE

Outside In: The Power of Putting Customers at the Center of Your Business

Harley Manning
Kerry Bodine

JAICO PUBLISHING HOUSE
Ahmedabad Bangalore Bhopal Bhubaneswar Chennai
Delhi Hyderabad Kolkata Lucknow Mumbai

Published by Jaico Publishing House
A-2 Jash Chambers, 7-A Sir Phirozshah Mehta Road
Fort, Mumbai - 400 001
jaicopub@jaicobooks.com
www.jaicobooks.com

Published in arrangement with
Amazon Publishing
www.apub.com

To be sold only in India, Bangladesh, Bhutan,
Pakistan, Nepal, Sri Lanka and the Maldives.

THE 6 DISCIPLINES OF CUSTOMER EXPERIENCE
ISBN 978-93-87944-74-9

First Jaico Impression: 2019

First published as
Outside In: The Power of Putting Customers at the Center of Your Business
by Amazon Publishing

Printed by
Print Plus Pvt. Ltd.
122, Shah & Nahar Ind. Estate (A-2),
Dhanraj Mills Compound, S. J. Marg,
Lower Parel (W), Mumbai – 400 013.

To the members of Forrester's customer experience team,
past, present, and future.

Contents

INTRODUCTION

Mastering the Outside In Challenge

YOU ROAM THE aisles of a drugstore, seeking a cold medicine. You hear, but can't quite make out, announcements at the gate as you wait to board your flight. You tap on a smartphone app seeking up-to-date information about your investments.

These experiences are the stuff of everyday life. They are the ways you experience the companies you buy from, trust your safe travel to, invest with — and they create a lasting impression that leads to whether or not you want to continue doing business with them. What I've learned from *The 6 Disciplines of Customer Experience* is that, more than any other factor, these customer experiences determine whether companies thrive and profit or struggle and fade.

The research in this book comes from Forrester Research, a company with over two hundred analysts dedicated to helping business professionals make better decisions in a world where technology is radically changing companies' relationships with customers. Among all of those insights, Harley Manning and Kerry Bodine's customer experience research stands out. Why devote a book to this topic? First, because after fourteen years of research, our customer experience practice can now effectively *prove* that customer experience makes a huge difference. (Check out the analysis in chapter 13, for example, which shows that stock in customer experience leaders yields the best stock market returns.) Second, because getting customer experience right is *hard.* Everything in your company contributes to it, from the way your call center employees talk, to your corporate email processes, to the policies your HR and legal departments put in place. (This is the customer experience ecosystem that we describe in chapter 3.) And finally, because the six central disciplines of customer experience, once you master them, can create a sustainable, hard-to-duplicate competitive advantage that sets your company apart from its competitors.

Here's a quick guide to the content in this book.

The first three chapters form Part I, which describes the value of customer experience. Chapter 1 defines what customer experience means, chapter 2 shows how it relates to the revenue your company brings in, and chapter 3 explains the customer experience ecosystem.

The heart of the book is Part II, which takes you into the six disciplines of customer experience: strategy, customer understanding, design, measurement, governance, and culture. There's a chapter on each discipline, illuminated with case studies that explain how to master it.

The end of the book, Part III, includes three chapters that explain the path companies take as customer experience becomes central to their business, the emerging role of the chief customer officer, and how customer experience will determine which companies succeed in the future.

Harley Manning, Kerry Bodine, and the customer experience team at Forrester have been working closely with companies around the world on all these elements of customer experience. They know what it takes to get real companies with real business challenges to change the way they do business. That's good news for your company, and it's great news for all of us customers, too.

—Josh Bernoff, Forrester Research
Cambridge, Massachusetts, May, 2012

PART I

THE VALUE OF CUSTOMER EXPERIENCE

1

You Need Your Customers More Than They Need You

KEVIN PETERS SAT alone in his car in the rain, watching the entrance of an Office Depot store. He was wearing a baseball cap and a well-worn pair of jeans.

Over the course of the last half hour he'd watched one customer after another emerge from the store. None of them carried a shopping bag. On their way out, they walked past an Office Depot employee leaning against a wall under the awning, smoking a cigarette out of the rain.

Kevin was torn. On the one hand, he didn't want anyone to know he was there. As the president of Office Depot's North American retail division, he'd come to this parking lot in New Jersey on a gray, dreary day to get a firsthand look at how customers experienced one of his stores. His method, already followed at dozens of other locations, was to observe customers coming and going, then enter, walk the aisles, and talk to customers about whether they were finding what they needed and how they liked the store in general.

The success of each visit hinged on the store manager not knowing he was there. Kevin wanted to see the store as a customer on a shopping trip, not as an executive on an inspection tour. But this situation was too much. Frustrated customers were leaving without products while one of his employees not only ignored them but laid down a cloud of tobacco smoke for them to walk through on their way out the door. Should he blow his cover by telling the manager to get his slacking employee back in the store to help shoppers?

Kevin made a decision: This couldn't stand. There was no way he was going to sit idly by and watch his business erode one customer at a time. He abandoned his undercover plans, got out of his car, and walked into the store on a new mission.

Because he'd planned to go incognito, Kevin hadn't bothered to find out the name of the store manager. But he knew that every retail location has a stanchion near the front of the store with a picture of the manager and, right under it, this service promise: "If you are not satisfied with your shopping experience, please see me or another manager on duty." Kevin walked over to the stanchion, looked up to see what the store manager looked like—and found a picture of the smoking employee outside.

When he tells this story you can see very real pain in Kevin's face and hear it in his voice. "The darn store manager! The person with whom we trusted our customer relationship." He pauses and repeats, "The person with whom we trusted our customer relationship."

What Went Wrong at Office Depot?

What underlying problem brought Kevin hundreds of miles away from his executive office in Boca Raton, Florida, and into one of his own stores—in disguise?

The story began months earlier when Kevin first got the job of president. It wasn't a great time to take over the helm of a retail chain. The economic downturn that began in 2008 had not been kind to retailers in general, and Office Depot's store sales had declined even more than those of its competitors.

What puzzled Kevin was that, even as sales declined, Office Depot's "mystery shopping" scores—compiled by a third-party research firm—were going through the roof. How could this be? How could customers be having a great in-store experience while not actually buying anything? The answer clearly didn't lie in Office Depot's Boca Raton headquarters, so Kevin set out to find it in the stores.

Kevin visited over seventy locations across the United States fully expecting to find a differentiated experience—one that set Office Depot apart from other office supply stores and big box retailers. He didn't. Instead, the experiences he found ranged from, in his own words, "poor to fair and, on a few occasions, good." But never good enough to truly differentiate Office Depot from its customers' other options.

By the time Kevin finished talking to hundreds of customers and watching them while they shopped, he'd begun to solve the puzzle. The mystery-shopping scores were actually correct—they were just asking the wrong questions: "Are the floors clean?" and "Are the shelves fully stocked?" As Kevin put it, "Who cares?"

Not his customers, as it turned out. They're mostly small-business owners who don't make money when they're not in front of a client or preparing work for a client. They want to find the office products they came for, quickly and easily. In other words, they want to get in, buy, and get out.

But Office Depot stores didn't help them do that. They were large and their signage was cluttered and confusing, making the stores hard for customers to navigate. Employees, both associates and managers, were neither as empathetic nor as helpful as they should have been. They had been coached all along to focus on tasks, not on building relationships with customers by listening carefully and responding to their needs. Wham, bam, thank you customer, and—oh, wait—did you forget to buy something? Sorry, I was so busy stocking the shelves and fixing the planogram that I missed that part.

Ultimately, Kevin knew that if he wanted to reverse the downward slide in sales, he needed to transform virtually every aspect of his in-store experience. Quickly.[1]

You Are in the Customer Experience Business—Whether You Know It or Not

This book is about customer experience, something that is fundamental to the success of every business. For most companies, customer experience is the single greatest predictor of whether customers will return—or defect to a competitor. It's so critical that even virtual monopolies like cable providers and health insurers suffer when they fail at it (which most do, as we'll see in the next chapter).

Customer experience goes to the heart of *everything* you do—how you conduct your business, the way your people behave when they interact with customers and each other, the value you provide. You literally can't afford to ignore it, because your customers take it personally each and every time they touch your products, your services, and your support.

So why are so many business leaders seemingly blind to the importance of customer experience? Primarily, it's because they don't know what they don't know—starting with what "customer experience" actually means. Sure, most executives have at least heard the term "customer experience," but they often believe it's just another way of saying "customer satisfaction."

That misunderstanding is a disaster in the making. Because if you *don't* understand what customer experience is and why it's important, you risk losing your customers to companies that do—think Apple, Amazon, Southwest Airlines, or USAA.

To appreciate what customer experience *really* means, let's start by clearing up a few of the more enduring misconceptions about it. We'll do that by listing some of the things that customer experience is *not*.

It's not soft and fluffy. *Of course* you love your customers—if not for them, you couldn't pay your mortgage. But loving your customers won't help you succeed unless you *do* something about it, like offering them products that meet their needs, and making it easy to find, buy, and use those products—all critical aspects of customer experience.

It's not customer service. People call customer service when they have a problem. So equating customer service with customer experience is like saying that a safety net is a trapeze act. Yes, the net is important to the act. But if the performer needs to use the net then something has gone wrong with the show.

It's not usability. Yes, people appreciate it when a product or service is easy to use. And ease of use has helped drive the success of products and services ranging from Apple's iPod to YouTube video uploads. But usability is just one piece of the customer experience puzzle—and not even the most important piece. Take your car, for example. Even if the steering wheel is easy to turn and the brake pedal feels just right, your driving experience will still be miserable if the car fails to meet your basic needs, like running reliably and stopping safely.

So if those are some of the things that customer experience is *not*—what, then, *is* it?

It's what products and services your company offers, how you manage your business, and what your brand stands for. It's what your customers think happened when they tried to learn about and evaluate your product, tried to buy it, tried to use it, and maybe tried to get help with a problem. What's more, it's how they felt about those interactions: excited, happy, and reassured, or nervous, disappointed, and frustrated.

Customer experience is how your customers perceive their interactions with your company.

Once you understand that, you can manage your business from the outside in, bringing the perspective of your customers to every decision you make.

Who are your customers? They're *both* the people who have purchased your goods or services *and* those who intend to buy your goods or services. Even if they don't actually buy anything, their active interest in buying puts them on our radar. That interest leads them to interact with you through your marketing efforts, your retail locations, your websites, and any other channels you support. And that leads them to form perceptions of their experience — perceptions that will determine what happens next.

What qualifies as an interaction? Here's how we think about interactions: they're reciprocal. Your customer takes an action such as visiting your store or website. Your company responds in some way. Maybe an associate walks up to your customer, or the website pops up an invitation to chat. Your customer then responds to your company's response — asking the associate a question or accepting the chat invitation — and so it goes until your customer achieves her goal, or gives up. When you string a series of these interactions together you end up with the steps in the customer journey (see figure 1-1).

Which brings us back to where we started: *Customer experience is how your customers perceive their interactions with your company.*

As it turns out, those perceptions matter a lot — as FedEx discovered.

CASE STUDY: FEDEX EASES CUSTOMER WORRIES

Looking out from within the FedEx world headquarters in Memphis, Tennessee, it might seem that the customer experience starts with logistics.

The company ships about 3.5 million packages per day in a mind-boggling ballet of planes. If you were to hang around its "Super Hub" at the Memphis International Airport for a month, you'd see about five thousand FedEx aircraft pass through. There are parking slots there for up to 175 aircraft at any one time. Handling all the packages that come off those planes takes twelve thousand FedEx employees and more than three hundred miles of conveyor belts that move hundreds of thousands of packages per hour. It's like magic.

But looking from the outside in, the customer experience begins when FedEx picks up a package or when the customer drops one off. For many customers, drop-off involves a trip to one of six-hundred-plus World Service Centers and FedEx Office locations. FedEx had always treated the FedEx World Service Center locations as convenient places for customers who want to fly in, drop off a pack-

Figure 1-1: The Customer Journey

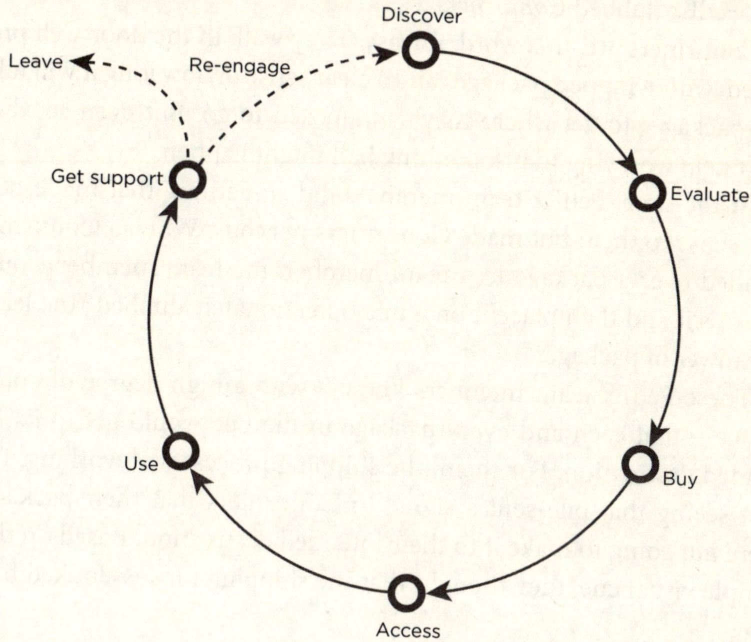

age, and fly back out again as quickly as possible. They even had a name for this type of customer—the Frisbee. FedEx thought that Frisbees accounted for the majority of walk-in traffic at these locations.

FedEx management believed they had been doing a pretty good job of serving these customers. But satisfaction surveys told them that not all customers were pleased with the experience. So in 2000, FedEx hired Ziba, a design and innovation consultancy, to help redesign the customer experience at the FedEx World Service Center locations. As part of that work, Ziba interviewed and observed FedEx customers to determine how they shipped packages and how they thought about shipping packages.

The results of the study were surprising. Only about 10 percent of the service-center customers were Frisbees. The rest fell evenly into three behavioral clusters based on how prepared they were when they walked in the door, and how much help they wanted from a FedEx employee. Of these groups, the most intriguing of all were the ones that FedEx dubbed *Confirmers.*

Confirmers are, in a word, uneasy. They walk in the door well prepared, with wrapped packages and a clear sense of how long it will take the packages to get where they're supposed to go. But even so, they can't help worrying that something bad might happen.

At the time, FedEx team members did something that made perfect sense to them but made Confirmers nervous. When a Confirmer handed over a package to a team member, the team member would process it and then place it on a pile (affectionately dubbed "the leaning tower of packages").

These FedEx team members knew—with a high degree of confidence—that each and every package in the pile would get to its intended destination. For them, the shipping process was working. But just seeing that pile sent a signal to Confirmers that their packages were *not* going to make it to their intended destination. Based on that simple visual cue, they thought that the shipping process looked broken.

As a result, Confirmers were on the verge of a panic attack because they believed something *with no basis in objective reality* ("My package will get lost because it's on that pile!"). And that made them highly at risk of taking their shipping business elsewhere.

The solution that transformed shipping into a great experience for Confirmers was elegantly simple. FedEx placed a wall with five presort windows behind the service counter. FedEx then trained their agents to take a package from a customer, say thanks, turn around, and slide the package through one of the windows. That sent a highly visible signal that the package was safe and sound and well on its way.

What was behind the agent wall? The leaning tower of packages.[2]

The Three Levels of Customer Experience

As we've already seen, customer experience is about customer perceptions. The research that Ziba conducted for FedEx reveals something fundamental about those perceptions. What was it about the shipping experience that disturbed Confirmers? After all, every time they used FedEx their packages got to the right destinations at the promised times — FedEx had optimized the shipping process with that goal in mind. Yet despite the fact that their needs were being met, quickly and easily, Confirmers were not having a good experience.

To fully understand why, you need to know that customers perceive their experiences at three different levels: *meets needs, easy,* and *enjoyable* (see figure 1-2). Every time they interact with a product, a service, a person, or an automated system, they judge how well the interaction helped them achieve their goals, how much effort they had to invest in the interaction, and how much they enjoyed the interaction. FedEx employees nailed the first two levels but blew it at the third when they failed to grasp how customers felt about the shipping process.

Figure 1-2: The Customer Experience Pyramid

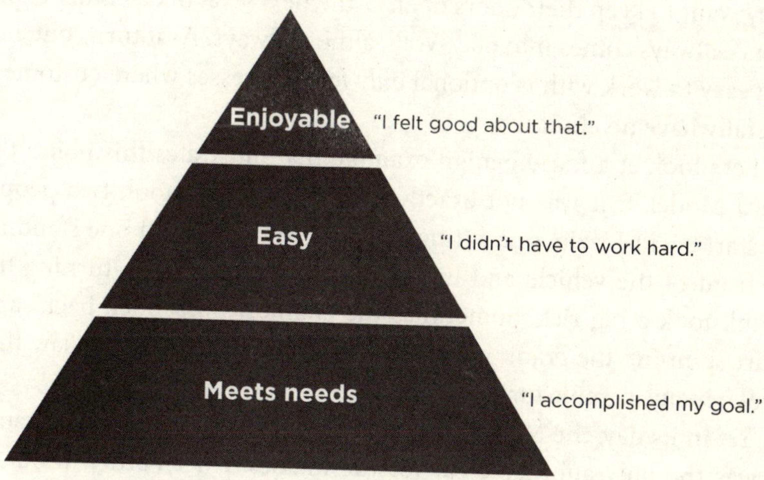

Kerry stumbled upon the original version of this model — the customer experience pyramid — in an academic paper by Dr. Elizabeth B. N. Sanders when she was getting her master's degree in human-computer interaction from Carnegie Mellon.[3] Like a lot of thinking that's ahead of its time, Dr. Sanders's 1992 paper hasn't gotten the attention it deserves. We've applied it in our own research for a number of years and tuned the version you see here as a result of our findings. It proves out beautifully in the real world — as we'll demonstrate in chapter 2.

Indeed, this model is so helpful when it comes to understanding customer experience that it's worth spending some time on. Let's start with the first level, meeting needs. That's at the base of the pyramid for a reason: It's the bedrock.

What if Office Depot never had printer paper or toner in stock? What if FedEx couldn't get packages to the right destinations? These would be company-killing failures beyond rescue by a sympathetic customer care representative. Game over, thanks for playing.

When "Easy" Offers Competitive Advantage

But when companies do meet basic needs — and all of them must if they want to keep their doors open — the next level of customer experience always comes into play. Well, almost always. As it turns out, being easy to work with is optional *only* for businesses where customers literally have no choice.

Let's look at a fairly benign example that illustrates this point: the Ford Model T. It was not exactly "user friendly." It took two people to start a Tin Lizzie: one sitting in the driver's seat and one standing in front of the vehicle and turning a crank. The person turning the crank took a big risk. Sometimes the engine would "kick back" and start spinning the crank in the opposite direction, a design flaw that broke many a crank-turner's wrist.

Yet in its day, the Model T was a huge commercial success because it was the only affordable car for the masses. It let Ford win out in the marketplace by owning the base of the customer experience pyramid.

Today Ford couldn't give away a vehicle that started with a crank and might break your wrist in the process. With tons of competition for low-priced vehicles, the company pays tons more attention to ease of use. Now for well under twenty grand you can buy a new Fiesta with touch-screen controls, a voice-activated navigation system, and a hands-free dock for your phone.

Who *can* get away with being hard to do business with in this day and age? Ironically, the best example we could come up with also has to do with cars: the Department of Motor Vehicles. And the only reason they can get away with it is because customers can't take their business elsewhere — yet.

In contrast, we've seen many examples where ease of doing business created a competitive advantage — or an entire industry. It was possible to upload video to the web, but not much consumer-created video was actually *on* the web until YouTube came along and made uploading easy. Digital music players didn't catch on because it was hard to get music onto them. Then Apple launched iTunes and iPods (which also led to iPhones and iPads and a market capitalization of $589 billion as of this writing). Netflix, eBay plus PayPal — there's real money to be made by lowering the barriers to customers using your product or service.

Meeting needs. Making it easy to buy a product or use a service or get customer service. It's not hard to believe that these are important aspects of a customer experience. But what about the idea that a company should make customer interactions enjoyable? Not everyone agrees that "enjoyable" is a key part of customer experience. Some people want to believe that only a few industries, like media or retail, need to worry about being enjoyable to work with, and not, say, manufacturing or shipping.

But remember our FedEx customer, the Confirmer. No offense meant to our friends in Memphis, but package shipping has got to be one of the least glamorous industries on the planet. Yet FedEx has an entire customer segment whose experience — and therefore continued business — hinges on positive emotional engagement. And FedEx does something about it. Because when it comes to customer experience, package shipping is also one of the most competitive industries on the planet.

Let's take a moment and see how these three levels of customer experience — meets needs, easy, and enjoyable — work together in a real-life scenario.

One Bad Experience Can Be All It Takes to Lose a Customer

Harley lives in Winchester, Massachusetts. Until recently, Comcast was his only option for cable service. Then competition came to Winchester. Verizon laid fiber-optic cables down Harley's street and soon afterward started aggressively marketing its FiOS service. The direct mail and television ads were relentless. Eager young Verizon employees knocked on his door every weekend looking to make a pitch. Soon friends began telling Harley that they'd switched and were delighted with the quality of their new Internet access, television package, and phone service.

However, none of this convinced him to switch — Comcast met his needs. The TV picture quality was good and the online service was fast. Plus, switching seemed like it would be a lot of effort.

Then something relatively minor happened. It started when Harley couldn't get online at his usual time: 5:30 a.m. The last time this had happened, just a month earlier, he'd wasted an hour trying to fix the problem before calling customer service to discover that there was a network outage. This time he immediately picked up the phone and dialed customer service. After navigating an unhelpful automated voice response system, he got through to a service representative. The rep, monosyllabic and grumpy, confirmed that the network was down — and failed to offer any insight as to when it might come back.

After Harley hung up, he had a delayed reaction. To be blunt, he got pissed off. He knew that the phone agent couldn't restore his service. But he sure as hell could have been polite, and an apology would have been nice. At that moment Comcast hit the customer experience nadir: It was not meeting Harley's needs because the service was down; it was not easy to use because he'd had to fight his way through its frustrating phone menu in order to get help; and it was decidedly not enjoyable because when he *did* get "help" it was from Mr. Grumpy. Later that morning, Harley called Verizon and made an appointment to have FiOS installed.[4]

It would be easy to dismiss this story as an isolated anecdote except for two facts. The first is that Comcast has an explicitly stated goal of becoming number one in customer experience. Its website includes this pledge: "Comcast will deliver a superior experience to our customers every day. Our products will be the best and we will offer the most customer-friendly and reliable service in the market." The second is that Comcast customers give it the lowest customer experience rating in its industry—and close to the lowest customer experience rating of any company in any industry we've studied. In other words, there are a lot of people out there having a similar experience to Harley.

If you juxtapose what Comcast says it wants to do with what its customers say it actually does, it's clear that Comcast could hardly do worse at achieving its customer experience goals.

Why Customer Experience? Why Now?

Based on our research with hundreds of companies, the challenges faced by Office Depot, FedEx, and Comcast are far from unusual. In fact, they're typical.

For decades, companies have been paying lip service to the idea of delighting customers while simultaneously disappointing them. That approach won't cut it anymore. Recent market shifts have brought us into a new era, one Forrester calls *the age of the customer*—a time when focus on the customer matters more than any other strategic imperative (see figure 1-3).[5]

Competitive barriers of the past—manufacturing strength, distribution power, information mastery—can't save companies today. One by one, each of these corporate investments have been commoditized. Now every company, and even enterprising individuals with smartphones, can tap into global factories and supply chains. And after huge IT investments, companies are realizing that the Internet cloud provides all of the computing resources they need.

Industry boundaries have dissolved. Automakers compete not just against one another but also against Zipcar, the wildly popular car-

Figure 1-3: We Have Entered the Age of the Customer

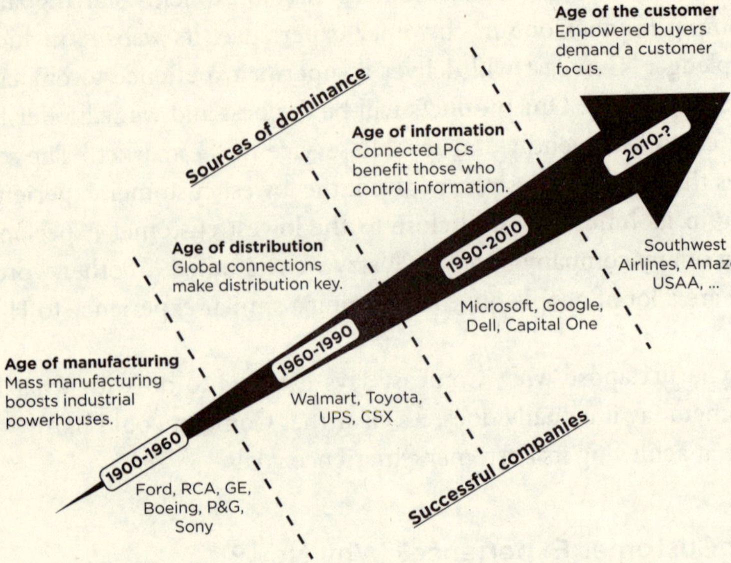

sharing service that makes the need for urban car ownership go away. Likewise, Google News, Expedia, and iPads undercut newspapers, travel agents, and laptop manufacturers, respectively. And eBay alone swallows massive amounts of profit from the retail industry as a whole.

Amid all of this, customers have more power than ever. With online reviews, social networks, and mobile web access, it's easy for customers to know even more than sellers about products, services, competitors, and pricing.[6]

The game has changed, and we all know it. Organizations sincerely want to deliver an improved customer experience, but overwhelmingly they fail to see the whole picture—how the back office, trusted business partners, incentive programs, and entrenched business processes undermine that effort.

The 6 Disciplines of Customer Experience aims to fix the problem by revealing the new imperative: creating and nurturing a system of interdependent, self-reinforcing practices that align employees, partners, processes, policies, and technology around customers. This is not just the same old "focus on the customer" message. It requires a new way to manage, looking deep into every process and incentive to see whether it supports the overall goal: *Deliver a great customer experience.*

In the next chapter, we'll show you the money — the economic impact of improving customer experience. Then we'll introduce you to a simple tool that reveals *where* you must focus your efforts in order to make those improvements. After that we'll describe the six disciplines that companies need to master if they truly want to take improving customer experience from a bumper-sticker slogan to a self-sustaining, competitive advantage.

Ready? Because it's time to do the numbers.

2

Customer Experience Means Billions to Business

PARRISH ARTURI IS senior vice president, customer experience, at Fidelity Investments, a company with a long history of taking customer experience seriously. In fact, the customer experience function that Parrish runs had been around for roughly six years when he took over.

Parrish raised his hand to run the customer experience organization in the middle of 2010 because he saw an opportunity. Up until that time the group had been narrowly focused on measurement — helping employees understand customer feedback and then put plans in place for making improvements. But Fidelity had recently upped the ante on customer experience by making it a major part of its five-year business plan. That led Parrish to believe that the time was right to expand the group's role at the enterprise level and take a more proactive approach.

He immediately began to focus on process improvement — going after systemic problems that got in the way of Fidelity serving its customers. Because some of the problems were big "rocks" and others just "pebbles," he introduced an innovative process improvement of his own. Instead of asking people to submit full-blown business requests for small projects, he got a pool of money dedicated to paying for little changes. By requiring appropriately lightweight justifications for these minor requests he was able to tackle more projects, faster.

One of these small projects began when a service rep noticed that a large number of people were having trouble logging in to their accounts through an automated phone system. The rep started a thread about the situation on a Fidelity discussion board dedicated to generating ideas for experience improvements. Parrish's team, the owners of the board, saw the thread and flagged it for attention.

The team then worked with the people who manage the phone system to identify the root cause of the login issue and quickly launch a solution. Although the total cost of that fix was less than twenty thousand dollars, it saves Fidelity $4 million a year by averting calls to customer service. It was just one of over one hundred and sixty projects that came through Fidelity's experience improvement system in 2011. Together those projects accounted for over $24 million in annual savings.

Fixing small problems and generating big savings is great. But over time Parrish realized that he could tackle more fundamental process changes by looking at key moments from the customers' perspective. His team identified problem resolution as one of these moments, and piloted an improved model for helping high net worth customers when they ran into trouble. Any time one of these well-heeled investors hit a snag, Fidelity assigned a case manager who followed their issue through to a solution. The program not only drastically reduced the amount of time to resolve problems — a benefit to customers — it was also a big hit with Fidelity employees such as the account executives, who liked having a single person working on their behalf to help resolve a major client's problem.

As promising as this sounds, Parrish didn't take it for granted that these efforts produced business results. Like all successful customer experience professionals, he carefully tracked the impact of the program and similar outreach efforts. As expected, there was a huge decrease in unhappy customers: The number of customers in the "detractor" category dropped by more than half.[1] Just as encouraging, there was a large increase in the number of happy customers.

Because his team could identify specific customers who'd become "promoters," they were able to determine how much more these people were investing with Fidelity. Clients who said they'd had a good experience put four and a half times more cash into their accounts than clients who said they'd had a poor experience. In total, this larger group of happy high net worth customers increased their investments with Fidelity by several billion dollars.

Did these results surprise his executives? "It didn't surprise them," Parrish explains. "This all makes intuitive sense. Having the specific numbers just puts the exclamation point on the business case."

When You Treat It As a Business Discipline, Customer Experience Leads to Profits

Here's the fundamental lesson of Parrish Arturi at Fidelity: *Customer experience leads to profits.* But not because it makes your customers feel warm and fuzzy, and not when it's just a slogan. Customer experience leads to profits . . . *if you treat it as a business discipline.*

In fact, customer experience is the greatest untapped source of both decreased costs and increased revenue in most industries—but only if you take the time to understand what underlies it and how you can benefit financially from improving it. And that is something that you *must* learn how to do. Customer experience fails to gain traction at companies that treat it like something soft and squishy.

We saw an example of this a few years ago when we were invited to run a workshop at a client's offsite meeting. The meeting had been called by the president of one of the company's divisions and included all of the president's direct reports. They had gathered because the CEO had issued a directive: The company was to become number one in customer experience for its industry.

Here's the catch: The directive had come down *two years earlier* and no one had done a thing about it. Now the division president, who had just stepped into the job, aimed to fix that situation.

There were about twenty people in the room, and after a while it became clear that the group had divided into two camps. The majority had shown up excited about improving customer experience and became even more excited as we got into specific ways to do that. But there were also three skeptics who became increasingly negative over the course of the day.

Finally, the most senior naysayer summed up his objections: "I have the funding to do two projects next year. One will bring us $5 million in annual revenue, and one will bring us $3 million in annual savings. Improving customer experience sounds great in theory, but what specific projects do you have that will earn more than $5 million or save more than $3 million? Tell me and I'll do one of those instead."

The pro–customer experience side of the room was outraged. Prioritizing customer experience projects was a "no-brainer," right? Every company needs customers, so it's obvious that customer experience is important. Besides, the CEO had decreed that they would be number one in customer experience!

As we stood at the front of the room, we watched the debate grow heated. Finally we interrupted and, to their evident surprise, addressed the most vocal customer experience enthusiasts. "Hold on a minute. He's right. You have got to learn how to build business cases for customer experience projects. If you show up with a business plan that has all cost and no benefit you will lose out every time to projects that show ROI."

We've seen similar situations many times. The customer experience champions in the room were enthusiastic, but lacked the business discipline needed to turn their excitement into action. Instead—after two years of inaction—they sat in that room debating what, if anything, to do about their situation. They were paralyzed because they hadn't approached customer experience from the perspective of the business results it delivers—unlike Dan Hesse at Sprint.

CASE STUDY: SPRINT'S CEO SAVES BILLIONS BY IMPROVING CUSTOMER EXPERIENCE

In June 2010, Sprint CEO Dan Hesse gave the opening keynote speech at Forrester's Customer Experience Forum. Tall, with a deep voice and a surprisingly open manner for someone who runs a major corporation, Dan leads the third-largest wireless telecommunications network in the United States.

"You may be wondering why someone from Sprint is giving a speech about customer experience," he began, essentially inviting everyone to reflect on their poor experiences with mobile operators. After a pause to let that sink in, he resumed. "Perhaps some of you have been that kid on a team who won the 'most improved' award." His punch line got a good laugh from the audience.

Dan had taken over as CEO in December 2007. Nobody was laughing then — Sprint had been bleeding red ink, losing customers faster than any of its major competitors. It had the lowest customer satisfaction scores of all of them.[2] In Sprint's internal presentations, managers highlighted the problem through customer complaints. These ranged from the polite ("Candidly, I encountered problems in almost every facet of my Sprint relationship") to the blunt ("Your service sucks").

Customers weren't shy about calling the company when they had a problem, and there were lots of problems. Even though Sprint employed an army of contact center agents to handle the calls, they could only cope with less than half of them. The remaining calls were outsourced to third parties at fees that rose in proportion to volume. To make matters worse, when service reps couldn't solve a problem — which happened a lot — they tried to make things right by giving customers credits. As Dan's director of customer experience, Tim Gay, put it, "When your customer experience is bad you buy off your customers — you give them a fifty-dollar credit." The result: Poor experience was taking a massive toll between call center outsourcing fees and customer compensation.

The deadly combination of fleeing customers and rising costs led Dan to set three priorities during his first week on the job: improve customer experience, strengthen the brand, and generate cash. "I always put customer experience first, then brand, then cash because it is a logical sequence," he explains. "You might argue that customer experience is first among equals. It really comes down to customers — attracting and retaining customers is how we generate cash."

And generating cash was an especially big deal for the cash-strapped wireless carrier. Dan reasoned that he had to focus everyone in the company not just on improving customer experience, but also on doing it in ways that would unquestionably benefit the bottom line. But how?

He settled on a simple yet effective strategy: Drive down the number of calls to customer service. He went with this approach for several reasons. For one, each call was tagged with a reason code such as "dropped call" or "couldn't understand the bill." That made it possible to create a list of the most frequent drivers of customer dissatisfaction. And this unambiguous data gave his team a starting point for tracing and attacking each problem's root cause.

Another reason was that Dan could hold the appropriate part of the organization accountable for fixing specific problems. "Most customer contacts had someone other than the person in charge of the call center who was responsible. Take dropped calls. I held the network person responsible for getting those calls to go down."

Here's how the process worked in practice. Having identified the biggest call drivers from the data, Dan's customer experience team traced their root causes. Then they worked with the responsible department—like marketing, IT, or billing—to resolve the underlying issues. For example, many calls were traced back to customer confusion about Sprint's large number of calling plans. The company responded by reducing the total number of plans even as it introduced a small number of unlimited "Simply Everything" plans—reinforcing Sprint's brand position as one of simplicity and value.

The real beauty of this strategy was that, even as it advanced the longer-term goal of reducing churn, it delivered near-term results by cutting costs. "Once we started knocking down these call reason codes," Dan explains, "we were able to close the third-party call centers, which made an immediate improvement to our bottom line."

This strategy of reducing calls to customer service was a smashing success. Even the near-term business results were staggering. The cost savings alone added up to over $1.7 billion *per year* as a result of fewer outsourced calls and fewer customer credits.

Unsurprisingly, Sprint's customer satisfaction scores rose as well. The once dead-last company came in first among major wireless carriers in the 2012 American Customer Satisfaction Index.[3] By early 2011, improved customer satisfaction had already brought Sprint's customer churn rate to its lowest level in company history.

As we write this, it's unclear how the Sprint story will *ultimately* turn out. In 2011, Dan Hesse moved into a new, more costly phase of customer experience improvements. He cut a deal with Apple to sell the iPhone — an expensive but necessary move given that his two major rivals offered the super-hot device. He also doubled his capital investment in Sprint's network in order to support increased data traffic from smartphone users.

While these were absolutely the right moves to make, the size of the total investment made the market skittish and threatened his support by shortsighted investors. Customer experience improvements can usually help, but can't always get you out of a crisis in time. Even so, despite the dip in 2011, Sprint's shareholder return for the total period from 2009 (when Dan began his efforts) to early 2012 (as we write this) has outperformed competitors.

Learn to Make the Business Case for Customer Experience

So if you believe in the business benefits of customer experience, how *can* you prove your point? The surefire way for most companies is to start with cost avoidance. In hard times, that's often the only way to get funding, and, even in good times, all firms love to save money.

The simplest way to prove savings is to do what Sprint did: Find customer experience problems, fix them, and measure the actual results. Then use your findings to continuously build support for your efforts over time. If you don't have your own version of Dan Hesse behind you, start with projects small enough to get funded by someone at a lower level of the organization. This approach works for any organization that delivers a less-than-perfect experience — and that's *every* organization.

To make a profit by spending on improving customer experience, you must first find places where the spending actually matters. Just as important, you should avoid spending on experience improvements that *don't* actually matter. Take, for example, Canada Post, the postal service for Canada. Canada Post is a crown corporation, which means that even though it's owned by the federal government of Canada, it operates much like any other business and is expected to make a profit — which it has for sixteen years in a row.[4]

A couple of years ago the customer experience team at Canada Post looked at the correlation between package scanning and customer loyalty. Packages get scanned as they pass through checkpoints on their way from whoever shipped them to whoever is receiving them. Customers use the data from these scans to track the progress of orders and get reassurance that they haven't been lost. For example, a shopper might follow along online as her package arrives in Canada from China, then gets put on a plane to Montreal, and so on.

Initially, Canada Post assumed that more scans were always better because customers would like to know every step that a package took along its route. To supply that information, the business would have to scan a package every time it changed hands. And that would add up to a lot of scans done by a lot of employees with a lot of expensive equipment.

But when the customer experience team analyzed the data, they found a clear point at which additional scans didn't increase loyalty at all. At that point other aspects of the customer experience became more important, offering a better return for Canada Post's investments. The end result was that Canada Post leaders saved money by not buying more scanning equipment than it needed.

Most Companies Have Lots of Room for Improvement

Does your company have customer experience problems? Almost certainly. We know this because we've been measuring the customer experience delivered by top brands since 2007 through our annual Customer Experience Index (CXi) — and the great majority of companies don't do well.

Here's how the CXi works. We ask more than seven thousand consumers to identify companies they do business with across thirteen industries. We ask them to tell us how well each firm met their needs, how easy the firm was to work with, and how enjoyable each was to work with (questions that correspond to the three levels of the customer experience pyramid that we described in chapter 1—meets needs, easy, enjoyable). Then for all three questions we calculate each firm's CXi score by subtracting the percentage of its customers who reported a bad experience from the percentage who reported a good experience. The overall CXi is an average of those three results.

We don't limit the survey results by just asking about a single channel like a retail location or a call center. Instead we take an enterprise-level approach and ask about the entire experience, which could span products, services, business units, and channels. This gives us the customers' holistic view of the brands they do business with.

Here's what we found when we ran this study in 2012—a pretty typical year. We collected statistically significant data samples for a total of one hundred and sixty U.S. brands. Based on their scores we categorized them into five different groups: Excellent companies were at the top of the charts, receiving scores of 85 points or higher. Good companies earned scores in the 75 to 84 point range, which is respectable—kind of like getting a B minus to a B in school. Then came the Okay companies with C student scores of 65 to 74. After that were the Poor companies (55 to 64 points) and the Very Poor companies (54 points or less).

So how did these major brands do in the eyes of their customers? Only 3 percent were Excellent, and just 34 percent were Good. That left almost two-thirds of the brands in disappointing territory: 31 percent were Okay, 23 percent were Poor, and 10 percent were Very Poor (see figure 2-1).

This tells us that mediocre customer experience is the norm, and that great customer experience is rare. What this means is that customer experience is a powerful differentiator for the very few companies that do it well.

This situation presents an incredible near-term opportunity for gaining a competitive advantage. We see entire industries where simply being *adequate* at customer experience makes a company stand out. For example, health-insurance companies have owned the cellar in our Customer Experience Index every year since we began the study,

Figure 2-1: Distribution of Customer Experience Index Scores, 2012

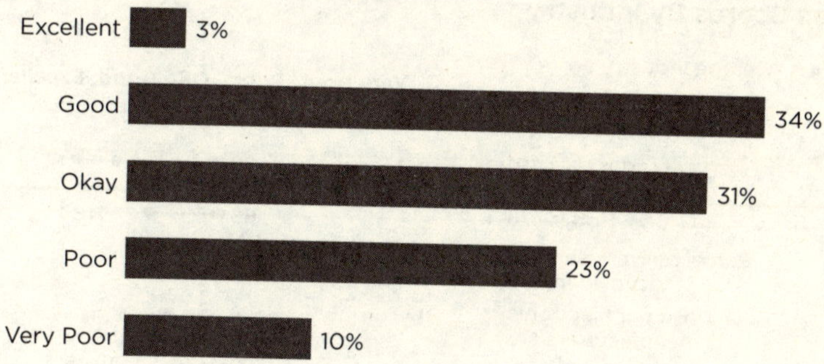

Base: 160 large North American brands scored in Forrester's Customer Experience Index, 2012, (percentages may not total 100 because of rounding)

Source: Forrester's North American Technographics Customer Experience Online Survey, Q4 2011 (US)

and 2012 was no exception (see figure 2-2). The industry average of 55 was at the very bottom of the Poor category. Top scoring companies, like Kaiser Permanente or Blue Cross Blue Shield of Illinois, tower over the rest of the industry with their Okay score of 72. They don't have to do customer experience better than firms in general — they just have to do it better than other health-insurance companies.

Other industries performed almost as badly in the eyes of their customers. The credit card and airline industries barely made it into the Okay category. Meanwhile, wireless service providers, TV service providers, and Internet service providers all had average scores that put them squarely in the Poor category, right alongside the health-insurance companies.

If you're not in one of those industries you can breathe a sigh of relief, right? No. We find huge gaps between the leaders and the laggards within virtually every industry. For example, the top company across all industries was a bank: USAA, with its impressive score of 89. Meanwhile, the bottom-ranked bank — Bank of America — earned a score of just 55. Also in that 64-points-and-below Poor category were HSBC, U.S. Bank, Citibank, and Wells Fargo.

Should you care if your industry is near the bottom of the CXi? Or if your company's customer experience is near the bottom of its indus-

Figure 2-2: High, Low, and Average Customer Experience Index Scores By Industry

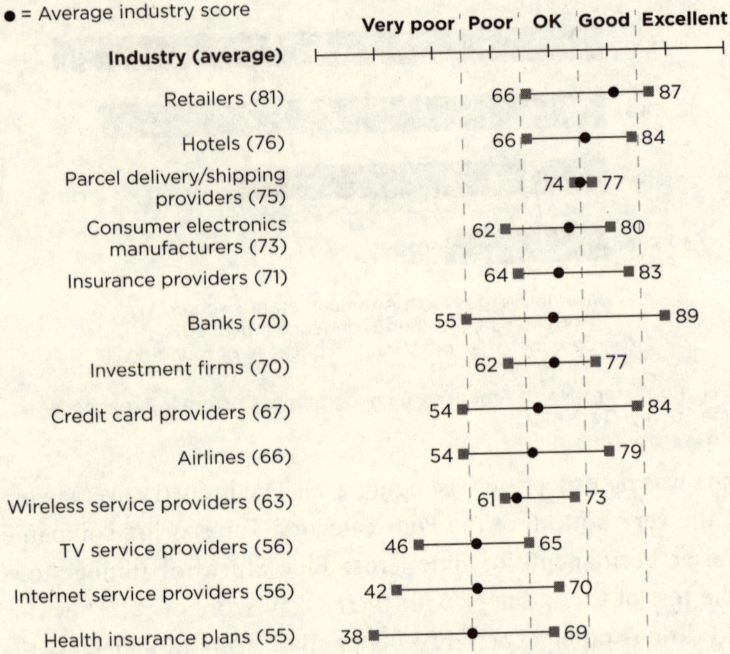

Base: US online consumers who have interacted with brands in these industries

Source: Forrester's North American Technographics Customer Experience Online Survey, Q4 2011 (US)

try? Yes, because it means you're not only bleeding money from unnecessary costs, you're leaving more revenue opportunity on the table than you can probably imagine.

Customer Experience Correlates to Loyalty

Parrish Arturi proved that customer experience drives revenue from Fidelity customers. You can't afford to ignore his example because this is the case for just about everyone's customers. Unless you work for a true monopoly, it is certainly the case for your customers. There's a simple reason why this is true: Customer experience correlates to loyalty. And that means that companies with higher CXi scores have

Figure 2-3: Correlation Between CXi Scores and Loyalty Metrics

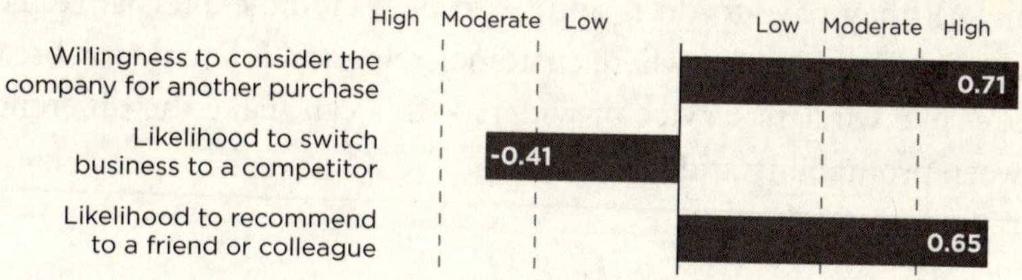

Base: US online consumers

Source: Forrester's North American Technographics Customer Experience Online Survey, Q4 2011 (US)

more customers who will buy from them again, who won't take their business elsewhere, and who will recommend them to a friend.

Here's how we know this for a fact.

When we field the CXi survey, we ask consumers to tell us three things: How willing they are to make another purchase from each company, how likely they are to switch business to a competitor, and how likely they are to recommend each company to a friend. Their answers let us calculate the relationships between customer experience and three of the most common loyalty metrics used in business today: purchase intent, churn, and word of mouth.

The relationships are impressively strong — about as strong as correlations get in the real world (see figure 2-3).[5] For purchase intent and word of mouth they're so high that *nothing else you do is likely to have more impact* on whether you'll get another sale or a recommendation from your customers. And that makes intuitive sense, doesn't it? Customers who've had bad experiences with your company won't be eager for more. Nor will they send their friends your way — not any more than you'd send *your* friends to a restaurant that served you a bad meal, or to a retailer that sold you a defective product and wouldn't take it back.

The correlation with likelihood to take business elsewhere is also significant.[6] Once again it's easy to see why. Giving your customers a bad experience — by not meeting their needs or just being rude — makes them wonder whether they wouldn't be better off buying from someone who isn't you. That's great for your competitors. They won't have to convince your customers to leave since you already did that for them. All they have to do is appear to be a credible alternative. For companies in industries where customer retention is a make-or-break issue—like wireless service providers—this can make the difference between profitability and failure.

The Eye-Popping Impact on Revenue

A good customer experience drives loyalty up, and a bad customer experience drives loyalty down. So what's the potential revenue benefit from driving customer loyalty up by improving customer experience? We answered that question by creating a model that predicts what would happen if a company with below-average customer experience for its industry improved to the point where it delivered an above-average customer experience for its industry.[7]

We modeled three types of revenue benefit from this improvement: incremental purchases from current customers, retained revenue as a result of lower churn, and new sales driven by word of mouth. When you add them up, the model shows that even small shifts in customer loyalty can translate into billions of dollars of incremental revenue per year for companies in two industries: hotels and wireless service providers (see figure 2-4).[8] And even the least affected industries like retailers and Internet service providers can see tens of millions of dollars in revenue benefits.

Major hotel chains have the most to gain: a total of $1.364 billion of revenue. The bulk of that money—$825 million—comes from retaining business that would have been lost to competitors. If you travel much yourself, you know that a hotel runs the risk of driving customers away when it delivers a subpar experience: You have no switching cost for taking your business elsewhere, and usually have many options when looking for a place to stay.

Hotels that go from providing a below-average experience to providing an above-average experience can also see a big revenue gain by grabbing business from their competitors. Our model shows that hotels that provide an above-average customer experience can earn an

Figure 2-4: Customer Experience Revenue Benefits

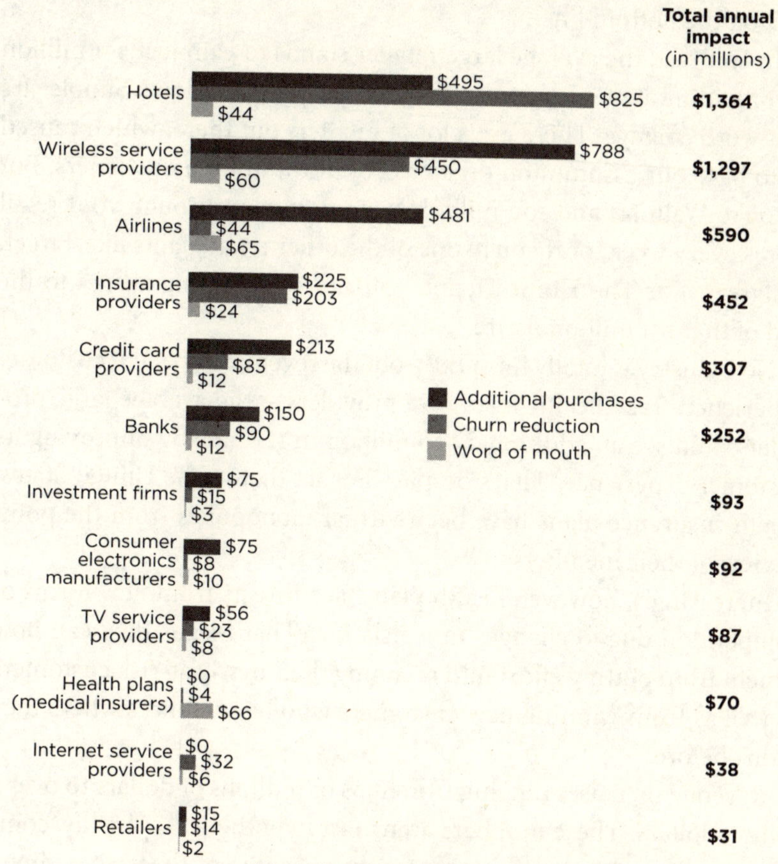

Base: US online consumers
(numbers have been rounded to the nearest whole number)

Source: Forrester's North American Technographics Customer Experience Online Survey, Q4 2011 (US)

incremental $495 million in revenue from additional night's stays by their happier, and therefore more loyal, guests.

The big wireless carriers also have a lot to gain: a total of $1.297 billion. That number includes $788 million from incremental purchases like adding a data plan or a second phone for another member of the family. It also includes $450 million of "retained revenue" — money the carrier would have lost but instead gets to keep because it lost fewer customers. Because these carriers have tens of millions of customers, keeping even a small incremental percentage of them makes a big impact on the bottom line.

In contrast, the average large retailer stands to gain just $31 million by providing better customer experiences. Why so low? Simple: It's that word *average*. There are a lot of retailers out there, which caused us to base our assumption on a base of just 4 million customers. But if you're Walmart and 100 million customers pass through your retail stores every week, or if you're one of the other retail giants like Target, Walgreens, or The Home Depot, you can start adding zeroes to the end of that $31 million figure.[9]

No industry is totally immune from the revenue impact of customer experience. Take health-insurance providers — the average large provider could see an additional $70 million in revenue by improving its customer experience. That's despite the fact that in the United States, health-insurance plans have been virtual monopolies from the point of view of their members.

Increasingly, however, health plans face threats from new forms of competition due to changes in legislation. That means they can now benefit from putting effort into retaining their newly at-risk customers as well as from winning new customers who have choices where they didn't before.

Revenue increases ranging from tens of millions of dollars to over a billion dollars: These numbers aren't just hypothetical. Already, companies that lead in customer experience — some of them your direct competitors — have turned the potential benefits shown by our model into reality. Let's look at some of them now.

Companies That Prove the Business Benefit of Customer Experience

USAA is a diversified financial services company that has the highest Customer Experience Index score in three industries: banking, credit cards, and insurance. This translates into strong financial performance in both good times and bad. As Wayne Peacock, executive vice president of member experience, points out, USAA retains 97 percent to 98

basis of customer experience. In fact, they already do — most just don't realize what that really means, what's at stake, or how to do it well.

This may seem overwhelming. With something this big and this important, it's hard to know where to start if you want to create change. That's why in our next chapter you'll learn about a simple but remarkably effective framework that can help you do just that: the customer experience ecosystem.

3

The Customer Experience Ecosystem

JOHN BIRRER IS enthusiastic and determined, just the kind of person you need to solve a big, persistent problem — like fixing the customer experience at a cable operator.

John is senior vice president of customer experience at Charter Communications, the fourth-largest cable operator in the United States. He came to Charter after eight years at T-Mobile, where he'd most recently been senior vice president of customer loyalty.[1] During his tenure at T-Mobile, the company won ten J. D. Power and Associates awards for customer service — six of them sit in a bookcase in John's office at Charter.

When he moved from T-Mobile to Charter, John knew what he was getting into. Although the wireless industry struggles to provide a good customer experience (remember Dan Hesse at Sprint?), the cable industry's struggles are worse.

What persuaded John to jump from the frying pan into the fire? After a financial restructuring, Charter's executive team had stabilized the company and was setting a new strategy for success. They'd picked customer experience as a key element of that strategy and started a search for someone to lead their improvement efforts. They'd found

John and convinced him that they were serious about transforming the business.

For his part, John was excited by the opportunity. "I thought Charter was the place to do something dramatic and make a big change," he explains. "I wanted to help make Charter not just the best company for customer experience in the cable space but one of the top-tier companies for customer experience, period."

But as John soon discovered, an underlying problem dragged down customer experience across the organization.

Charter employees had developed a culture of compliance. From a naïve perspective, this made them look hard-charging and dynamic: "Tell me what you want me to do and I'll go do it!" But from John's perspective, this behavior caused unneeded customer pain. He saw frontline employees salute and execute any directive even if their own experience told them it was wrong for the customer.[2]

This situation drove a host of cascading problems. It started with unhappy customers. In turn, frontline employees felt miserable about what they were doing to make customers unhappy. Meanwhile, management was frustrated that the Charter customer experience was bad.

Here's just one example of how this played out. Charter's small-business customers were struggling to install the company's new and improved software on their routers. They'd bought and paid for the software, confident that they could get it to work. But when they tried to do just that, they were surprised to find that they couldn't.

As unhappy as that left them, Charter's technical support specialists were even more frustrated. They had the skills and tools needed to fix the software problem, but doing so would require them to touch their customers' routers. They weren't allowed to do that because those routers had been purchased from third parties, and a company policy prohibited the techs from touching customer-owned hardware. Consistent with their culture of compliance, the support specialists followed the policy even though it left them feeling miserable.

What would it take to resolve this situation? John was determined to figure that out. He started by writing down each step of the customer's journey. He began at the moment they purchased the software and ended at the point where they called for help but didn't get it. Then he carefully listed each Charter employee, process, and system that the customers touched along the way, either directly or indirectly. He drew lines between the players to show how they were connected.

By the time he finished, John had filled up a large sheet of poster paper with a complex web of relationships. It was mind boggling. To help make sense of it, John color coded each step of the journey. He placed a green dot on steps where people in the diagram were happy. He placed a red dot to indicate where people were unhappy.

When he was finished, he stepped back and saw a sea of red dots associated with customers, starting soon after the sale. Service techs who weren't allowed to finish the installations had their own red dots. None of that was a surprise. The surprise was the sea of green dots associated with most other Charter employees, who were largely unaware of the serious problems the customers and techs faced.

The small-business sales reps were happy because they got their commissions based on sales, not installations—even though they'd contributed to the problem by not communicating tech requirements during the sales process. The human resources managers who'd approved the sales reps' compensation plan were also happy, unaware that the plan had a flaw. And Charter's lawyers, who had created the policy prohibiting the technicians from fixing the problem, were happy because they had protected the company from potential liability. They were blind to the poor customer experience that resulted from their efforts.

John Birrer was looking at a map of an interdependent set of relationships we call the *customer experience ecosystem.* He could see at a glance that this one was way out of balance and, as a result, it had failed—failed Charter's customers, failed his fellow employees, and failed his senior management.

What Natural Ecosystems Teach Us About Customer Experience

A customer experience ecosystem is the complex set of relationships among a company's employees, partners, and customers that determines the quality of all customer interactions. It is the single most powerful framework for diagnosing and then fixing customer experience problems in ways that make the fixes stick over time.

To understand customer experience ecosystems, it's helpful to look at a parallel system: a natural ecosystem. Specifically, let's examine the natural ecosystem in Zion National Park in southwest Utah. As it turns out, there aren't nearly as many butterflies in the park as there used to be, and that's because of a long chain of events.[3]

The development of Zion National Park in 1918 brought an influx of tourists to the area. As people flocked to see the natural beauty of the park firsthand, their ever-increasing numbers scared off some of the wildlife—not the butterflies, but the cougars. When the cougars retreated from the areas most frequented by tourists, they left the park's mule deer with no natural enemies. This resulted in a mule deer population explosion. The deer started gobbling up everything in their path including one of their favorite delicacies: cottonwood tree saplings.

Now to you and me a cottonwood sapling looks like a bush. But to a deer it looks like a salad bar. So the saplings turned into lunch specials and never grew into trees. That was bad for the stream banks where the cottonwoods grew. Without the root systems of the adult trees, the banks eroded. Eroding banks caused the streams to widen out and wash away topsoil, leaving large areas of exposed gravel where wildflowers could no longer take root and bloom. And with fewer wildflowers, the butterflies had little nectar to eat, and so they left (or died).

Keep in mind that Zion National Park started out with a healthy, self-sustaining ecosystem. Then a chain of events occurred: tourists arrived, cougars fled, deer multiplied, cottonwood trees became scarce, stream banks eroded, wildflowers died off, and butterflies mostly disappeared. That left the park with an unhealthy ecosystem and a lot less natural beauty (and natural beauty is kind of the point of having a national park in the first place).

This chain of events might seem obvious the way we just laid it out. But it took scientists decades to determine the root cause of the butterfly problem. That's because natural ecosystems consist of complex interdependent relationships that change over time. Understanding them and restoring them to health requires certain tools and skills: you can't just air-drop a ton of butterflies into Zion National Park and solve its butterfly problem. Yes, that would increase the park's butterfly population in the short term. But if you really want to solve Zion's problem and make those changes stick over time, you've got to understand the root cause of the butterflies disappearing—tourists—and start your work from there.

Are you trying to solve customer experience problems without understanding your customer experience ecosystem? You might as well be air-dropping butterflies into Zion National Park. You're going to spend a whole lot of money and end up right where you started.

Make no mistake: If you have customers, you have a customer experience ecosystem. And if you're wrestling with a big, thorny customer experience problem—like the ones that confronted Kevin Peters at Office Depot and Dan Hesse at Sprint—then something has gone wrong with its complex and interdependent relationships.

If you want to fix your customer experience problems, you need to identify their root causes and then create a new equilibrium for your customer experience ecosystem. That's exactly what John Birrer did to solve the software installation problem at Charter.

Creating a Healthier Ecosystem at Charter

The customer experience ecosystem for Charter's failed small-business software installation had its own chain of events and multiple root causes. To nurse it into health, Charter took a number of steps. For one, the legal team reversed its policy so that service techs could work with customers on a fix, even if it meant touching non-Charter hardware. The product team worked with the software provider to eliminate the need for a fix in the first place. And the company is rolling out a new, more consultative sales approach so that potential problems get surfaced at the beginning of the customer journey, not toward the end.

Despite Charter's problems, don't think for a second that its unhealthy ecosystem was due to employees who don't care about customers. As John puts it, "People don't come to work thinking 'How can I make customers unhappy today?'"

The real root cause was more subtle. At Charter—and probably at your company, too—it stemmed from a lack of connectedness: across silos, across departments, and back to customers. "The customer was falling through the cracks," John explains. "It's because we were compliance driven. When people saw the customer falling through the cracks, there was no hand reaching down to stop them from falling." Fortunately, John delights in finding those cracks and moving the organization to close them — as he also did with Charter's monthly bill.

The project around the bill started with customer pain. "Our customers call us about twice a quarter," John says. "We did an analysis, and the number-one call driver was our bill. So we looked at the bill. We had gone to black-and-white printing to save money, but color helps you navigate by calling your attention to what's important. I looked at the bill and I couldn't understand it, so how would a customer?"

When John reviewed the bill, one problem leapt out. "We had a full page of legal mouse type. How does that make us look to customers? Do you trust a company that gives you a full page of six-point font?" Then John realized that the legal disclaimer page might be an opportunity in disguise. Because paper and ink are expensive, he thought, "If I could get rid of that one page of legal jargon that no one reads, I could pay for a color bill."

John set out to get rid of the disclaimer. First he asked the billing team why it was there in the first place. "They told me that this is what the legal team asked to put on the bill. So I sat down with the billing team *and* the legal team." John handed the disclaimer to the lawyers. "We identified paragraphs that we had needed for a legal action that was already settled, and other language that was no longer necessary. We ended up going from a full page of legal language to just an inch or an inch and a half of legal language."

The new color bill came out in January 2012, fully funded — with money left over — by the savings from cutting a page that customers didn't want or need.

A solution that hadn't been clear from the inside-out perspective of his fellow employees became obvious once John looked at the problem from the customer's perspective — from the outside in. Starting from that perspective, he took the time to understand the complex, interdependent relationships behind the broken experience. That told him what needed to change and who had to be involved in the change. And by bringing the disconnected parties in the customer experience ecosystem together, he was able to fix a problem that the billing team thought impossible to touch and the legal team didn't know existed.

This approach can solve problems even when the ecosystem includes parties you normally wouldn't think of—people who don't work for you and aren't your partners, but who nonetheless have a profound impact on the experience your customer has with you. Vanguard found this out when they tackled a particularly emotional journey for some of their clients.

CASE STUDY: VANGUARD TRANSFORMS A LIFE-CHANGING CUSTOMER JOURNEY

Shannon Nutter-Wiersbitzky is head of the market research and voice of client team at the Vanguard Group. Vanguard is one of the world's largest investment management companies, with assets of roughly $1.8 trillion in U.S. mutual funds.[4]

Shannon leads a team of researchers and analysts focused on finding out why clients do the things they do and how they're feeling about Vanguard products and services. Not long ago, they discovered that some of their clients were struggling with a particularly sensitive life event: specifically, the loss of a loved one and the inheritance process that followed. Clients had to deal with multiple people at Vanguard, which was frustrating. And the process was so complex that there were high error rates.

The reality is that the process of transferring assets when someone passes away *is* complex, for a variety of valid reasons. Those reasons, including legal requirements and tax implications, mean that each step of the process is best handled by the appropriate experts. And at each handoff of any process, there is an opportunity for error.

But here's a different and more compelling reality: Clients going through an extremely emotional time in their lives don't want to retell their story to one expert after another or deal with any more problems than they've already got.

To improve this client journey, Vanguard brought in process experts from its Center for Excellence. These experts quickly realized that the ecosystem that supports the journey extends to professionals outside of Vanguard, like the lawyers and accountants who do work on behalf of their clients. To make life easier for their clients overall, not just when they're dealing with Vanguard, the team needed to understand those relationships, as well.

The process team met with a law firm to understand how Vanguard's actions impacted attorneys when they dealt with Vanguard clients. They also met with a funeral director to understand how people feel and act during various stages of grief. As a result of their findings, Vanguard completely transformed the customer experience ecosystem that supports this particular journey. They eliminated the need for talking to multiple Vanguard employees by assigning each client a single point of contact: one person from a centralized group of experts responsible for making sure that everything goes smoothly for the family.

The result is a faster process with fewer errors. But that's not what their customers focus on most. By early 2011, when the new process had been in place for only a short time, Vanguard had already received more than two hundred letters from clients saying what a fantastic experience they'd had during such a tough time. Shannon read us quotes from some of the letters. They don't start out by saying that Vanguard got everything right. Instead, they start with comments like this one: "You were compassionate and had obvious care and concern for my welfare."

If you want to solve your most sensitive customer experience problems and turn your customers into advocates, then you must also learn how to nurture your customer experience ecosystem, as Vanguard did. Right now we're going to take the critical first step on that path by understanding the components of a customer experience ecosystem and how they interrelate.

Customer Experience Ecosystems Deconstructed

Just like a natural ecosystem, your customer experience ecosystem consists of living beings. These are the customers, employees, and

Figure 3-1: The Players in Your Customer Experience Ecosystem

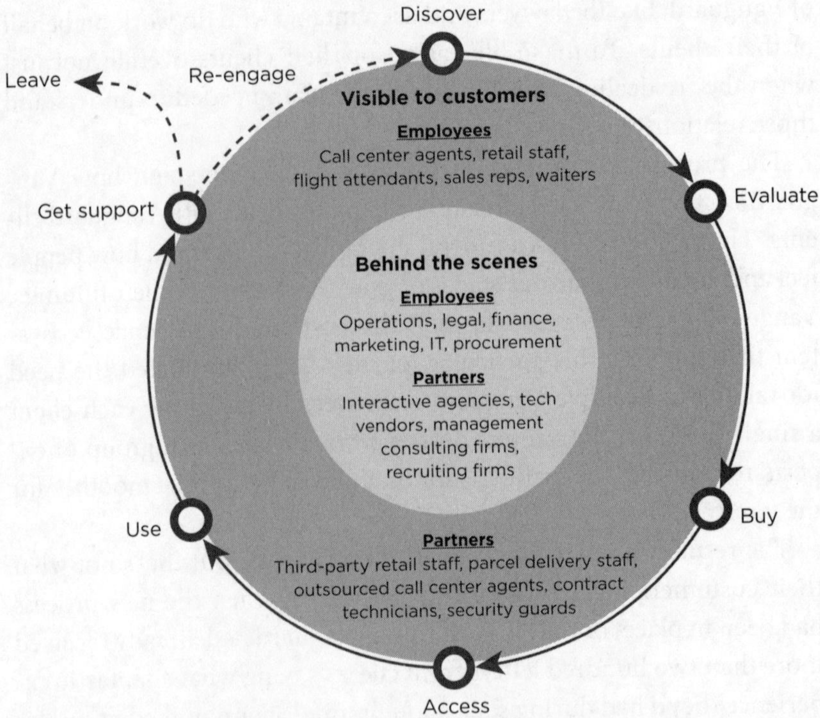

partner companies who interact with each other, either directly or indirectly, along a customer journey (see figure 3-1). The ecosystem also includes nonliving components, like the policies, processes, and technologies that lay down rails for how people interact.

In a healthy customer experience ecosystem, each of the parties' actions benefit the other parties in the system. That leads to balance — think Zion National Park before the tourists arrived. But here's your challenge: All of the parties have unique needs that can bring them into conflict with each other.

To John Birrer's point, this conflict isn't driven by malice. Many of your employees and partners simply don't understand how their actions affect others in the ecosystem and, ultimately, the customer experience. Yet without this understanding they'll focus on getting their own needs met regardless of the impact on others. Ironically, this self-defeating behavior drags them down as well.

For example, your executives need to drive revenue growth and profitability. That can lead them to pursue policies that chase customers away, like fees that seem reasonable from their perspective but infuriate the people who must pay them. That's what happened in September 2011, when Bank of America officials proposed what they probably believed to be a modest five-dollar monthly fee for the use of debit cards.

From the insider perspective of a bank executive, debit-card transactions cost the bank money to process. Why shouldn't consumers pay those costs plus markup in return for the convenience? Fair's fair, right? Except that consumers didn't see it that way. From their outside-in perspective, debit cards had long taken the place of cash in daily customer journeys like buying a cup of coffee or a bag of groceries. Why should they pay for access to their own money sitting in their own accounts any more than they'd pay to take cash out of their wallets? Consumers rose up in protest and Bank of America dropped the proposed fee a month later — after an upsurge in closed accounts.[5]

Companies can avoid embarrassing mistakes like this one by making sure that everyone in the ecosystem understands the needs of the other players and how their actions impact customer journeys. That's true no matter who those players are. They could be middle managers seeking to cut costs, frontline staff hoping to get through the day without battling angry customers, partners looking to meet their contractual obligations — or the customers themselves.

How can you help those players understand the ways in which their own actions ripple through the broader ecosystem? The best way is to deconstruct the ecosystem by mapping it.

Ecosystem Maps: A Systematic Approach to Improving Customer Experience

Ecosystem maps systematically uncover the customer experience ecosystem's hidden dynamics. What's more, they avoid the pitfalls of other methods used to accomplish the same task. For example, the simplest and perhaps most common technique for digging into any given customer experience problem is to pick a single instance of customer pain and then look for its root cause with the "5 Whys" method: Just start with a problem and work back to the problem's root cause by repeatedly asking "why?"[6]

But the 5 Whys have a severe limitation as they're applied by most people. Take the Charter software installation dilemma, which could have gone something like this. Problem: The router software can't be installed. Why? It's incompatible with our customers' hardware. Why? The third party that makes the software didn't account for all the possible hardware configurations. Why? We didn't tell them about all of our customers' hardware configurations. Why? We didn't think of it. Solution: Let's tell the third-party software provider about the hardware configurations and they'll fix the problem. Great! And we didn't even need all five of our whys!

If that sounds good to you, consider this: If John Birrer had taken that straight-line approach, he would have missed the fact that the service technicians *could* have installed the software — if they hadn't been prohibited from doing that by the legal department. Which means that the situation John was able to improve almost immediately would have instead waited for the new software release from Charter's partner.

Worse, John might not have realized that the legal department — as well as the sales department and the finance department — were complicit in this problem at all. That would have left most of Charter's ecosystem in the unhealthy state that caused the problem in the first place *and would have no doubt caused similar problems in the future.*

In contrast, a customer experience ecosystem map is simple enough for the average business person to create, understand, and use. At the same time, it's powerful enough to uncover the complete network of interconnected relationships that impact your customer experience each and every day.

One reason the tool works so well is that it starts small. It has to: Realistically, you won't be able to map the entire customer experience ecosystem for every type of customer you support and every single journey they take. That would be like trying to map the natural ecosystem for planet Earth.

Instead, begin by mapping the ecosystem that supports a single but very important customer journey.

How to Create a Customer Experience Ecosystem Map, Step by Step

In May 2011, we brought seven chief customer officers together as part of a networking event. They worked at companies with names you'd know, in a variety of industries, both business-to-consumer and business-to-business. We introduced them to the concept of ecosystem mapping by having them create their own maps. We'll use their experience to show you what to do to create your own map.

This introductory exercise took our participants just under two hours. To try this out for the first time and get a sense of how the process works, you'll want to reserve about that much time for yourself. You won't need sophisticated tools: poster paper, three packs of colored sticky notes (in different colors), several sheets of colored stickers, and some markers. When you're done, you'll have a basic understanding of the concepts involved as well as a simple but sound ecosystem map that you can put to immediate use. And even though you'll develop a more advanced understanding of how to create and use ecosystem maps in the future — and invest far more than two hours to create maps of far more complex customer journeys — the fundamentals you're about to learn will remain the same over time.

First, pick an important target customer and think of a problematic journey for that customer. It doesn't matter whether that customer journey involves buying a product or service, using that product or service, getting support, or whatever — just so long as the journey causes significant pain for an important customer. You'll also want to make sure that the journey you select is one you understand well, otherwise you won't be able to complete the exercise without running off to do research.

Next, write down the series of actions that the customer takes as part of that problematic journey. For example, "opens bill and reads it," "sees charge that looks wrong," and "calls customer care to get billing details." Write each of these actions on a separate blue sticky note and place the notes in a row across the top of the sheet of poster paper (see figure 3-2). In working with our chief customer officers, the journeys were remarkably similar in length, despite the diversity of industries, customers, and problem types — ranging from eight to eleven steps. That's about the right number of steps for a journey you're tackling in your first outing, especially in a compressed time frame like this two-hour exercise.

Next, write down all the people and groups that your customer interacts with at each step, like a call center agent or someone in the billing department. Do the same thing for objects or systems that the customer touches — like a mobile phone or a paper bill. We had our chief customer officers put the people or groups onto pink sticky notes, the objects or systems on yellow sticky notes — use whatever color scheme works for you, as long as you're consistent. Then place both sets of notes on the poster paper, lined up under the relevant steps in the process (see figure 3-3).

Draw a horizontal line across the middle of the poster paper, below the notes you've placed on it so far. This is the "line of visibility." Your customers can see everything above it — the people, products, systems, snail mail, email or whatever — that they interact with. Everything you're about to put below the line is completely invisible to your customer, despite the fact that what they don't know is often the thing that hurts them.

Using sticky notes in another color, post the actions, people, groups, objects, and systems that support the above-the-line parts of the ecosystem (see figure 3-4). These should include people and things like your bill designer, your bill printer, the action of printing the bill, the IT system that supplies the data that goes into your bill, your IT department that maintains the system that provides the data that goes into the bill . . . you get the picture. That process will take a little longer than the previous steps — it took our chief customer officers about a half hour.

Then the fun begins. You're going to need to put colored dots on the sticky notes. With our chief customer officers, we used little colored stickers so we could make changes on the fly by moving them around. In a pinch, you can just make do with colored markers (you'll just end up rewriting some sticky notes). Put green dots on each part of your ecosystem — each sticky note — that is working well *from the perspective of the person who was touching it.* Tag parts of the ecosystem that are making people unhappy with yellow dots, and parts of the ecosystem that are making people very unhappy with red dots.

The results we got with our chief customer officers were very much what we described for John Birrer at the beginning of this chapter (see figure 3-5). It's almost certainly what you'll see as well. Customer interactions with people, objects, or systems along their journey turned red well before employee or partner interactions did. Some employee and partner interactions stayed green despite the fact that they were a root cause of customer grief.

We had expected something like this outcome. But even we were surprised by the consistently repeated pattern of unhappy customers let down by happy, oblivious employees and partners. Since that first session we've repeated this exercise with other groups, and the result is *always* thc samc.

By using the process we just described, you can get started *today* on finding and fixing customer experience problems. Don't hesitate to take this first step — it will help you right now and start you down a path to something even more powerful in the future.

How far can you take ecosystem mapping over time? As you develop a deeper understanding of your customers and their journeys, and as you involve customers and other people in your company in this process, you can use your map to help transform every aspect of the customer experience. That's what Virgin Media is doing in the U.K. today.

CASE STUDY: ECOSYSTEM MAPPING AT VIRGIN MEDIA

Sean Risebrow is director of customer experience for Virgin Media in the U.K., the largest Virgin company in the world. It's also

Figure 3-2: Customer Journey

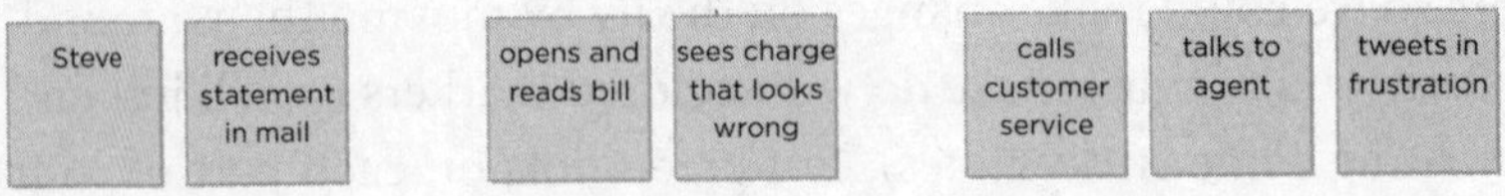

Figure 3-3: What the Customer Sees Along the Journey

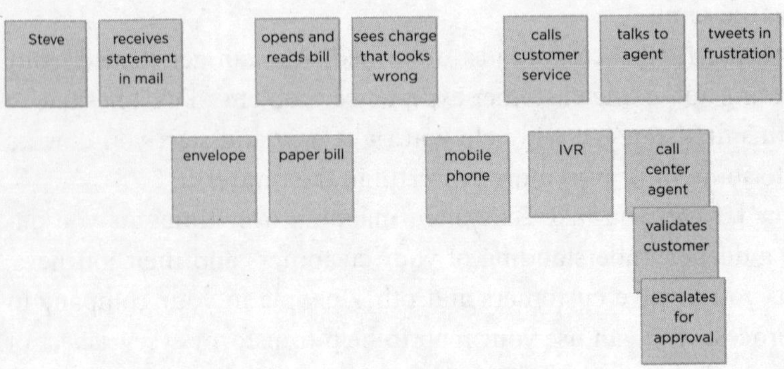

Figure 3-4: What the Customer Can't See That Affects the Journey

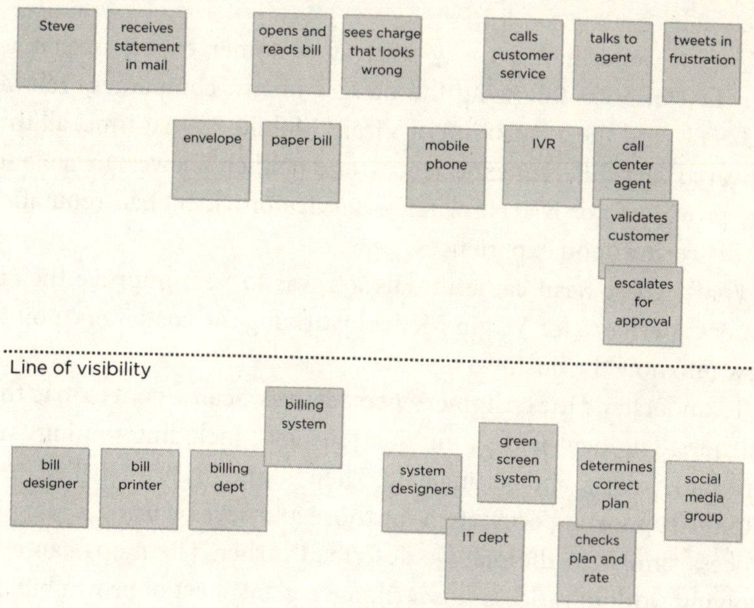

Figure 3-5: What's Wrong With This Picture?

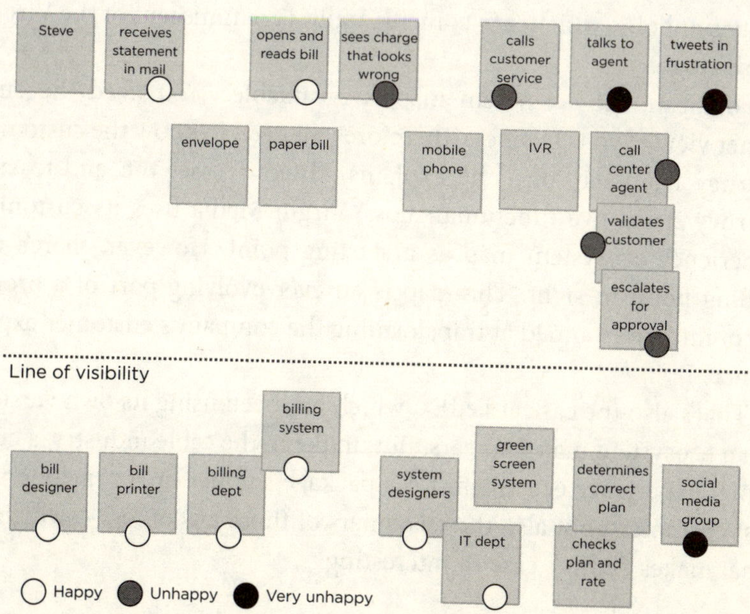

the U.K.'s largest mobile-network operator, and its second-largest provider of residential broadband, home phone, and pay TV services.

Virgin Media had a rocky start at customer experience. It was launched in 2007 following the merger of two companies, Telewest and NTL, and the acquisition of Virgin Mobile. At that time, all three delivered very different experiences, and neither Telewest (a cable service provider) nor NTL (a wireless service provider) had reputations for delivering good experiences.[7]

That's where Sean came in. His job was to help improve the customer experience for Virgin Media by driving the customers' point of view into how the business operates.

To understand the customers' perspectives, Sean set out to map their journeys. He identified six unique journeys, including joining (subscribing), paying, and getting help. Then he and his team drilled down into the supporting ecosystem for those journeys by using a mapping process similar to the one we described earlier. The map—an ever-evolving work in process—is striking: a giant sheet of brown butcher paper covered in red pieces of tape and multicolored sticky notes. It links all six journeys together in a continuous flow shaped like an infinity symbol—which, not coincidentally, is reminiscent of the Virgin Media logo.

For Sean, the ecosystem map is invaluable. "You need the customer view of your business, therefore you need to know the customer journey from day one," he explains. "In our case, the end-to-end journey spans five functional silos." Virgin Media uses its customer experience ecosystem map as a starting point. However, there's no ending point in sight. The map is an ever-evolving part of a broad set of initiatives aimed at transforming the company's customer experience.

That's also the case at FedEx, which has been using its own version of an ecosystem map for years. But unlike in the cable industry, a customer experience ecosystem for a package shipper might include not just customers, but also the customers of those customers—which is what makes FedEx's case so interesting.

CASE STUDY: FEDEX TAKES CHARGE OF ITS EXTENDED ECOSYSTEM

Debbie Newport leads the channel strategy and orchestration team at FedEx. As we mentioned in chapter 1, FedEx has a long history of taking customer experience *very* seriously: The shipping giant has a customer experience steering committee that meets monthly, chaired by its founder, chairman, president, and CEO, Fred Smith.

Although it doesn't call it "ecosystem mapping," FedEx conducts what is essentially an ecosystem mapping exercise. It's been doing it for over a decade. The way it works is that the shipping giant created a map of its customers' journeys, which it refers to as the "customer corridor" — the path customers go down as they interact with FedEx.

Every year, FedEx conducts research to determine what moments matter most to customers as they move along the corridor — moments like receiving a delivery. FedEx drills down to fully understand how what it does determines the quality of the customer experience during those moments. When they find problems, they launch projects to fix them. Those projects get reviewed by the customer experience steering committee, so you had better believe that the problems get resolved.

In 2008, Debbie Newport's group was created to solve a specific kind of problem. These problems occurred when customers moved from one channel to another, like going from a website to a phone agent. One of the hardest parts of tackling this challenge was knowing where to start. "You just don't change the ecosystem in a week," Debbie explains. "We were boiling the ocean with two hundred and fifty touchpoints. So we backed up to the forty-eight touchpoints that customers use most often. Then we took the time to map out those forty-eight in extreme detail across all customer segments."

Her team was able to determine logical bundles of touchpoints that customers cross regularly, like going from a "track a shipment" page on a website to a phone agent who can tell them why they didn't see their package information online. Next they brought in the customer corridor research to identify opportunities for improvement. By analyzing the emotional drivers of customer loyalty, they were able to determine which improvement projects offered the greatest opportunities for moving the loyalty needle.

The next step for Debbie's team was to engage the business owners of the touchpoints in her improvement projects. If you've ever shown up at a colleague's door to help fix a business problem, you know it can be a sensitive situation. You run the risk of saying, "Hi, I'm here to help," and having that heard as, "Hi, I'm here to force you to change." And in the words of the immortal Scott Adams, creator of *Dilbert*, "Change is good. You go first."

But that sensitivity to change didn't materialize. In fact, Debbie's reception within FedEx was extremely positive. According to Laurie Tucker, senior vice president of corporate marketing and Debbie's ultimate boss, "You might have expected that other departments would have been resistant to Debbie showing up to help them improve their experience. But the other departments were thrilled. They'd say, 'I always knew I had this problem but I can't go to my peer and say you need to make these changes to solve my problems.'"

As part of a natural evolution, Debbie's team recently extended the scope of its work. This involved reaching out to other companies with which FedEx shares customers — like retailers who ship products to consumers through FedEx. This turned out to be tricky, but they had to do it. Here's why.

One of the biggest customer experience challenges FedEx confronts is the problem of what happens when a residential customer — a consumer — misses a delivery. The easy part for FedEx is putting a sticker on the door that notifies the customer. The hard part is actually getting the package to the customer after that happens.

Although FedEx has made substantial improvements to the missed-delivery experience on their end, there was a limit to how much they could do. That's because in order to really solve the problem they needed to change a part of the ecosystem that wasn't under their control. They had to design a solution for a problem that started when the consumer ordered a product from a retailer or a manufacturer that offered them delivery options and collected delivery information.

This was a "crossing the channel" problem on steroids. If the retailer or manufacturer didn't collect the right information via phone or website — like the hours when the recipient would be home — and then pass it to FedEx, the delivery failed. But FedEx had little leverage to get the right information collected and passed along because the retailer or manufacturer was one of their business-to-business customers — someone who paid FedEx, not the other way around.

Analysis showed that a small number of very large FedEx business customers accounted for a disproportionate number of missed deliveries to consumers. These were the businesses that were *not* getting needed delivery information to FedEx. It was clear that to get more packages into the hands of the intended consumer recipients, FedEx needed to fix the part of the ecosystem controlled by its business customers. But when FedEx account managers first offered their business customers help with reorchestrating their part of the ecosystem, they hit a brick wall. Unlike what happened *inside* FedEx, this time the message that got heard really was something along the lines of, "Hi, I'm here because I need you to change."

That's when Debbie's team swooped in with a different approach — the same one they'd proved inside FedEx. According to Laurie Tucker, "When the channel management team showed our business customers how failed deliveries were costing them money — because their customer was not getting the benefit of their service or product — then it was 'Aha! Now I see why I need your help.'"

After that, the result was all upside. Consumers had a better delivery experience. FedEx won loyalty from its business customers. The business customers got products to *their* customers — consumers — as intended.

And it all started with understanding the customer experience ecosystem.

If You Want to Be in the Game, You Must Understand Your Ecosystem

We can't emphasize this strongly enough: If you want to make major improvements to the customer experience offered by your company, you must start by understanding your customer experience ecosystem.

Otherwise you'll only solve part of your problem. That's what *would* have happened to FedEx if it hadn't included its business customers in its efforts to solve the failed delivery problem. And that's what *is* happening at companies all across the globe, right now.

Understanding your customer experience ecosystem is a necessary first step if you want to be in the game. Winning the game—by delivering a customer experience that's superior to the one offered by your competitors—takes more. If you want to win more customers, keep them longer, and maximize the resulting profits, you'll need to master the six disciplines of a mature customer experience organization.

We'll introduce you to those six disciplines in our next chapter. Then we'll show you how smart organizations have gained a sustainable competitive advantage by moving up the customer experience maturity curve.

PART II

THE SIX DISCIPLINES OF CUSTOMER EXPERIENCE

4

From Bumper Sticker to Business Discipline

In January 2010, USAA flipped the switch on a radical reorganization that had been in the works for two years, placing all nine thousand customer-facing employees — including its marketing, channel management, sales, and service functions — under its executive vice president of member experience, Wayne Peacock.

To the outside world this might have seemed like a puzzling move. USAA, which provides insurance, banking, and investment products to 8 million U.S. military families, wasn't reacting to a downturn in its business. In fact, when it made the decision to reorganize, its business was strong and growing in the midst of a recession.[1] So why risk messing with success?

The answer is that although USAA was already a leader at customer experience, its executives viewed it as somewhere in the middle of its journey to become fully customer-centric.[2] They were right — they'd hit a limit with the approach that had worked so well for them in the past.

Up until that time, USAA's success at customer experience had been driven mainly by its customer-centric culture. That culture is defined by the company's mission to improve the financial well-being of its members for generations to come.[3] When Wayne addresses new hires in the company's financial foundation boot camp, he tells them: "We have a calling that is bigger than ourselves. We have a purpose that is more important than the products and services that we sell."

When you've got a culture like that, employees do the right thing for customers by reflex. And when they're performing well-understood tasks within a single line of business — settling insurance claims — it's not hard for them to know what the right thing to do is.

But it's *not* always easy to know what to do, because USAA members *don't* interact with the company from the perspective of simple tasks that fall neatly within a single line of business. Instead they interact with USAA around messy, complex life events, like relocating to a new city.

"When an army colonel graduates war college at Carlisle, Pennsylvania, and moves to Fort Carson," Wayne explains, "the story is much bigger than homeowner's insurance and a new mortgage. In six to eight weeks, he will most likely be deployed to Afghanistan. And oh, by the way, this is the second time in twelve months that he has uprooted his family and moved them."

As USAA more fully understood the full range of what was going on in this member's life, it became clear that the officer needed help with a series of challenges that included getting a Realtor, finding a home, buying that home at a good price, getting a mortgage, and getting insurance — all in under two months, while helping his family adjust to a new city. Unfortunately, most USAA employees didn't understand that end-to-end customer journey. Their business wasn't designed to help them understand members from a perspective that crossed product lines. And even if employees *had* understood the members' journeys, USAA products and services weren't designed to support those journeys. The organization just wasn't built that way.

USAA concluded that in order to be fully customer-centric, it needed to operate from the perspective of its members. That required a world-class voice-of-the-customer program so USAA could understand member needs in new and deeper ways. It required a customer segmentation scheme based on those needs to guide the design of products and services. It required an organization and governance structure that would let USAA go to market in a radically different fashion that spanned traditional product silos. In short, what USAA needed was a radical transformation in the way it did business.

Wayne sums it up this way: "We iterated on customer experience over a five-year period. We made incremental progress. But you come to an inflection point where, if you want to go farther and you want to go faster, you have to make a change." In this case, a *big* change.

Customer Experience Grows Up

Is the lesson of USAA that you must reorganize and put everyone under a customer experience czar? No, although that can be very helpful under the right circumstances. The lesson of USAA is that to achieve the full potential of customer experience as a business strategy, you have to change the way you run your business. You must manage from the perspective of your customers, and you must do it in a systematic, repeatable, and disciplined way.[4]

It's easy to miss this point. As we've seen, so many companies fall short at customer experience that being barely competent can make you a leader in many industries. And we've seen how mapping a customer experience ecosystem and fixing the problems you find can save a large company billions of dollars, increase its revenue by billions of dollars, or both. You might easily decide that ecosystem mapping, combined with a find-and-fix approach, is all you'll ever need to maximize your potential.

But that's not true. Ultimately, you'll want to break out of the find-and-fix cycle by changing the way people in the ecosystem operate, so you can avoid creating these problems in the first place. You'll also want to find ways to differentiate yourself that can't be easily copied. To do both of these things, you need to make a leap. You need to go from ad hoc efforts to improve customer experience all the way to a comprehensive solution where you systematically envision, design, implement, and manage the customer experience that you deliver.

The Six Essential Customer Experience Disciplines

All mature companies routinely perform a set of sound, standard practices that result in a high-quality outcome.[5] That's just as true for the accounting firm that does your books as it is for the utility company that supplies your power. It's true for manufacturers — they don't get up in the morning and start pondering how they'll produce high-quality widgets that day. Similarly, retailers have practices for keeping their supply chains flowing and their shelves stocked, and media companies have practices for getting the news online and into print. That's how grown-ups do business.

Companies that want to produce a high-quality customer experience also need to routinely perform a set of sound, standard practices. These practices fall under six high-level disciplines: strategy, customer understanding, design, measurement, governance, and culture (see table 4-1).

Megan Burns, Forrester's lead analyst on customer experience maturity, uncovered the six disciplines by reviewing Forrester's customer experience research going back to 1998. She also studied programs at firms that get high marks in our Customer Experience Index. "My goal was to create a framework that summarizes known best practices in a way that's easy for anyone to understand," she explains. "It gives people who are new to customer experience a vision of the future that's realistic but not overwhelming. And for those practitioners on the customer experience journey, it offers a way to organize everything they have to think about into manageable chunks."

These disciplines represent the areas where companies that are consistently great at customer experience excel. If you want to deliver a great customer experience, they are where you need to focus, too.

Table 4-1: Mature Customer Experience Organizations Excel at Six Disciplines

STRATEGY PRACTICES

- **Define** a customer experience strategy that describes the intended customer experience.
- **Align** the strategy with overall company strategy.
- **Align** the strategy with the organization's brand attributes.
- **Share** the strategy with all employees (e.g., distribute documentation, conduct training sessions).

CUSTOMER-UNDERSTANDING PRACTICES

- **Solicit** feedback from customers about their experiences with the company (e.g., through surveys or interviews).
- **Collect** unsolicited feedback from customers about their experiences with the organization (e.g., by mining calls, email, or social media posts).
- **Gather** input from employees about their experiences with customers and their role in delivering the customer experience.
- **Conduct** observational research studies in customers' natural environment (e.g., in-home observations, shadowing).
- **Analyze** customer insight drawn from across research techniques and organizational boundaries to identify key customer pain points and opportunities.
- **Document** customer understanding in a way that is easy for employees to understand and use (e.g., personas, customer journey maps, and role-based voice of the customer reports).
- **Share** customer understanding with all employees (e.g., distribute documentation, conduct training sessions).

DESIGN PRACTICES

- **Follow** a defined customer experience design process any time a new experience is introduced or an existing experience is changed in a significant way.

- **Use** customer understanding deliverables and insights to focus and define requirements for projects that affect customer experiences.
- **Engage** customers, partners, and employees as part of the experience design process (i.e., co-creation).
- **Use** iterative ideation, prototyping, and evaluation as part of the experience design process.
- **Identify** the set of complex interdependencies among people, processes, and technologies that shape interactions with customers (i.e., the customer experience ecosystem).

MEASUREMENT PRACTICES

- **Define** a customer experience quality framework that aligns with how customers judge an experience and is consistent across the organization (e.g., channels, lines of business).
- **Define** the subsets of customer experience metrics that show how each group, role, and individual in the organization contributes to customer experience quality.
- **Measure** how customers perceive their experiences with the organization based on the criteria in the customer experience quality framework.
- **Collect** descriptive metrics about each experience (e.g., length of interactions, errors encountered) that provide context for customer perceptions.
- **Analyze** customer experience metrics to determine differences in experience quality among key customer segments, tasks (e.g., buying a product, getting service), or aspects of the experience (e.g., friendliness of staff).
- **Model** the relationship between drivers of customer experience quality (e.g., speed, accuracy); customer perceptions of their experiences (e.g., easy, reliable); and business outcomes (e.g., increased sales, calls to care centers averted).
- **Share** customer experience metrics and models with all employees (e.g., distribute reports and dashboards, conduct training sessions).

GOVERNANCE PRACTICES

- **Define** a consistent set of customer experience standards across the organization.
- **Include** alignment with the customer experience strategy as a criterion for evaluating project funding and prioritization decisions.
- **Include** impact to customer experience as a criterion for business decisions about policies, processes, technology, and communications.
- **Maintain** a dedicated queue of customer experience improvement projects.
- **Review** customer experience program status and metrics regularly to monitor progress toward business goals, adjusting tactics or resource allocations if needed.
- **Assign** role-specific customer experience management tasks to employees as a requirement of their positions.
- **Evaluate** employee performance against role-specific customer experience metrics.
- **Facilitate** the necessary coordination across groups that share responsibility for a given experience.
- **Whenever** a change is approved to a policy, business process, product, technology, or other system that affects the customer experience, proactively redesign that experience to reflect the change.

CULTURE PRACTICES

- **Screen** candidates for customer-centric values as part of the hiring and selection process.
- **Screen** candidates for the specific skills needed to deliver on the organization's customer experience strategy as part of the hiring and selection process.
- **Provide** training to help new and existing employees build and maintain the skills they need to deliver on their part of the organization's customer experience strategy.

- **Communicate** the importance of customer experience to employees, customers, and other stakeholders (e.g., shareholders, partners).
- **Collect** and share stories of customer experience best practices across the employee base.
- **Perform** rituals and routines that reinforce the importance of customer experience and what it takes to deliver it.
- **Use** informal rewards and celebrations to highlight exemplary customer-centric behavior.
- **Connect** formal reward structures (e.g., raises, bonuses, promotions) to performance on customer experience metrics.

1) Strategy

The strategy discipline is your game plan. It's a set of practices for crafting a customer experience strategy, aligning it with the company's overall strategy and brand attributes, and then sharing that strategy with employees to guide decision making and prioritization across the organization.

The customer experience strategy defines the intended experience. For example, the experience at Costco—a warehouse store in the United States where customers push giant carts through huge aisles stacked high with value-priced products—is very different from the experience at an Apple store, where customers see a comparatively sparse selection of pricey products and get expert assistance with picking the right one. Costco's experience aligns with its overall strategy as a cost leader; Apple's aligns with its strategy of innovation.

The strategy discipline is critical because it provides the blueprint for the experience you design, deliver, manage, and measure. Without it, you, your employees, and your partners won't know whether to deliver an experience like the one at Costco, at Apple, or somewhere else entirely. Worse, you could deliver a Frankenstein experience of mismatched parts, like putting an Apple genius bar in the middle of a Costco store where customers wouldn't care about it but would worry that prices were going up to pay for it.

2) Customer Understanding

The customer understanding discipline is a set of practices that creates a consistent shared understanding of who customers are, what they want and need, and how they perceive the interactions they're having with your company today. In other words, it's the thing that replaces everyone's best guesses about customers with real, actionable insights about customers.

The customer understanding discipline includes a number of research practices such as conducting observational research studies (think of it as studying customers in the wild), collecting feedback (both solicited and unsolicited), and gathering input from employees about their interactions with your customers. The discipline also includes the practice of analyzing the information you collected through research. A third set of practices involves documenting your findings in ways that are easy for employees to understand and sharing those insights with your employees, through workshops and other methods.

The customer understanding discipline is bedrock. Without this level of insight, you're liable to frustrate and annoy your customers with your well-intentioned efforts to serve them. When Geek Squad, the U.S.-based computer services company, interacts with its customers, it deals with them differently depending on which customer archetype they correspond to. A customer could be "Jill," a suburban mom who uses her computer and other information technology daily. To her, technology is like plumbing and Geek Squad is like a plumbing company that she calls when she wants a leak fixed.

However, a Geek Squad customer could also be "Daryl," who loves getting his hands dirty but sometimes gets into trouble when one of his tech projects goes awry. Trying to engage a Jill in the same way as a Daryl would be disastrous. When Geek Squad is at Daryl's house he enjoys chatting about the gory details of the latest innovations, a conversation that would bore Jill senseless.[6]

3) Design

The practices in the design discipline help organizations envision and then implement customer interactions that meet or exceed customer needs. It spans the complex systems of people, products, interfaces, services, and spaces that your customers encounter in retail locations, over the phone, or through digital media like websites and mobile apps.

Design spells the difference between a symphony orchestra performance and a garage band jam session. The orchestra performance is carefully arranged, rehearsed, and executed — like the customer experience at top companies. The jam session just sort of happens, with varying levels of quality — like what we've all encountered at companies we've stopped doing business with over time.

Practices in the design discipline include following a formal design process. Other practices include using the insights from the customer understanding discipline to focus and define requirements; identifying the interdependencies among people, processes, and technologies that shape interactions with the ecosystem; engaging customers, employees, and partners as part of the experience design process; and using iterative idea generation, prototyping, and evaluation.

Design weeds out bad ideas early and focuses your customer experience efforts on changes that really matter to customers. By leveraging expertise and ideas from customers, employees, and partners, it encourages creative solutions — and helps avoid missteps by grounding those solutions in reality.

Kevin Peters has implemented many of the practices in this discipline at Office Depot. To envision and define the store experience his customers want to have, Office Depot built a "planogram lab" — a prototype store in a nondescript office complex near company headquarters in south Florida. That lets him bring in customers to help design the shopping experience that's just right for them, and then test those designs out on other customers. Everything from the amount of floor space to where products appear on shelves to where employees stand when they stock those shelves was designed from the ground up.

4) Measurement

The measurement discipline is a set of practices that lets organizations quantify customer experience quality in a consistent manner across the enterprise, and deliver actionable insights to employees and partners. This is how you put customer experience metrics on par with traditional business metrics such as sales and profitability.

The practices that let organizations quantify customer experience quality include choosing the specific metrics they'll use to conduct their measurement, then defining the subsets of those metrics that are relevant for each group, role, and individual in the organization.

Practices that help firms deliver actionable insights to the employees and partners include: measuring how customers perceive their experiences with the organization based on the criteria in the framework; collecting descriptive metrics (e.g., length of interactions, errors encountered); analyzing customer experience metrics to determine differences in experience quality among key customer segments, tasks (like getting service), or aspects of the experience (like friendliness of staff); modeling the relationship between drivers of customer experience quality (like speedy delivery), customer perceptions of their experiences (like ease or reliability), and business outcomes (like increased sales); and sharing customer experience metrics and models with all employees.

This discipline is key because it lets companies understand the current state of the customer experience they provide, uncover opportunities for improvement, and track progress over time. It connects the dots starting with what needs to be done to improve customer experience, all the way to the business benefits of what has been done.

The customer experience team at technology giant EMC has a sophisticated measurement framework. It first identifies the aspects of the customer experience that drive the most loyalty, like ease of doing business. It then prioritizes those drivers based on customers' satisfaction with each driver and the impact of each driver on the overall experience. That tells EMC which things to fix immediately, which to improve over time, which to maintain at current levels, and which to promote as strengths.[7]

5) Governance

The customer experience governance discipline is a set of practices that helps organizations manage customer experience in a proactive and disciplined way. If your customer experience strategy is your game plan, then the governance discipline supplies your referees and your rule book. It does this through a mix of assigning responsibilities and changing business processes.

The practices related to assigning responsibilities include giving customer experience management tasks to specific roles within the organization, and facilitating coordination across groups that share responsibility for a given experience.

The practices related to processes include defining a consistent set of customer experience standards; including impact to customer experience as a criterion for major business decisions; including alignment with the customer experience strategy as a criterion for evaluating project funding and prioritization decisions; maintaining a dedicated queue of customer experience improvement projects; reviewing customer experience program status and metrics regularly; evaluating employee performance against role-specific customer experience metrics; and proactively redesigning an experience to reflect changes in policies, business processes, products, technologies, or other systems that affect the experience.

The governance practice is essential because it holds people accountable for their role in the customer experience ecosystem, and helps keep bad experiences from getting out the door. It also gives a boost to initiatives that improve customer experience.

Customer experience management practices hold people accountable in a number of ways. These range from executive oversight, like what the customer experience steering committee does at FedEx, to day-to-day coaching of frontline employees.

Processes help force customer experience concerns into the mix when making day-to-day business decisions. For example, Canada Post requires all funding requests from any department to answer ten customer-focused questions in the business case. This ensures that all leaders think not just about how their projects will affect the bottom line, but also about how they'll impact the customer experience.

6) Culture

The culture discipline consists of practices that create a system of shared values and behaviors that focus employees on delivering a great customer experience. You might think of it as the way you shape what your employees do when you're not in the room.[8] Practices in the culture discipline fall into three categories: hiring, socialization, and rewards.

Hiring practices include screening candidates for customer-centric values, and screening candidates for the specific skills needed to deliver on the organization's customer experience strategy. Of these two, the most important is screening for values — like commitment to helping customers. We've often heard this expressed as "hire the will, train the skill," which is shorthand for "it's easier to teach someone a skill than it is to change their core beliefs or personality."

Socialization practices include communicating the importance of customer experience to employees, customers, and other stakeholders; training new and existing employees in the skills they need to deliver on their part of the customer experience strategy; collecting and sharing stories of customer experience best practices across the employee base; and performing rituals and routines that reinforce the importance of customer experience. Of these, rituals and routines are the least understood yet most intriguing. You see them at companies like Umpqua Bank, where employees at all branch locations get together for five minutes each day for "motivational moments," taking turns sharing lessons they've learned that connect back to the customer.

Rewards practices include connecting formal rewards (e.g., bonuses, promotions) to performance on customer experience metrics and using informal awards and celebrations to highlight customer-centric behavior. Informal awards are often overlooked but they can be powerful motivators. For example, Starbucks encourages personal recognition with M.U.G. Awards, which partners give to employees as a thank-you for "moves of uncommon greatness."[9]

The culture discipline is perhaps the most powerful of all the disciplines because it embeds practices from the other five disciplines into employee DNA. Companies like Disney, Zappos, Southwest Airlines, Ritz-Carlton, and FedEx all point to their customer-centric cultures as key to their success. That's because this discipline turns customer experience excellence into a habit and makes future change easier by creating an ecosystem that's receptive to customer experience improvement efforts.

To understand how powerful a customer-centric culture can be, you don't have to look farther than the company we've already praised for its culture, USAA. When storms ravaged much of the United States in the spring of 2011, USAA representatives deployed to the devastated locations for twelve-hour shifts, seven days a week, over the course of eight weeks. USAA executives visited with them in the field, and employees at the home office connected with them to create a sense of teamwork. This behavior stemmed from the deeply held, shared belief that the field team was doing the most important work at the company: taking care of its members in their hour of need. As they like to say at USAA meetings, "We do the right thing because it's the right thing to do."

It's Commitment Time

Mastering the six essential disciplines of customer experience takes time and effort but *it's something that you have to do.* As we told you in chapter 1, this is the age of the customer. You're not going to succeed through manufacturing strength, distribution power, or information mastery—those have all been commoditized. And you can't win by controlling the flow of information about your products and services, either. Often your customers know more about your products, services, competitors, and pricing than you do — courtesy of the information age.

If you want to succeed, today and in the immediate future, you have to decide — right here, right now — to roll up your sleeves and do the work of building competence in these six disciplines. That may scare you. But what should scare you more is the thought of becoming irrelevant to your customers, which is what will happen if you don't take action.

You can take heart from knowing that many of your competitors don't even realize that the game has changed. Fewer still will understand, let alone undertake, the transformation process needed to get into the game. This hit home with Office Depot's Kevin Peters when he spoke at an investor's conference in mid-2011. On stage, he told the story of the transformation he was leading at Office Depot. The auditorium full of people included all of his competitors, from office-supply superstores to big-box retailers. As he was leaving the auditorium he overheard someone from a competitor say to a colleague, "That was really interesting. We have to send a memo out to our employees next week to tell them to treat customers well."

We hope it's clear to you by now that it's going to take a lot more than a memo for you to transform your business. But it's our intention to make your transformation process as easy as possible. Over the next few chapters we'll show you how to develop your capabilities in the six essential disciplines of customer experience. For each discipline, we'll give you examples of companies that have implemented best practices successfully. And we'll tie them all together with insight into how they relate to each other.

It's time to get started. Your customers and your company will be glad you did.

5

Strategy

FRANCISCO PITA WAS in a tough spot. The Airport Service Quality group had just published the results from its latest European passenger survey, and Faro airport in southern Portugal was at the bottom. So were some of the other airports managed by ANA Aeroportos de Portugal, the airport operator Francisco works for.

Many ANA managers were disappointed with the news, but as Faro airport's head of marketing and customer service, Francisco was especially troubled. "People today compare the service they get at an airport with the service they get at a hotel or retail store," he explains. Faro airport wasn't keeping up with their ever-growing expectations.

This wasn't just a matter of pride for Francisco — it was matter of profits. To understand his dilemma, you first need to understand an airport's business model. It makes money by bringing more passengers through its doors each day and getting those passengers to spend more money on goods and services throughout its terminals. It accomplishes this by attracting more airlines to fly more routes in and out of it. That's because an airport's real customers *aren't* travelers, they're the airlines that pay for using its gates and terminals. So for decades, Francisco and his ANA colleagues had focused primarily on airline relationships and infrastructure initiatives—think baggage transfers and runway maintenance.

Francisco knew that tending solely to behind-the-scenes logistics wouldn't cut it any longer. To compete in the fierce European market, he needed to turn his focus to the thousands of airline passengers that passed through his airport each day. But how?

Developing a better airport experience is a complicated matter. Air travelers might arrive at the airport in a taxi or via public transport, or they might park their cars in an off-site lot. Once in the airport, they may make purchases from any one of a large number of coffee shops, sit-down restaurants, and souvenir stores. They must make their way through a maze of security guards. And of course, the airlines themselves employ throngs of check-in and gate personnel. Past research showed that travelers saw the airport experience as a whole, and often didn't know where the airport's services ended and other companies' services began.

Two questions kept Francisco up at night: What role should the airport operator play in this complex ecosystem? And what type of passenger experience should it provide? He couldn't just start adopting random best practices from other airports—even if executed flawlessly, this approach would at best get him to parity with Faro's competitors. To draw passengers from other European airports while avoiding missteps that could waste millions of euros in facility changes, he needed a plan. He needed a passenger-experience strategy.

It turned out that Francisco wasn't the only one losing sleep. When he proposed to develop a strategy for improving the passenger experience in Faro, ANA's board of directors jumped on the opportunity to extend the initiative to all of ANA's eight airports. So Francisco engaged Engine Service Design in a multiphase project to help his organization understand passengers' needs and expectations throughout the travel experience and to translate those insights into a new vision for airport passenger services.

The team conducted in-airport interviews, studied passengers as they moved about the airport, and ultimately identified a set of commonly held needs and desires. For example, travelers wanted to feel prepared and enabled to make any necessary decisions about their onward travel, but even seasoned flyers felt a sense of stress and disorientation the moment they stepped off the jet bridge and into the terminal. Passengers also wanted a better sense of place, an environment that authentically reflected Portuguese culture.

From these discoveries, Engine and ANA identified three roles that defined how the airports should behave.

- **The advisor:** a knowledgeable resource that helps passengers arrive at the airport prepared and informs them of key information during and after their journey
- **The companion:** a helpful guide who knows what passengers like and creates a pleasant airport experience through tailored airport facilities
- **The hero:** a friend who provides help when passengers run into trouble, providing reassurance and helping them to get back on track

Once they had their passenger strategy in place, Engine and ANA were able to design a set of service offerings and airport interactions that supported these three behavioral roles. For example, they enhanced the airport's advisor role through open lounges with interactive monitors that provide travel information. To fulfill the companion role, the team developed concepts for breastfeeding facilities, vending machines filled with diapers and baby food, locker and stroller rental stations, and children's play areas that help reduce stress for families traveling with small children.

This strategy work has completely transformed ANA. Its airports are now equipped with solutions for specific passenger segments, such as families, groups, and premium travelers. And the passenger experience has become one of the main factors that Francisco and his colleagues take into account in a variety of business decisions.

Great Customer Experiences Don't Happen by Accident

Could Francisco and his colleagues have penned a list of new airport services without first developing an overarching strategy? Of course. Would those services have met passengers' needs, generated additional revenue for ANA, and attracted more airline routes? Perhaps, if they were lucky. Would those services have created a cohesive and consistent passenger experience, one that helped travelers know what to expect whenever they flew into Portugal? Definitely not.

Great customer experiences don't happen by accident. They're the result of countless deliberate decisions made by every single person in your customer experience ecosystem on a daily basis. To align those decisions, employees and partners need a shared vision: a customer experience strategy. Without that beacon, employees are forced to set out on a random walk, and their decisions and actions will inevitably be at odds with each other, despite all best intentions.

That's what happened recently at a large Internet company. The head of customer experience discovered three simultaneous projects in the support organization: one to move more customers to chat support, one to move customers away from chat support, and one to extend chat support to three additional languages. The three well-meaning project leaders sincerely believed that their individual initiatives would improve the support experience, yet none of them had any idea the other projects were even happening.

This scenario unfortunately repeats itself ad infinitum at companies across the globe. Why? Because most firms lack a customer experience strategy.

You wouldn't suggest that your company add headcount in a particular department, launch a new product line, acquire another firm, or approve a marketing campaign without knowing what its overall corporate strategy is. You shouldn't make decisions about how to interact with customers without a strategy, either.

Your Customer Experience Strategy Must Support Your Corporate Strategy

So what's the right customer experience for your company?[1] Unfortunately, most companies don't take the time to properly answer that question. They simply try to emulate one of the most famous customer experiences on the planet: Apple's.

Ever since the original iPod was introduced in 2001, companies in every industry have had Apple envy. For over a decade, executives have been asking us how they can become "the Apple of term life insurance" or "the Apple of retail auto parts." Citibank even went so far as to hire the same architectural firm that designed the Apple store concept for its flagship "branch of the future," a retail banking space that bears a striking resemblance to today's Apple stores.[2]

Here's the problem with that approach: Blatantly ripping off another company's customer experience — no matter how good it is — isn't just rude, it can be downright disastrous. Sure, the Apple customer experience fits Apple's relentless focus on design and innovation down to a T, but that doesn't mean it's the right customer experience for any other company. Is your corporate strategy the same as Apple's? If you answered no (and 99.99 percent of companies should fall into this category), then you need to focus on defining the customer experience that best aligns with the corporate vision your executive team has put forth — your company's target market, value proposition, unique strengths, financial objectives, and core values.

Consider car-sharing company Zipcar, whose business model is built around cost optimization through self-service. Members use the service as a cheaper alternative to buying a car, but far from feeling cheap, the Zipcar member experience feels fast and efficient. Members make reservations from the company's website or mobile apps, which also let them unlock the doors and honk the horn remotely — fun! A universal Zipcard enables members to access any of the company's cars in Canada, Spain, the U.K., and the United States. And the firm automatically posts details of every reservation to members' online accounts.

Contrast this customer experience with that offered by Box Home

Loans, a U.S.-based mortgage company that's driving growth by creating deep connections with a select customer group. Box Home Loans only targets customers with high credit scores who want to purchase owner-occupied property, and appeals to this select group by offering an empathetic and personalized customer experience along with its low rates. The same loan officer who provides the original quote stays with the customer throughout the application process and calls or emails every two to three days to provide a status update.

What would happen if Zipcar sent a concierge to greet customers every time they picked up a truck for a quick trip to IKEA? What if Box Home Loans made its customers complete every step of the loan process through self-service applications and get help from an online community? The wrong customer experience would confuse their customers at best, and send them racing off to a competitor at worst. That's why *your customer experience strategy must match your corporate strategy.*

In addition, your customer experience strategy must align with your brand attributes. That might seem obvious, but at many companies it's not — as a major retailer recently found out.

Your Customer Experience Strategy Must Align with Your Brand

The head of customer service at a major U.S. retailer called us for help with crafting a customer experience strategy for the store's nationwide contact center. We immediately asked him — and about ten of his direct reports, who were also on the line — what the company's key brand attributes and values were. Their response: dead silence. Not a single manager from the retailer's customer service organization could articulate what this well-known and beloved brand stood for, and they eventually admitted that none of them had ever spoken with the marketing or branding groups, which were located across the country.

We ended the phone call quickly and sent them off with homework to forge these new relationships and learn about their brand, and we were pretty adamant about not proceeding until they had done that step. Here's why: The retailer's marketing team spends millions of dollars to advertise every year, and each advertising message includes implicit (and sometimes explicit) promises about the experience customers can expect in stores, online, and on the phone. But the customer service team wasn't tuned into these messages. As such, they had no way to assess whether the decisions they made on a daily basis — like who to hire, what to say when they picked up a call, or how to resolve customer complaints — supported or undermined the company's promises. They had no way to determine what kinds of customer interactions were appropriate for their brand. And if they didn't know that, they'd almost certainly end up squandering that huge advertising budget.

You need to be able to guide the activities and decision making of employees at every level of your organization so that they can deliver on your company's brand promises. That's why *your customer experience strategy must also match your brand attributes and values.*

Executives at Holiday Inn understand this well. They translated the iconic hotel brand into a customer experience strategy before embarking on a major lobby-redesign initiative.

CASE STUDY: HOLIDAY INN'S NEW LOBBY EXPERIENCE REFLECTS THE HOTEL'S BRAND VALUES

"The hospitality industry is offering the same exact thing that it did a hundred years ago," laments Eric Nicolas. "A roof, a bed, and a meal." As director of global brand management for Holiday Inn, part of the InterContinental Hotels Group, he knows this won't fly in the age of the customer. "Today you have to give consumers more reasons to stay with you."

Holiday Inn recently completed a $1 billion brand refresh that included changes to bedding, bathroom products, and even the scent that greets guests as they walk into the brand's more than three thousand franchised hotels. But in the majority of its seven hundred and fifty properties with on-site restaurants, the hotel chain was still losing dinner customers to casual restaurants like Outback Steakhouse and Chili's Grill & Bar, which typically flank its properties. And in the

made to our customers and to each other." And Apoteket, Sweden's largest pharmacy chain, created a five-minute video showing how its new at-home and in-store health-checkup service should feel for customers.

Executives at multinational bank BBVA also found success with these approaches—and then they took things to a whole new level.

CASE STUDY: BBVA MAKES ITS CUSTOMER EXPERIENCE STRATEGY COME ALIVE

Many of today's banking practices are rooted in inside-out thinking. "Our ways of banking and our customer experience represent the ideal solution for the bank based on current technologies, existing processes, and how we've worked internally for decades," says Beatriz Lara Bartolomé, chief innovation officer at BBVA, one bank that's not content with the status quo. "What we want to do is develop a system that represents the ideal future solution for *customers*—and then find a way to make that system work for the bank."

BBVA engaged Continuum to help develop that strategy. After months of customer research, data analysis, workshops, and brainstorming, the team developed a set of guiding principles such as this one: "Human understanding—Instead of just selling to our customers, BBVA staff will work more closely with them, to help them understand what they really want from their financial futures and map out the steps they'll need to get there." They sketched out new interactions that would enable customers to share the same digital screens as advisors (instead of looking at the back of advisors' computers) and to get cash from existing pharmacies and bodegas with their mobile phones. They indicated how these scenarios related to key brand attributes like "transparency" and "convenience." They created beautiful diagrams depicting the entire strategy, complete with visualizations of information in the cloud, social networks, and an array of existing and new distribution channels.

The team created a radically new customer relationship and distribution model—and they had gigabytes of slide decks documenting the new strategy and all of the activities that had led up to it. But two big questions remained: Would BBVA's employees interpret the strategy consistently? And, if so, would they know what actions they needed to take to move toward the vision? BBVA wasn't about to take any chances. To pull off a change initiative of this scale and execute the strategy as planned, the bank needed more than a small handpicked team at headquarters. It needed the help of the company's more than one hundred thousand global employees. And for that, BBVA had to make the strategy come to life.

Continuum came up with a compelling way to do it: Turn ten thousand square feet of office space in downtown Madrid into the banking equivalent of a concept car.

Imagine walking into a pharmacy. Everything is white. The floor, the ceiling, the walls. The shelves and the countertops. Every single pill bottle and tube of ointment. The room's only blue (BBVA's brand color) is on several rows of debit cards hanging on the wall, a small touch-screen device standing on the counter, and a large sign encouraging you to "turn your phone into your bank."

What kind of pharmacy is this?

It's a full-scale working mockup inside BBVA's Madrid Center for Innovation. Peek around the wall and you'll find a completely white living room, bodega, and bank branch, too. As you walk around this white wonderland, projected videos temporarily focus your attention on the otherwise empty walls, explaining how Camilo—an archetype representing one of BBVA's target customer groups—will deposit and withdraw money in this particular space. After each video, specially trained employees play out key interactions in front of you using smartphones and countertop kiosks.

In just twenty minutes, you've been completely immersed in BBVA's strategy to become *the* customer-centric bank. You understand, deep in your bones, exactly what the company's vision is for the future of every single customer interaction. Even if you don't work in financial services, you can probably start to make a list of things that need to change in order for the bank to start moving in this direction. And as you walk out the door, you'll no doubt feel a touch of excitement and inspiration.

Since the mockup's construction, thousands of visitors ranging from bank executives to branch tellers have toured the space. It became so effective at bringing BBVA's strategy to life that the bank asked Continuum to create smaller, portable versions that now travel the globe with members of the strategy team and help them to bring the vision to employees in Europe, the United States, Mexico, and South America. The mockup's success also expedited the launch of a radical new branch design that BBVA is now piloting in Madrid.

Set Your Organization on the Right Course

You have a choice. You can continue to let your employees and partners wonder what they should do to improve the customer experience and flounder as they try to coordinate their own activities with those of other departments. Or—like ANA, Holiday Inn, and BBVA—you can guide them toward a common vision and facilitate concerted efforts by crafting a customer experience strategy that clearly defines the intended experience.

You've got several of the building blocks right within your own walls. Even if they're not immediately at your fingertips, a little digging will undoubtedly uncover your company's corporate objectives and brand attributes—the foundation of your customer experience strategy.

But how can you know what will really differentiate your customer experience in the minds of buyers? How can you align your strategy with customers' real needs, behaviors, and motivations? This is where the discipline of customer understanding comes in, with practices like social-media listening, ethnographic research, and customer journey mapping that help companies get into the heads of their customers. That's what we'll describe in the next chapter.

6

Customer Understanding

FOR SEVERAL YEARS in a row, customers had rated Virgin Mobile Australia the country's top mobile operator in customer satisfaction. Matt Anderson, Virgin Mobile's chief operating officer, should have been happy with those results. He wasn't.

Virgin Mobile had edged out the other three major telecom companies down under—but in reality, Matt knew, its customer experience was basically indistinguishable from the others. For a company operating under the Virgin brand name, that was a big problem. As Matt explains, "We weren't interested in being up to par with industry standards. We wanted to create a differentiated customer experience: one that was uniquely Virgin."[1]

To make that happen, Matt needed to understand what Aussie consumers really wanted and needed from a mobile operator. As a first step, a team of business analysts examined the company's customer satisfaction scores, Net Promoter survey results, and financial data.[2] This quantitative data pointed them to two areas that tied strongly to customer loyalty but where Virgin performed poorly on customer satisfaction but that tied strongly to customer loyalty: the processes of picking a mobile plan and getting a problem resolved. Then they confirmed that improving these experiences would be a worthwhile investment by quantifying the lifetime value of a "promoter" versus a "detractor."

But the picture was still incomplete. "The business analytics showed us where to play," says Matt. "But they didn't show us how to win." For that, the team needed to understand what the Virgin brand values meant from a customer perspective and how those values connected within the context of customers' daily lives. Matt called on two service design firms, Proto Partners in Australia and Zilver Innovation in the Netherlands, for help with a completely different kind of customer research.

The team asked a selection of current Virgin Mobile customers to create online diaries.[3] Each day for a week, the customers responded to several questions related to Virgin's brand values, such as "What is unfair?" and "In which situations do you feel in control?" The customers shared stories about their home and work life, added personal photos of themselves and loved ones, and annotated their personal diary pages with icons that expressed their emotions.

At first blush, this exercise might sound fluffy. But these online diaries got Virgin Mobile directly to the emotional insights that it needed to be successful. "One very powerful insight was the deeper meaning of 'control' in customers' lives. We thought control meant giving customers options to modify their contracts based on their individual needs," says Matt. To that end, the company was about to move from nineteen standard billing plans to a system where customers could slice and dice hundreds of individual plan features any way they wanted. But the diaries indicated that infinite options weren't what customers wanted *at all.* One participant said, "If you give me the best deal, and make me understand why it's the best deal, I feel in control."

The insight that customers wanted greater understanding of a smaller number of choices wasn't lost on the Virgin Mobile team, who quickly reversed their approach to helping customers choose the right plan. They halved their number of available plans, which resulted in immediate positive feedback — both from retail staff, who found the new plans easier to sell, and from customers. In just the first seven months after this change, Virgin saw a 10 percent jump in customer satisfaction.

What You Think You Know About Customers Is Probably Wrong

Thinking you know what customers want is risky. *Knowing* what they want leads to customer experience improvements that matter. Virgin Mobile thought it knew what its customers wanted. In fact, Matt and his colleagues had planned major initiatives based on those assumptions. They were headed down a perilous path—one that wasn't illuminated by customer insights. But by tapping into a variety of different research methods, they were able to understand what customers really needed, and what type of mobile-operator experience would best embody the famous Virgin brand. This made all the difference.

Without someone like Matt at the helm, most companies neglect to build a foundation of customer understanding before they develop product, service, and experience strategies—and then proceed with costly initiatives. With millions of opportunities to connect to customers every day, how is it even possible that companies lack deep customer insights?

First, employees and managers often fall into the seductive trap of assuming that what *they* want is what customers want. After all, *they're* customers, too! A few years ago, when we asked the lead designer from a kiosk software vendor about his process, he told us, "Well, I really just figure out what I like and what works for me. Then I think about what my mom and my dad would need. Sometimes I'll mention a project to them in passing and get their feedback." This type of inside-out thinking is self-centered at best, and dangerous at worst.

Second, many companies view customers only through a numerical lens. Given the quantitative focus of most modern management practices, this shouldn't come as much of a surprise. We recently spoke with the head of consumer insights at a major cosmetics manufacturer, who was building a repository of shopper purchasing patterns from retailers' point-of-sale systems. Although he insisted that he wanted to create "a true three-hundred-and-sixty-degree view" of his customers, he wouldn't even consider our suggestion to study how women actually use his company's products in the bathroom every morning. Women (and drag queens) of the world should be outraged that a guy in a suit has the audacity to think he understands them based solely on when and where they shop for makeup.

Third, many companies use qualitative research methods inappropriately. The most frequent offender: focus groups, which simply aren't good at uncovering existing customer behaviors and needs — the types of insights required to design the customer experience. An anecdote from Holiday Inn's Eric Nicolas demonstrates this point: "We did an online food diary where we asked travelers to tell us what they were thinking about having for breakfast, what they actually had, what snacks they bought, and how they felt before and after they ate dinner. One lady told us she wanted to eat healthy. But then she bought a pizza at four p.m. and ate four slices. At ten p.m. she ate another slice. The last slice was her breakfast. That would never have come through in a focus group."

The good news is that you can avoid these pitfalls. In this chapter we'll introduce you to a range of research techniques that will help you understand who your customers are, how they perceive the interactions they're having with you today, and what they want and need from your company tomorrow. Then we'll show you how to document these insights in evocative ways and create a shared understanding of customer needs throughout your company.

The kinds of insights you can expect to glean by following these practices are often unexpected. As you saw, Virgin Mobile learned that it needed to change its product offering. E.ON Energy, a gas and electricity provider serving twenty European countries, found out that it just needed to communicate better.

CASE STUDY: E.ON ENERGY DIGS INTO CUSTOMERS' EMOTIONS

"People thought we were liars!" That's just one of the eye-popping realizations that Adam Elliott, E.ON's head of customer insights, found when he started surveying customers about the experience of switching to E.ON from another energy provider.

Here's how that switching process works: "A prospective customer calls us to ask about our service, a sales rep tells the customer that E.ON is cheaper than what they currently have and makes the sale right there on the phone, and the customer is left with a set of expectations about how big the bill will be," explains Adam. Now fast-forward several months to the day that the customer gets their first E.ON bill. Sometimes, it's actually *higher* than what they had paid with their previous provider—but not because the sales rep misled them. "It could be that the first bill is a winter bill and the customer is comparing that to a summer bill. Or it could be that the first bill is delayed and covers four months of consumption rather than three."

The surveys also revealed another important insight: Those customers who didn't think E.ON was lying thought it was boring. Maybe this isn't too surprising, given that we're talking about a utility company. But it didn't sit well with Adam. "We want customers to get the first bill and love us. If they don't have a strong positive opinion of us after three to four months, we haven't sufficiently engaged with them."

Why is Adam so concerned with customers' emotions? "The way that we make a customer feel will dictate how they behave—whether they stay with us as their energy provider, whether they call us up, and whether they shout at us when they do call," he says. For example, the churn rate for new customers—those who had been with E.ON for a year or less—was much too high. But when and how did customers want to be engaged? And what kinds of emotions did new customers have during the switch-over period? "These things have huge cost and revenue implications," says Adam. "But typical management information doesn't address how our customers feel."

To get to the bottom of these questions, Adam enlisted the help of Andrew Franklin, E.ON's head of service design. Andrew asked a group of brand-new customers to keep every communication they received from E.ON over the six weeks that it took to get them switched over from their old provider. He also asked them to create a graph of how they felt about the switching experience each day.

active confirmation emails to customers the night before. The result? One hundred thousand deflected calls per year.

Accor, the parent company of over four thousand hotels including luxury brands Sofitel and Novotel and budget brand Motel 6, layers manual human analysis on top of natural language processing to find out what customers are saying about its properties. Accor's partner, social media monitoring company Synthesio, determines the sentiment of comments posted on sites like TripAdvisor.com and Booking.com and categorizes them among thirty different topics including hotel location, ease of parking, check-in, food, drinks, cleanliness, and pricing.[8]

Individual hotel managers receive daily customer insights that help them detect problems with their properties. For example, one Novotel hotel manager recently noticed a surge in negative reviews pertaining to hotel keys. Yves Lecret, Novotel's marketing director in France, explains, "We identified a problem with guests' room keys being demagnetized by their smartphones. We reported this problem to our supplier, who was able to make the technical changes necessary to correct this issue."

Go Deep with Ethnographic Research

If you want to find out what your customers *actually* do, what motivates them, and what opportunities exist to better meet their needs, you need to conduct some form of ethnographic research.[9] Ethnography, which has roots in the field of anthropology, is simply about observing your customers' behavior in a natural setting. That's why ethnographic research methods like diary studies, in-home observations, and one-on-one interviews can help you understand how to create experiences that fit within the context of your customers' personal or professional lives.

"You need to get away from your desk and into the field," says Conor Brady, chief creative officer at Organic, the interactive agency that recently helped an upscale chain of fitness centers redesign its website and mobile app. At the start of the project, each member of the agency team received a temporary membership so that they could get a feel for the gym's premium experience and see how people interacted in the space.

As in most big-city gyms, workout traffic peaks at this location before and after the nine-to-five workday. But this club's wildly popular yoga, cardio, and spinning instructors drive additional spikes at class times. "A bunch of the team showed up one night. We were on the floor using the fitness machines, and we saw a queue of about thirty people start to form along the wall next to one of the studios." Conor approached one of the members and casually asked what the deal was. To get into the classes, he learned, members had to stand in line.

But that wasn't all. The members explained that certain spots in the studios were more desirable than others, depending on personal preferences. "Some wanted to be near the instructor to show off or see what was going on, while others wanted to hide in the back." Members wanted certain spots so badly that they were willing to stand around for a half an hour to get them.

"It was kind of ironic," says Conor. "These customers each pay thousands of dollars a year to work out on some of the best fitness equipment in the world. Yet here they were, standing perfectly still as they waited in line — not daring to actually go exercise for fear of losing their spot in the queue."

Based on these insights, Organic developed functionality that enables members to reserve a specific spot in a class from the web or a mobile device. Now they only need to show up ten minutes before class to claim their place. "If the gym's executives had said, 'We have a lot of demand for our classes,' that wouldn't have gotten us very far," says Conor. "We wouldn't have discovered this need if we hadn't gotten away from our desks."

Tap Internal Knowledge and Expertise

The majority of customer insights should come from customers themselves. But you shouldn't overlook the vast amount of knowledge held by call center representatives, retail staff, service technicians, account managers, and the like. Each of these frontline employees talks with dozens or hundreds of individual customers each day and routinely witnesses both good and bad customer experiences in action. This front-row seat enables them to spot problems and unmet customer needs long before those issues surface in traditional research.

That's why many companies have created voice of the employee programs.[10] For example, accounting software developer Intuit created an online community for its employees called Brainstorm, where employees can submit ideas for improving the customer experience, vote on others' ideas, and track ideas from submission to implementation.[11] Investment firm Vanguard supplements a similar online tool for its employees with a low-tech approach: whiteboards placed in prominent locations throughout its operations and call centers.

In addition to surfacing customer insights, frontline and behind-the-scenes employees can help you understand how internal operations, policies, processes, and systems negatively affect the customer experience.

Dann Allen, head of experience design and improvement from AAA Northern California, Nevada, and Utah, discovered this on his first day on the job. That's when his new boss gave him an important assignment. Members were unsatisfied with the automobile club's product renewal experiences. Dann needed to figure out what was broken — and he only had four days to do it.

There was no way to execute a customer research study in that time frame, so he quickly started chatting with his coworkers from across the organization. That turned out to be a good thing, because AAA members simply wouldn't have been able to identify the nearly one hundred different variations in renewal scenarios that Dann uncovered internally. "What customers got from us depended on what level of membership they had, how long they'd been with us, what type of insurance they had, and what state they lived in." Dann also discovered that each of the organization's marketing programs, insurance products, and membership products ran on separate and often unconnected systems. This meant that the company would often bombard its customers with a slew of uncoordinated communications. "We were bugging our customers a lot."

Document Your Research Findings in Easy-to-Digest Formats

Dann could have documented his findings about AAA's product renewal experience in a slide deck or spreadsheet. Instead, he pinned up each and every email, bill, reminder, outbound call script, and direct marketing piece that a high-value customer would receive come renewal time on a wall-sized timeline.[12] Dann shared the visualization — which quickly became known as "the wall of shame" — with employees from the company's call centers, branches, auto insurance, home insurance, IT, and marketing departments and asked them to verify the experience. "People were flabbergasted. They asked, 'This is *really* what we do to our members?'" says Dann. It was this wall-sized visualization that helped his colleagues to understand the customer experience as they hadn't been able to before.

Like Dann, you've got to take your customer data and turn it into a compelling picture or story — something that will make it easy for your colleagues to understand and share. Two tools are especially effective for this purpose: personas and journey maps.[13]

Personas Help You Document Who Your Customers Really Are

Personas are fictional characters that embody your target customers' key behaviors, attributes, motivations, and goals. Unlike market segmentations, which typically remain nameless and faceless, personas come to life with first and last names, photographs, and vivid narratives that describe day-in-the-life scenarios.

Financial services firm and credit card issuer Discover has a set of six personas that represent key customer behaviors. "Valerie," Discover's primary persona, is a recently divorced forty-two-year-old woman living in Seattle. She's got two college-age kids and, like many Americans in the "sandwich generation," she also takes care of her aging parents. After sixteen years as a stay-at-home mom, Valerie got divorced, found a job, and built a new life that she'd never really imagined for herself. Now she's a librarian at the University of Washington, earning

$40,000 a year. "She's being squeezed by all of these things, trying to keep it all together and build some financial security," says Steve Furman, Discover's director of e-business. "If we can take care of Val, then other people will most likely get the tools that they need as well."

To give the personas some texture, Steve added each one's favorite brands, like Gap, the *New York Times*, ESPN, or Six Flags. He assigned each persona a real credit score, which has helped his internal business partners recognize how the personas fit into their product development and marketing plans. Steve also listed the devices that each persona uses. "That helps us understand how they're spending their time with us and what kind of messaging works for different groups, like email, SMS, or push notifications from an app."

Journey Maps Help You Document What Your Customers Really Do

Journey maps are documents that visually illustrate a particular persona's activities over time. Many journey maps plot the entire course of a customer's relationship with a company—all of the steps that customers take as they discover, evaluate, buy, use, and get support for a product or service—and all of the touchpoints that they interact with along the way. Others zoom in to just one particular part of the journey. As Jonathan Browne, Forrester's expert on journey mapping, explains, "The scope of the journey map, the exact visualization, and the degree of detail it contains vary based on how the organization wants to use it."

One person using journey maps is Carol Pudnos, the customer experience director at Dow Corning, a global supplier of silicones that show up in everything from shampoos to solar panels. She recently helped employees from the company's specialty chemical business in China understand the needs of "Eric," one of Dow Corning's primary personas. Eric's a formulating chemist, the guy who's ultimately responsible for developing new products for his company to launch in a particular market.

"We had gotten some feedback that our product offering wasn't as broad or robust as our customers needed it to be, and that it didn't meet their performance specifications," explains Carol. To get a better understanding of what Eric was looking for, she organized a two-day journey mapping workshop in Shanghai with representatives from sales, marketing, channel management, and research and development. The team created a horizontal timeline and plotted the specific steps that Eric takes as he considers what silicone products to buy, like attending a trade show, asking for a sample, and calling for lab analysis.

"When we peeled back the layers of the onion through journey mapping, we realized that our product offering wasn't too narrow. The problem was that the touchpoints and people interfacing with Eric weren't able to help him use our products effectively." Armed with a more holistic view of the problem, the team is now following up faster with highly skilled technical experts on critical touchpoints and revamping its product information, training, and technical materials.

Craig Lee, senior manager performance development at the airline Emirates, created a very different type of journey map. It's a detailed illustration depicting a sea of customers as they travel from their hotels, through the airport, onto planes, and to their destinations. The drawing portrays hundreds of real-world customer interactions. One customer is shown getting a text message about a chauffeur service that's arriving to pick him up, while an Emirates employee in another part of the map informs a customer about a departure delay.

This journey map is the centerpiece of Emirates' customer experience education programs. Craig prints it onto huge pieces of fabric and then lays it on a conference room floor. During the training sessions, employees walk around the map and describe, discuss, and enact different aspects of the customer experience that they see. Training tools like playing cards and posters provide additional context, like what customers need at key touchpoints.

A Cautionary Note

Personas and journey maps have caught on like wildfire over the past several years. That's a great thing for firms that want to get a better understanding of who their customers are and what they do. However, many companies and interactive agencies have gotten so caught up in the persona and journey map hype that they skip the research phase and go straight to crafting these documents based on what they *think* they know about customers. Don't make that same mistake. Your end goal isn't the personas and journey maps themselves. Your end goal is deep customer insights, which just happen to be encapsulated in these particular formats.

That's one of the lessons from Boeing, a company that conducted extensive customer research and then created personas and journey maps that helped rescue customers from its own website.

CASE STUDY: BOEING'S PERSONAS AND JOURNEY MAPS CREATE BROAD UNDERSTANDING

Dustin Cox manages the e-business customer experience for Boeing Commercial Aviation Services (CAS), the aerospace manufacturer's support and services arm. "Historically, when a customer would take possession of an aircraft, they'd receive reams and reams of documentation in the belly of the plane," he explains. But in 2000, the organization changed all that with the launch of MyBoeingFleet.com, a portal that distributes maintenance and repair information digitally.

Over the next decade, the site mushroomed to more than 180 different applications that deliver mission-critical data, process e-commerce transactions, take service requests, and provide training. But, as happens with so many websites, the explosion in content and functionality brought on customer complaints about a disjointed experience. "Our customers are under extreme cost pressures, and we wanted to make this a more efficient site for them," says Dustin. He also realized that Boeing could reduce its own costs and drive additional profits by developing and maintaining a more streamlined site.

Dustin reached out to interactive agency EffectiveUI to help him launch a major redesign. The agency, in turn, urged him to kick off the project with an ethnographic research study—a major departure from business as usual for the engineering-driven company. "Historically, our 'research' was to listen to sales and support teams when they came back from client engagements, or to talk to one-off customers at a conference," says Dustin.

Dustin jumped on board and the research team began a whirlwind tour of fourteen customer companies including passenger and cargo airlines, maintenance providers, and leasing companies in ten different cities across North America, South America, Europe, and Asia. "Our research team has donned hard hats in airplane hangars, acquired security badges to access airline personnel, and walked with engineers, maintenance planners, and equipment purchasers through their typical days at work," says Joel Flom from EffectiveUI.[14] Altogether, they spoke with nearly one hundred and fifty people who buy, fly, and fix Boeing planes and parts.

Dustin describes a typical research session: "We sat down and asked them to tell us about their role, their duties, and the systems they use. Then we'd ask them to perform some of those activities as we shadowed them for three to four hours. We allowed them to go about their work, but asked them to think out loud so that we could accurately record what they faced in completing their tasks. Then we wrapped up with questions about how they did certain tasks or why certain tools presented challenges for them."

Along the way, the research team shared quotes, videos, and screenshots from the sessions with the broader CAS community. "We had a lot of converts," Dustin says through a huge smile. "Even the veteran employees who had been wary of the research in the first place said, 'Oh, I didn't know *that* was the case' or 'Wow, those two things are used together?'"

The research insights pointed to a new way to segment Boeing's customers. CAS traditionally thought about its customers in terms of their specific job titles, assuming that each role performed a unique set of tasks. But the research showed that many functions overlapped. In addition, there were few differences among people who worked at large airlines, small airlines, leasing firms, and regulatory agencies.

These insights led the team to create a set of personas based on core behavioral patterns. The personas — which include a technical service engineer, a buyer, and a technical librarian — describe each functional role's general work context (what their work environment looks like and what technical systems they use) as well as their specific context for using MyBoeingFleet.com (things like their job responsibilities, site usage patterns, most important tasks, and key pain points). The team also developed journey maps depicting two or three key scenarios for each persona.

"They're really powerful tools," Dustin explains. "We initially thought that several stand-alone areas of the site worked just fine. But when we connected them in a journey, we found that days elapsed between some of the key steps in a process. In those gaps customers were sitting around, unaware of what was happening to their requests." With another journey map, the team discovered that they were providing all of the right tools, but not in a way that supported customers' work flows. "We'd show a maintenance procedure that required three different parts, but we didn't link that to the availability of those parts. And once customers found the information on availability, they had to step out of that area to actually make the purchase."

Dustin says the research project and its deliverables created a huge shift at Boeing. "When you work on something for ten years, you kind of forget that you can do something differently." The personas have helped CAS employees understand who they're designing the portal for and what data and functionality those customers need. The journey maps got previously fragmented teams to look past the parts of the customer relationship that they owned and focus on the end-to-end experience. "They helped us understand that we can't look at delivering experiences from point to point. Customers go through fluid processes and we need to think of our solutions in that way."

Share Your Customer Insights Early and Often

Customer insights are worthless when they're locked in your head or squirreled away in a database. Like Dustin, you need to share your customer research with people across your company. Personas and journey maps help to facilitate those conversations. But there are other effective ways to share customer insights, too.

Lambert Walsh, vice president and general manager of global services at software company Adobe, has experimented with a bunch of them.[15] "We started with a video to show our CEO and his staff that it was impossible for customers to purchase an upgrade for an individual product within Adobe's Creative Suite." After watching a seven-minute reenactment of a customer going from screen to screen on Adobe.com with no success, one of the senior execs was silent — and then simply said, "You've got to be kidding me." Those six words compelled the responsible business unit to change the underlying policy that had prevented the purchase.

Spurred on by the power of the video, Lambert created a physical listening post in Adobe's headquarters. Flat-screen panels, each displaying a different type of input, dominate one wall of the room. Screens on the far left show insights from Facebook, Twitter, and other social forums; the middle screens pipe in real-time video from the company's call centers in Asia, Europe, and North America; and the right-hand screens display the top issues bubbling up in Adobe's customer relationship management (CRM) system and customer surveys.

"It's a centralized location for us to expose people to the overall experience," says Lambert. Product management groups have used the listening post to find out how recently released products are resonating with Adobe's customer base, while engineering teams have gone in to replay customer service calls that mention a particular error code. (Lambert's team is also developing a tablet app that will enable employees to access the listening-post content from anywhere.)

Lambert next created a customer-immersion program that regularly exposes Adobe's leadership to the experiences that cause the most pain for their customers. The one-day program, which takes place onsite in one of Adobe's call centers, includes an overview of customer feedback focused on one of four targeted areas — marketing, sales, IT, or engineering — depending on the audience. Then the senior leaders attempt to complete a defined scenario as if they were Adobe customers.

Lambert describes how this works: "In one session, we asked the execs to pretend they worked in procurement and that someone in their company had just come back from a marketing event and wanted to purchase an Adobe product they saw. Their job was to find the product on our website and purchase five licenses." Then the facilitators watched as the immersion program participants navigated the website, made decisions about which version of the product was best, and tried to make the purchase. "We knew that particular scenario was impossible. You could only buy one license at a time. But if we had just talked with execs about the issue, the importance and urgency of spending time and money to fix it just wouldn't have resonated."

Paul Weiskopf, an executive responsible for Adobe's corporate strategy, agrees. "I was asked to play the role of a customer and go find some information about the range of products we offer for web conferencing. Going through that process awakened me to the degree of complexity that exists for customers."

Lambert says that the immersion program has significantly changed the company's conversations and priorities. "The senior leaders who have been through the program want to take accountability and they want to create additional awareness throughout the company to help drive change."

Customer Understanding Is the Foundation of All Customer Experience Efforts

If you want to harness the power of putting your customers at the center of your business, you have to start with a complete picture of who they are and what they want from you. This view will come into focus when you analyze customer data that spans multiple research techniques and organizational boundaries, just like Virgin Mobile, E.ON, and Adobe do.

Many companies have the in-house know-how required to conduct quantitative research. But many of the qualitative research techniques we've discussed in this chapter, such as ethnographic research and text mining, require specialized skills or technology. That's why you'll likely need to partner with outside experts who can help you set up your research studies, ask the right questions, collect data, and synthesize the results into meaningful insights.

If you try to skimp on this part of the process — and continue with assumptions about what you *think* customers need and want — you'll not only fail to create true customer understanding, you'll also put the rest of your customer experience initiatives at risk. That's because the insights you glean from this practice will, in turn, lay the groundwork for the other five customer experience disciplines.

Customer insights ultimately drive your customer experience strategy. They should form the cornerstone of your metrics and governance programs. They need to be tightly woven into the fabric of your culture. And, as we'll see in the next chapter, they're the primary input into your customer experience design process.

7

Design

WHEN YOU THINK about hotbeds of design, the utility industry probably doesn't jump to mind. But in the southeast of England, Darren Bentham from Southern Water tapped into the power of design to overhaul a critical customer-facing process.

New government regulations in the U.K. require that every home get a water meter, a complete change for the majority of homes — millions — that now pay for water based on a provider's estimate of usage. Mandatory meter installation had the potential to be a downright terrible experience for Southern Water's customers, not to mention a customer-relations headache. Homeowners faced periodic water shutoffs, blocked sidewalks, dug-up front gardens, and the hassle of figuring out an entirely new bill.

But Darren, Southern Water's universal metering program director, saw an enormous opportunity. He wanted to get customers onto meters as quickly and easily as possible so that people could start to establish the link between the size of their bills and their water consumption and ultimately reduce the amount of water they use. This was important, because the districts Southern Water serves actually have less water available per person than the desert countries Sudan and Syria.[1]

Darren had a vision. He knew exactly where he wanted to go. The problem was that he had no idea how to get there. "Traditionally we've built large-capital projects, like treatment plants and pipes," explains Darren. This was a very different type of project. "This was about how people thought about their water use."

Darren started with research that revealed customers' various motivations for saving water (or not) — like protecting the environment, saving money, or seeking convenience without much regard for environmental or financial implications. In Darren's words, "It got us thinking about customers as individuals with different needs, rather than this homogeneous group we labeled 'customers.'"

The research also revealed a key insight: Meters alone weren't going to be enough to get Southern Water customers to use less water. This was bad news. Darren knew he needed help, so he turned to Design Council U.K., a non-profit organization that provides design advice to industry, communities, and all levels of government. The Design Council connected Darren with a number of agencies that could help him change his customers' behavior. Among them: design and innovation firm IDEO.

IDEO's designers identified the steps in the meter-installation experience, from learning about the meters and getting one installed, to receiving a new bill and transitioning to pay-for-use billing. In journey maps, they detailed how customers would interact with Southern Water depending on whether or not customers would be home and whether or not they cared much about the installation process — factors that research showed would greatly influence an individual customer's needs and questions. IDEO then created communication materials and water-saving tools — ranging from a list of the top ten water-saving tips to water calculators — that they thought would be helpful at each step of the process. They shared these items with Southern Water customers to get feedback and make sure that they'd feel informed and empowered at each step of the meter-installation journey.

IDEO also organized a workshop with employees from Southern

Water; Balfour Beatty, the construction firm doing the installations; and Groundwork, a group of contractors who would be going door-to-door to provide information about customers' new bills. "Even though they're all unique organizations with their own skills to bring, they were going to be seen as a single entity and associated with Southern Water," says Andrea Koerselman, service design lead at IDEO London. "It would have been easy for each of them to get caught up in their own remit, but they all needed to be prepared to address customers' needs and concerns at any time. So we jointly developed agreed-upon roles and responsibilities for the installation period and discussed customer insights that they could incorporate into their own training programs."

In the end, the collective team — Southern Water, two external implementation partners, and multiple design consultancies — created the Meter-To-Me installation process, a completely new way to roll out water meters and encourage homeowners to start saving water.[2]

It was carefully designed with the customer experience in mind: Three months prior to the meter installation date in a given area, Southern Water placed ads in the local press, met with neighborhood watch groups, and dropped off leaflets at post offices and public swimming pools. All of these communications shared one common message: *Save water, save energy, save money.* Six weeks out, the company sent customers a welcome package to let them know their meters were coming and where they could go to get more information. Then, one week before installation, employees put up street signs to remind neighbors of the impending work.

When installation day finally arrived, Southern Water parked a mobile information unit on the street so that people could come in, ask questions, and talk about their specific issues. They also handed out water-saving showerheads and coupons for other water-saving products.

After all this, Southern Water didn't actually switch customers over to pay-for-use billing. The up-front research had shown that customers would need some time to adjust their thinking around how they used water, so Southern Water continued to bill them as before while the meters collected data. After three months, the company sent customers a communication that showed their daily consumption and what their water bill *would* have been for that period under the new program.

At that point, they also gave customers a choice: switch over to the new billing system immediately or transition to pay-for-use billing over a three-year period. Customers whose bills were going to go down could therefore see immediate savings, while those whose bills were going to go up had time to learn how to conserve water.

Halfway through the five-year meter-rollout plan, both Southern Water and its customers are happy with the results. It's no surprise, really. The Meter-To-Me process was *designed* to succeed.

Customer Interactions Need to Be Designed, Not Left to Chance

The new Southern Water meter installation experience is a dramatic improvement over the utility-industry status quo. But it didn't magically spring into existence, and it wasn't the accidental result of unrelated decisions. Darren and his agency partners meticulously engineered the experience through nearly a year's worth of structured activities that represented a new way of working and thinking. They created the Meter-To-Me installation experience by following a human-centered design process.

Design isn't just about picking the right shade of blue for the company logo. It's a problem-solving process that incorporates the needs of customers, employees, and business stakeholders. And it's a way of working that creates and refines real-world solutions.

Design is the secret weapon of companies such as Fidelity Investments, Virgin Atlantic, the telecom company Orange, and the BBC. It gives them a strategic advantage in figuring out what products and services their customers truly need and in defining the exact characteristics of every customer interaction, whether it's how call-center agents talk to customers, what functionality should be on the website, or how to best assist in-store shoppers.

Design is the most important business discipline that you've probably never heard of. But how, exactly, does design work?

Design Demystified

Design *as a business discipline* can be a tough concept to grasp for folks who typically deal with spreadsheets and bullet points. And while it *is* a departure from the way most companies work, it's actually not all that mysterious. At its core lies a pretty straightforward methodology.

Consider computer programmers for a moment. Skilled coders wouldn't (or at least *shouldn't*) attempt to develop a new piece of software — or make an upgrade to an existing one — without defining the system specs or testing their code. And they certainly wouldn't do these tasks in an arbitrary or haphazard way. They'd follow a predefined set of steps. Why? Because adhering to an established development process increases the likelihood that they'll create something that adds real value and works the way they intended.

A human-centered design process accomplishes exactly the same thing.

As the *human-centered* part of the name implies, a typical design process starts with research to understand customer needs and motivations. It's the kind of in-depth ethnographic stuff that we talked about in the last chapter: interviews with customers, in-home observations, diary studies, and the like. If the project doesn't involve direct customer-employee interactions — like a website redesign — that might be all that you need to do. But if it's the type of project requiring changes to internal processes or behaviors, you'll also need to dig into the needs and motivations of employees and external partners.

Analysis is next. This is when teams create artifacts like personas, journey maps, and other visual models to synthesize the research data. During this time, the team may need to reframe the project focus. Why? Project teams often set out to solve one problem, but research insights lead them to discover that there's actually a bigger (or just different) problem that's more valuable to tackle. That's what happened to

Figure 7-1: Sketches for a Mobile App

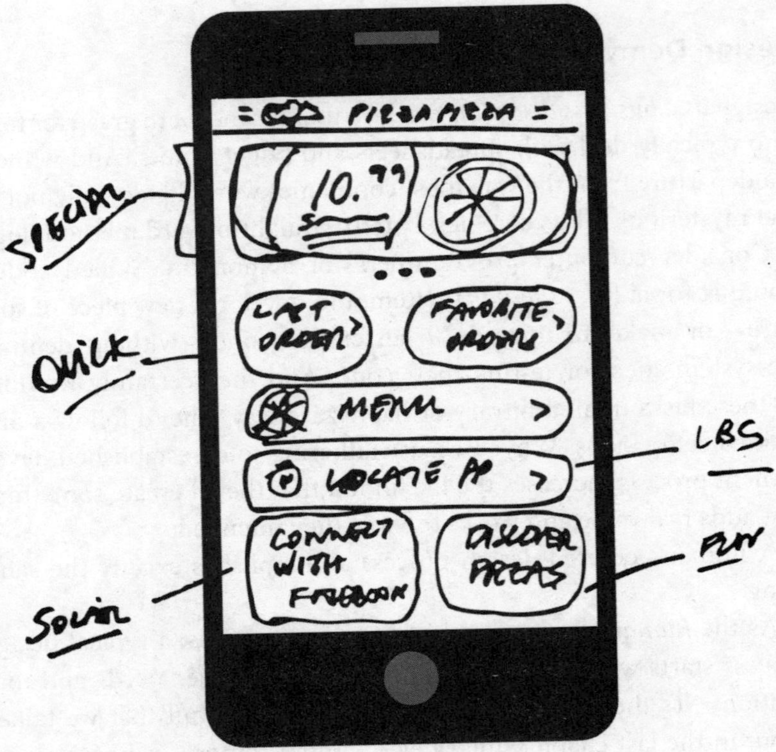

Source: Pizza Pizza and Plastic Mobile

Eric Nicolas from Holiday Inn, as we described in chapter 5. He started his project with the goal of increasing revenue in hotel restaurants and found that food and drinks were only part of what Holiday Inn guests were looking for. And so the design team reframed their work around an integrated lobby experience.

The next phase is ideation, which is just a fancy word for coming up with ideas. Any seasoned designer will tell you that their first idea is almost never the right one. That's why good design teams push themselves to come up with tens, if not hundreds, of possible solutions. At this point, they may also temporarily throw the realities of logistics and operations out the window. As Fred Leichter, chief customer experience officer at Fidelity Investments, explains, "It's easier to make a profound idea reasonable than to make a reasonable idea profound. We start with stuff that's out there, wild, and aggressive, and figure out if it has merit. Smart people will figure out how to get great ideas implemented."

Next the design team creates prototypes, which can take a variety of formats. For example, designers from Plastic Mobile drew rough pen-and-paper sketches of a mobile app for Pizza Pizza, one of Canada's largest pizza chains (see figure 7-1). For its lobby redesign project, Continuum built Holiday Inn a full-scale hotel lobby out of foam board in an empty warehouse. And McDonald's employees work with consulting firms like Dramatic Diversity/DD+D to act out new ways to perform actions such as taking a customer's payment and presenting a food order.

At this point, prototypes go out in front of real customers and employees for feedback. Not just once — multiple times. Designers take the feedback from each round of testing and incorporate it into increasingly refined prototypes that quickly converge on what customers and employees really need.

Finally, the team documents the features of the resulting product or service and the intended interactions. As with prototypes, this documentation can take many formats. For Pizza Pizza, Plastic Mobile created wireframes that outlined the various pieces of content and functionality in the mobile app and how those elements should behave (see figure 7-2). And service design firm live|work developed a conversation guide for claims agents at Gjensidige, Norway's largest insurance company, to refer to when speaking with callers (see figure 7-3).[3]

Designers often describe this end-to-end process as a double diamond (see figure 7-4).[4] It starts at a singular point — the initial focus for the project — but quickly diverges as the research uncovers new insights and potential problems to solve. The process converges to the midpoint as teams synthesize the research findings and reframe the project focus. The process diverges again as teams brainstorm a broad

Figure 7-2: Mobile App Wireframe

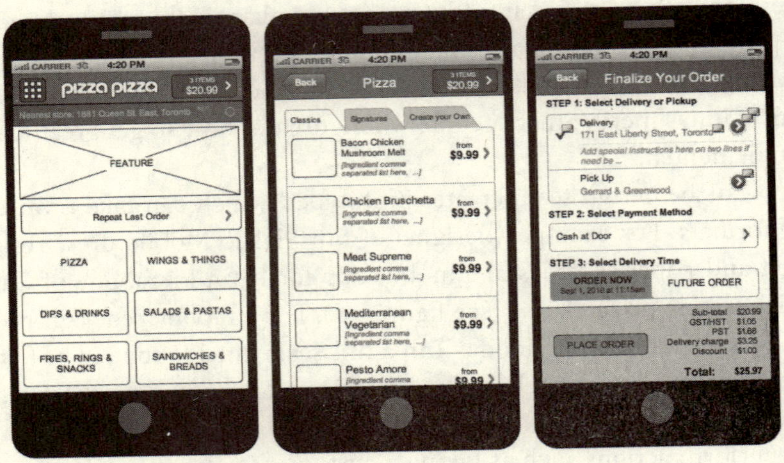

Source: Pizza Pizza and Plastic Mobile

Figure 7-3: Conversation Guide

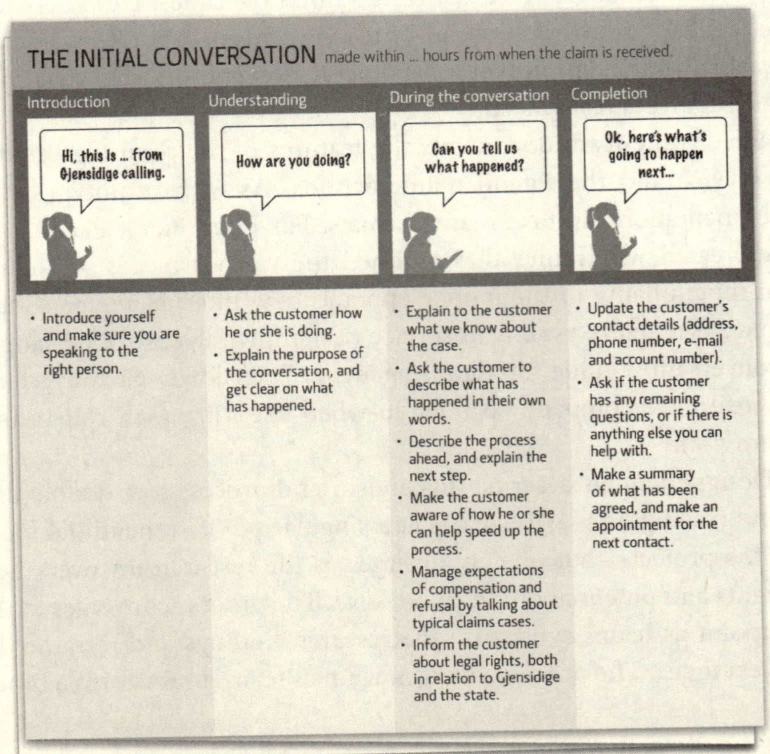

Source: Gjensidige and live|work

Figure 7-4: Design Process Double Diamond

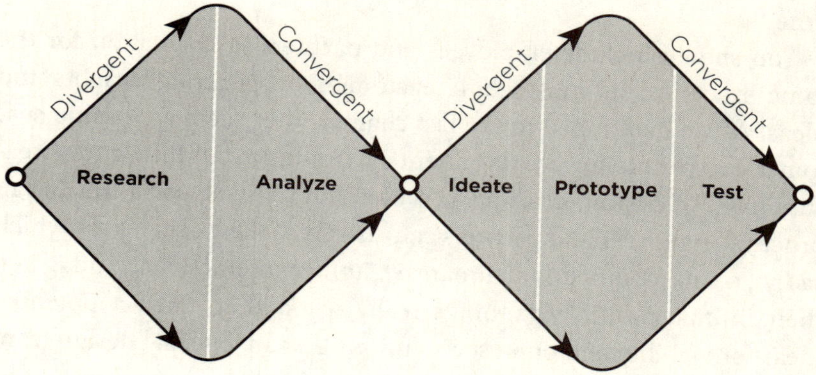

range of possible solutions and start to prototype. Lastly, refinement through multiple rounds of prototyping and testing converges the process to its final point: the design solution.

The Role of Cocreation in the Design Process

As Oliver King, cofounder of Engine Service Design, says, design is an activity that's best done *with* people, not *to* them. In other words, it's a participatory process — not something to be decided by one person in a locked room and delivered on a silver platter. The most effective design processes include people from across the entire customer experience ecosystem — customers, employees, and external partners — to help synthesize research data, ideate possible solutions, create prototypes, and provide feedback. Designers call this *cocreation*.

Henry Ford famously quipped that if he had asked customers what they wanted, they would have said, "A faster horse." So what if customers aren't always skilled at telling you exactly what they want? We bet Ford's customers would have also said they wanted a horse that kept them dry during rainstorms and carried multiple suitcases — and Henry would have connected the dots. The same thing goes for your customers. When they're face-to-face with the rest of the design team, customers *can* provide valuable input, including firsthand accounts of what they need and want, the seeds of ideas for others to build upon, and feedback that can be incorporated into prototypes in real time.

You should include employees and partners in cocreation for the same exact reason you include customers: to generate insights and ideas. As we mentioned in the last chapter, after seeing the same customer complaints surface day after day, frontline staff turn into a treasure trove of customer insights. When they're involved in the design process, employees and partners can also voice their *own* needs, which sadly go unaccounted for in many customer interactions. And, given their intimacy with how things really work, they can vet potential ideas for viability and often see solutions that an external design team would otherwise miss.

There's one other reason to cocreate with employees and partners. At some point, you're going to need to make changes to existing systems, processes, and policies. If key stakeholders haven't been involved with the design process from the start, they'll react to your changes like antibodies attacking a newly transplanted liver. Cocreation will lead to employees who will happily evangelize the design process and its outputs on your behalf.

Your company might already be doing something similar to cocreation: crowdsourcing. Companies like Verizon, Starbucks, and—yes—Ford have picked up on this trend over the past several years and now use social technologies like Facebook contests, public communities, and ideation websites to generate new product and service ideas.[5] While crowdsourcing can certainly provide useful insights, it's not a substitute for what we're talking about here: active collaboration among employees, partners, and customers throughout the entire design process.

Leaders at Fidelity understand this. They're using cocreation to improve customer interactions across their business.

CASE STUDY: FIDELITY COCREATES THE CHARITABLE-DONATION EXPERIENCE WITH DONORS

"I'm a designer." That's how Fred Leichter describes himself. It sounds like a pretty odd statement when you learn that Fred majored in math, worked as a systems developer on Wall Street, and wears a tie to the office on most days. But Fred insists that design isn't just for those of the black turtleneck persuasion. "Design is simply a different way to think that hits upon the things we need to do in order to be faster, more innovative, and more empathetic."

Over the last several years, Fred has partnered with the Institute of Design at Stanford (often referred to as "the d.school") to embed design thinking throughout Fidelity. His approach loosely follows the design process he's learned from Stanford: empathize with customers, define the problem, ideate solutions, prototype, and test. And, as often as possible, include real customers at each step.

Fred's the first to admit that not all projects and processes are a good fit for this approach. "For Y2K, we didn't need to get tons of customer feedback to figure out if date fields were going to stop working," he explains. "But when we're asking what people need in terms of financial security, that's a much more open-ended question." So on projects ranging from the redesign of a complex online financial-portfolio product to envisioning the 401(k) of the future, Fred steps in.

Recently a group from Fidelity Charitable, an independent public charity that helps people maximize the effectiveness of their charitable giving, asked Fred to help test a new mobile app they'd designed. They believed that donors wanted to be able to support charities quickly and easily and that a mobile app was just the thing to fill that gap.

"In the past those types of ideas would be off to development for coding and we'd just do some last-minute usability testing," Fred says. Rather than take that path, he encouraged the Fidelity Charitable team to back up, broaden their perspective, and rephrase the problem from the donor perspective. So instead of "What kind of mobile app will enable donors to make donations quickly and easily?" they started asking, "What are the needs of charitable donors when they're on the go?" Through this new lens, they saw that their mobile app was just one of many possible answers.

To explore the full range of other possibilities, Fred orchestrated a cocreation workshop. In the morning, he gave Fidelity Charitable employees just one hour to create pen-and-paper prototypes for ideas that they thought would fill a particular donor need.

Donors then joined the group. The employees asked the donors to tell them about the last time they made a charitable donation. What did they do? Why did they make the decisions they made? What tools did they use? As the donors told their stories, the employees quickly formed a composite picture of real donor needs and wants.

That's when the fun really started and the session became, in Fred's words, "not your father's focus group." To make the workshop setting as realistic as possible, Fred and his team mocked up a fund-raising cocktail party, served virgin cocktails, and solicited fake donations from the participants. They asked donors to act out different scenarios they'd envisioned in their prototypes, like bumping their smartphones together to make a donation transaction, and watched how they responded to the ideas.[6] At the end of the party, the Fidelity Charitable team showed the participants their rough sketches and asked for their direct feedback.

Then, while the donors got a tour of Fidelity's headquarters followed by a sit-down luncheon, the Fidelity Charitable team got just ninety minutes to refine (or completely redo) their original sketches based on the donor interviews, role play, and feedback. After lunch, the employees engaged in another round of donor feedback and discussion.

"When these sessions go well, the customers become part of the design team and become incredibly engaged in making things better," Fred explains. "They help to craft something that meets their needs." And that's exactly what happened. The donors gave Fidelity Charitable constructive feedback on the original mobile app, and they also voiced their desire for other digital solutions: a customizable website homepage that would enable individual donors to see immediately the content or functionality that was most important to them; data and articles on each charity that would help them make better grant decisions; and a community that would connect them with other generous, qualified donors so that they could learn how others felt about giving to particular charities.

"With the workshop focused on the mobile app, we weren't expecting to learn how we could transform the online donor experience," says Andus Baker, senior vice president of service delivery and technology at Fidelity Charitable. "That was really powerful. Up until the co-creation session, we knew there was an opportunity to make improvements to the website — it *is* the primary way we interact with donors — but this workshop catalyzed us into action. The donors told us things that would help us take it to the next level, and we're using those insights to inform our strategy."

The Role of Prototyping in the Design Process

One other thing drove Fidelity's success on this particular initiative: its prototypes. Fred and his colleagues didn't let their ideas for interacting with customers remain abstract concepts. They brought them to life in the physical world by drawing them and acting them out. This approach has multiple business benefits.

"What keeps me up at night is rolling out the same mistake fifteen hundred times globally," says Eric Nicolas about his work at Holiday Inn. Referring to full-scale models like his foam-board hotel lobby, he explains that "prototypes help us figure out the major design issues that we couldn't see on paper." And that means finding out what works — and what doesn't — before he sinks time and money into implementations built on flawed thinking.

It might initially feel scary to put something unfinished in front of your customers, but the roughness of the prototype is actually paramount to this objective. Fred Leichter explains, "If you present customers with something that looks polished, most people will tell you what they think you want to hear, which is, 'I like it.'"

As we saw with BBVA's banking mockup in chapter 5, prototypes also make ideas tangible and help organizations to create a shared understanding of the intended experience. This gives prototypes an incredible power to build consensus among groups of stakeholders with different motivations and priorities.

And because they exist in the real world, not in a presentation that's more easily filed away and forgotten, prototypes can also help you keep ideas alive and top of mind while you create buy-in. Let's face it:

It can take a while for large organizations to come around to the idea of interacting with customers in a new way.

Mayo Clinic designers routinely build prototypes as part of their day-to-day work — and have reaped every single one of these benefits.

CASE STUDY: MAYO CLINIC PROTOTYPES NEW DESIGNS FOR OUTPATIENT ROOMS

In 2011, Dr. William Mundell, an internist at Mayo Clinic, got the job of configuring his division's outpatient facilities in a new building. Aside from occasional updates to furniture and décor, the clinic's outpatient examination rooms in Rochester, Minnesota, hadn't really changed since early in the twentieth century. In 1954, Mayo facilities staff moved the rooms' couches from one side to the other so that doctors and patients could sit side by side. (Yes, that was a big deal at the time.) During the 1990s, the IT department installed computers on the physicians' desks.

William wasn't starting from scratch, however. In 2005, a team of designers from Mayo's Center for Innovation had kicked off a project to improve care in the clinic's outpatient practice and, as part of that work, had studied patient-physician interactions in the hundred-year-old exam room configuration.

What did they find? The computer setup forced doctors to turn away from patients in order to look at the screen — and if patients wanted to see on-screen X-rays or charts, they had to sit at odd angles and crane their necks. The room provided limited space for patients' family members and personal items. And the equipment for physical exams — the reclining exam table, dressing area, sink, and tools like scopes and blood-pressure cuffs — dominated the space, even though the bulk of each appointment was simply a conversation about patient history and symptoms.

To address these and other outpatient care issues, the innovation team brainstormed concepts that included new space layouts, technologies, processes, and roles. Then they found a large open space in the hospital and built a full-scale prototype of a new outpatient floor—complete with cabinets, exam tables, and computer monitors—constructed out of foam board. Over a two-month period, patients, physicians, nurses, hospital administrators, facilities personnel, and IT staff toured the space and shared their feedback.

One solution in particular resonated with the group: the creation of separate consultation and examination rooms. The idea addressed all of the issues uncovered in the research. It sounded perfect—obvious, even. But would it work in a real clinical context? The innovation team needed to find out.

Months earlier, they had permanently secured one corridor of outpatient exam rooms for an experimental, yet fully operational, lab space. So they quickly removed the medical equipment from one of these rooms and outfitted it with a round table, four chairs, and a computer monitor mounted to the wall on an articulated arm. When they observed real patient-physician interactions in the newly configured space for thirty days, they found that patients were more comfortable and relaxed, asked more questions, and helped to create their at-home action plan—key factors for getting on the road to recovery.

While the consultation-only room gained wide praise, the clinic didn't have resources to completely overhaul all of its existing examination rooms. Now, with the blank slate of building a new space, William saw an opportunity to implement the consultation-only rooms on a broader scale. But one big problem stood in his way: There wasn't enough floor area in the new space to accommodate the number of separate consultation and exam rooms required to serve all of his division's patients.

He approached the innovation team, and together they brainstormed alternative floor plans. Inspiration finally struck from the least likely of places: The *Brady Bunch* bathroom. Technically referred to as a "Jack and Jill," the bathroom on the iconic 1970s TV show had two doors, each leading to a bedroom on either side. In the Mayo version, the team proposed, two consultation rooms could share one inner examination room. It sounded intriguing, and William began to socialize the concept with his colleagues.

All was going well until one of Mayo's physicians, an outsider to the project, observed: "It won't work. You'll be able to hear voices through the doors to the shared room." With patient privacy and confidentiality at risk, this single statement had the potential to kill the entire project right then and there.

But rather than let the project die or get into endless debates that would have had the same end result, the innovation team asked clinic facilities staff to install doors in the walls of three adjoining exam rooms in their experimental corridor — that night. And by the following morning, William had his answer: No sounds or voices escaped through the closed doors. "Nothing looks the same on paper as it does in real life," says William. "We had to create full-scale mockups and throw some arrows at them to see if they'd stick or not."

With doors now cut, the innovation team converted the three rooms into the Jack and Jill configuration and, as before, invited several doctors to start seeing their patients there. Over the next several weeks, Mayo employees suggested modifications like lighting the exam room more brightly and turning up the heat a few degrees. They also realized workflow efficiencies they hadn't anticipated. Physicians could type up their notes in one room as patients changed clothes in the other, and support staff could clean the exam room while patients chatted privately with their doctors.

They also found that patients' companions — friends, spouses, language translators — appreciated the ability to stay in the consultation space while the patient had a private exam. Many patients even opted to leave the door ajar so their companions could listen in, and this unexpected behavior further helped to improve their care. One doctor asked an older male patient if the moles on his back were new. The man, who had never actually seen his own back, had barely gotten the word "no" out of his mouth when his wife chimed in from the next room, "Honey, those are new!" That quick exchange, which might never have happened in the old exam-room configuration, enabled the doctor to make a more accurate diagnosis.

Ultimately, William was able to go to the clinic's space-planning committee with an arsenal of data that supported his Jack and Jill floor plan. "It was a big investment. Having all that data gave the committee a level of comfort that they wouldn't have had otherwise. They knew it would work."

You Need a Dedicated Customer Experience Sandbox

The Mayo innovation team largely attributes the success of its prototyping efforts — and, ultimately, the redesign of the outpatient experience — to its experimental patient corridor. In that space, they're free to make just about any changes they want. "If we had to ask for permission every time we wanted to prototype something, it would take a hundred years," says Maggie Breslin, one of the project leaders.

But what if your company doesn't have a physical space like a hospital ward where customers come to visit? Can you still create a customer experience sandbox that gives you the freedom to test new customer interactions? Absolutely.

In 2011, the customer experience team at Rogers Communications, Canada's largest telecom carrier, identified five journeys that had the greatest potential to impact both the customer experience and company financials: adding a product, changing a product, changing hardware, getting support, and moving to a new home.

Rather than slowly make incremental improvements to these five journeys across the entire company, they drew a circle around a geographical area in north Toronto that's home to seventy thousand customers and got executives to sign off on designating this as an experimental area for one year. With free rein, the team redefined employee behaviors, introduced new capabilities, and retrained over five hundred employees and partners on the five customer journeys in just four weeks. Customers in this area, dubbed the "Hot House," then began to talk to agents in a different call center, meet with specially trained technicians, and have access to service capabilities in local retail stores.

Just six months into the initiative, average revenue per user for new customers in Rogers' cable and wireless businesses had risen between \$3.00 and \$3.50 more in the Hot House than across the entire Rogers network and churn was between 0.5 and 0.7 percent better comparatively. The Hot House also produced significant drops in inbound calls, repeat truck rolls, and employee absenteeism and significant increases in store foot traffic and sales conversions. As happened at Mayo, data from the experimental zone gave Rogers executives confidence to roll out the program to its most competitive districts and, eventually, to its entire customer base.

The Design Discipline Means Mastering a New Way of Thinking

The *right* customer experience changes, implemented the right *way*, won't just fall into your lap. You must actively design them. This requires learning — and then sticking to — the steps in a human-centered design process. Don't worry, you don't have to do this alone. Interactive agencies, service design firms, and innovation consultancies appropriate for the scale and scope of your customer experience initiatives can teach you the ropes and help you build design competencies within your company.

Design will stretch your skills and challenge your old ways of working. At times, it will require that you make a leap of faith and put something you're not quite sure about in front of customers you value. But we guarantee, it will be fun — and it will help you create the great experience your customers are looking for.

What happens next? Once you design new customer interactions, how can you tell whether or not they're having the effects you intended? That's where the measurement discipline comes in, and that's the topic of our next chapter.

8

Measurement

Bonny Simi sounds a little like a character in a made-for-TV movie — almost too over-the-top to be true. She's a three-time Olympian and a ten-time National Champion in the sports of luge and bobsled. She's worked as a television sports reporter in a major U.S. market and as an Olympic commentator for the NBC and CBS networks. With that background, you might expect to find her working at ESPN or Nike. But no, these days she's putting her master's degree in business management (from Stanford) to good use at JetBlue Airways. There she's a vice president and, believe it or not, a pilot.[1]

Bonny started working as a pilot for United Airlines in 1990 but moved to JetBlue in October 2003. Although JetBlue had only been flying for a couple of years, the industry was already buzzing about its customer experience. That experience was designed to "bring humanity back to travel" with features including more legroom, seat-back televisions, and tasty snacks that people wanted to eat instead of cardboard meals that they wanted to avoid.[2] It seemed like a winning value proposition to Bonny, who was passionate about customer experience.

When Bonny began her orientation training at JetBlue she was enthusiastic. When she finished her training she was still enthusiastic, but also puzzled. There'd been a lot of talk about the importance of delivering the JetBlue experience. However, the young company didn't train employees on how to deliver that experience, or measure how well they delivered it. How could Bonny, or any other crew member, know what to do and whether they were doing it well?

Bonny continued to fly while also working her way up through a series of management jobs at the airline. She eventually got a director-level position in charge of customer support planning in the call center, where she discovered the existence of a small measurement team that tracked Net Promoter Scores but didn't do much with them. She approached her boss with a proposal to build a bigger, better team that would collect a broad range of data, analyze it, and get it out to the rest of the company where it could drive improvements. She got the go-ahead to create a program from scratch and became the new director of customer experience and analysis.

Over time, Bonny implemented a comprehensive set of measurement tools. The workhorse of the program is an email survey that determines the key drivers of customer experience on each flight—the outside-in view of what matters to customers. The survey asks passengers to grade each part of their end-to-end process, starting with making a reservation and continuing on through the end of a flight.

When survey responses come back, an internal system attaches operational data, such as what channel each customer used to book his or her flight and whether there were any problems with the plane they were on. That lets JetBlue analysts correlate satisfaction scores with the likely reasons that the scores rose or fell. For example, if a previously loyal customer who took flight 637 now says that he wouldn't recommend the airline to friends, how would you know what had soured him? If operational data showed that the customer's seat-back TV wasn't working, you have a likely culprit for his change of heart.

Bonny makes sure that the right people get the data she collects. "At the executive level, we highlight the top three things that the COO or CMO need to be concerned about. Is it service in airports? How our fares and fees are doing? That analysis can drive the big million-dollar projects we're going to do and how we measure the success of those projects." For example, the public address system at the Los Angeles International Airport terminal that JetBlue flies out of had such poor sound quality that passengers couldn't understand announcements. That wasn't a million-dollar project, but it did require management intervention. Ultimately, JetBlue executives sought — and got — permission to put in their own PA system to solve the problem.

At the department level, measurement typically focuses on tracking the success of the projects that are already underway. For a project targeted at improving the airport experience (like the new PA system at LAX) the measure of success might be how passengers rate the helpfulness of airport crew members now that they can understand their announcements.

At the individual level, metrics help supervisors coach employees to develop a better experience. Bonny makes a compelling case for why this is so powerful: "Sharing positive customer feedback directly with the crew members is a fantastic motivator, and a far better way of reinforcing the JetBlue experience than a supervisor providing negative feedback."

JetBlue continues to improve its customer experience measurement practices, which Bonny deems mission critical. "If your strategy is bringing humanity back to travel, then the measure of success — besides profit — is what our customers say." Those improvements include a new measurement platform that will replace the homegrown systems the company created. The platform will consolidate all customer feedback, whether it's solicited through surveys or unsolicited — like the insight gathered from call center transcripts and posts on social media sites.

As it turns out, though, the new platform will be rolled out by Bonny's successor. She recently got promoted to vice president of talent, where she can use her *other* master's degree from Stanford, this one in human resources management.

Measurement Keeps Customer Experience on Track

Bonny Simi's measurement program takes the guesswork out of managing the JetBlue experience. It does this by capturing what actually happened during a customer interaction (such as a flight), how the customer felt about the interaction, and whether the customer is willing to recommend JetBlue afterward. That tells employees and partners what's going right (or wrong), what, if anything, to do about it, and what business impact to expect as a result.

When you adopt measurement practices like the ones at JetBlue, you'll (1) know with certainty how your customers felt about the experiences you provided, (2) understand the drivers of a good or a bad experience, (3) get actionable insight to the relevant people in your customer experience ecosystem, and (4) connect the dots between customer experience quality and business results.

In the rest of this chapter we're going to walk you through what it takes to implement customer experience measurement practices in your organization. We'll start by explaining how to lay the foundation for your efforts. To do that, you'll create something that many companies neglect: a customer experience measurement framework.

The Customer Experience Measurement Framework

A customer experience measurement framework strings together cause, effect, and business outcomes into a coherent story for your company. It's a tool that helps you decide what to measure, how to measure it, and what your findings mean to your business.

To begin creating your own framework, choose which customer experiences you want to measure. You need a two-tier system here. The first tier will give you the big picture, a broad view of your overall customer experience. That tier includes your customers' perceptions of their experiences with your company as a whole over a given period of time, like a quarter or a year.

The second tier will capture perceptions of discrete, end-to-end customer journeys, like all the steps in planning and taking a trip if you're an airline, or all the steps in finding and buying a product if you're a retailer. It should provide details about customers' specific experiences with individual touchpoints that they encounter along each journey. For JetBlue, those touchpoints might include the travel reservation website or the seat-back TV, each of which represents a potentially important experience for their customers. If you haven't already identified your list of touchpoints, you will when you conduct the customer journey mapping exercise we described as part of the customer understanding discipline in chapter 6.

Here's how this two-tier system works in practice at Royal Bank of Canada (RBC). Its first tier measures satisfaction with overall experiences like how easy the bank is to do business with and how well it communicates. In its second tier, line-of-business and channel managers measure perceptions of the touchpoints that are most important to their specific customers, whether that's ease of navigating online banking tools or satisfaction with financial advisors. RBC's second-tier metrics also include operational data, like average wait time in a branch.[3]

Some companies find that the complete list of touchpoints in their second tier feels overwhelming. For example, FedEx identified roughly two hundred and fifty customer touchpoints. Measuring all of them felt like boiling the ocean, so FedEx trimmed back its efforts by focusing on the forty-eight touchpoints that its customers use most often, like a drop box or a mobile tracking app. That allowed the shipping giant to study each of the forty-eight "in extreme detail" across all customer segments and identify loyalty drivers for each touchpoint by segment.

Picking the customer experiences that you want to measure is half the battle. The second half of the battle is deciding *how* to measure those experiences. We're now going to show you the three types of metrics you need to do just that: perception metrics, descriptive metrics, and outcome metrics (see table 8-1).

Table 8-1: Three Types of Customer Experience Metrics

Descriptive Metrics	Perception Metrics	Outcome Metrics
What happened?	What did the customer think about what happened?	What will the customer do as a result of what happened?
• Customer called to resolve problem with bill • Was on hold for 5 minutes • Spoke with phone agent 998 in Manila for 2.5 minutes • Trouble ticket opened • Trouble ticket closed	• Opens bill and sees that it's wrong—again! • Searches for customer service number and finally finds it • Waits on hold forever • Frustrated that phone agent needs so much information • Incorrect charge reversed • At least the agent was pleasant	• Complains to friends about the faulty billing • Won't purchase more from this company any time soon • Starts noticing offers from competitors
Common Metrics		
• Call and email volume • Average call time • Calls lost before answered • Website visits • Average pages per visit • Average transaction value • Average calls per customer per year	• Customer satisfaction with the overall experience • Customer satisfaction with specific aspects of the customer experience • Call resolution rate • User goal completion rate (web, mobile, tablet)	• Likelihood to recommend • Likelihood to purchase • Likelihood to switch to a competitor • Actual purchases made • Policy renewals • Churn rates
Captured through . . .		
• Analytics systems	• Surveys and text mining	• Surveys and/or analytics
Common Data Sources		
• Contact center logs and analytics • Web and mobile analytics systems • Point of sale systems • Billing systems • CRM systems • Business intelligence systems	• Enterprise Feedback Management (EFM) systems • Online feedback and survey tools • Contact center call transcripts • Customer letters and emails • Social media posts and comments	• EFM systems • Online feedback and survey tools • Contact center logs and analytics • Web and mobile analytics systems • Point of sale systems • Billing systems • CRM systems • Business intelligence systems

Perception Metrics: The True Measure of a Customer's Experience

If you remember back to chapter 1, we defined customer experience as how your customers *perceive* their interactions with your company. Therefore, to measure customer experience is to measure customer *perceptions* — which *only* exist in the minds of your customers. You'll get this insight out of your customers' heads and into your hands by asking them how satisfied they were with various aspects of each experience that you're measuring. Did it meet their needs? Was it easy? Did they enjoy it?

Like JetBlue, virtually every organization that measures customer experience collects perception metrics primarily through surveys. That's because surveys let you put numbers on what you're measuring, a main goal for any measurement system. They do that by forcing customers to respond on scales that you determine — for instance, from very dissatisfied (1) to very satisfied (5). That level of precision lets you track your progress over time *and* build models that correlate your progress with business benefits like those we described in chapter 2. This contrasts sharply with the ethnographic research techniques we described in chapter 6, which are great for uncovering qualitative insights but much too imprecise to use as a measurement tool.[4]

Surveys have another potential benefit worth noting: If you pick a standard methodology — like the American Customer Satisfaction Index or Forrester's Customer Experience Index — you can benchmark your performance against other firms that use the same approach.[5] That's particularly useful for making apples-to-apples comparisons within your industry, and across all industries.

Your only potential alternative to surveys is still in its infancy: software tools that *deduce* customer perceptions. These tools are similar to the ones we described in chapter 6. By analyzing unformatted text like call center transcripts and social media posts, the software determines the customer's satisfaction level — either with a particular interaction or overall.

This is a promising new source of insight that can supplement survey data but can't replace it for the foreseeable future. That's because the tools have a ways to go before they can accurately gauge sentiment about specific customer interactions as precisely and consistently as a survey. You should consider this option when your measurement program matures, but start out with the tried-and-true approach of fielding surveys.

Descriptive Metrics: What Happened in the Real World

Descriptive metrics consist of operational data about your customers' interactions, like call center records of when they called you and how long they were on the phone, or billing system records of what they bought from you and what channel they used for the purchase.

These metrics provide context for customer perceptions by telling you what happened in the real world. For example, a telecommunications company we worked with told us how they were once flooded by calls from customers complaining that their bills were wrong. Normally that would trigger a project to fix the billing system. But descriptive metrics showed that the customers' bills were correct for the plans they'd purchased. That led the company to conduct root cause analysis, which revealed the real problem: Customers were confused about which service packages they'd bought. Because their bills didn't align with their expectations, the bills just *seemed* wrong.

To gather descriptive metrics you'll need to get help from your IT department. They'll mine internal systems like contact center logs, billing systems, and CRM systems with a tool like SAS, SPSS, or ClickFox. Although this type of data mining can be tricky to set up initially, it's something you need to do. Otherwise, your guess as to what actually happened — was the bill *really* wrong? — won't be any better than that of your customers.

Outcome Metrics: The Insight That Predicts Business Results

Outcome metrics tell you what customers intend to do — or actually did — after interacting with your company. These metrics let you connect a customer perception like being satisfied with a shopping trip, to a business result like getting another purchase from the same customer. Outcome metrics come in two varieties: self-reported data about a customer's *intended* behavior, and historical data about a customer's *actual* behavior.

Outcome metrics about *intended* behavior ask customers to predict what they'll do in the future. Net Promoter Score (NPS) is by far the most popular metric of this kind.[6] NPS is based on customer responses to this question: "How likely is it that you would recommend [company name] to a friend or colleague?" Many companies find Net Promoter Score so compelling that they use it as both an outcome metric *and* a perception metric, assuming that people who plan to recommend them must have had a good experience. Our own research proves that's a reasonable assumption most of the time.[7] However, there is a cost: Companies that use NPS for this dual purpose trade off a detailed understanding of the experience in return for simplicity.[8]

The other outcome metric consists of data about *actual* customer behavior. Its advantage is that actual behavior equals reality, whereas intended behavior—which is based on what people *think* they might do—is one step removed from reality. For example, with intended behavior, customers may say they're going to buy from you again, but will they? And if they do, when? And how much will they spend? If you want to build a business case that shows ROI from incremental purchases, and all you've got is data about intended behavior, you'll have to make assumptions about the answers to all those questions—and defend those assumptions if they're challenged. If that troubles you, your alternative is to look up data about what customers really did, when they did it, and how they did it.

You can gather data about actual customer behavior in the same way you collect the data for your descriptive metrics. In both cases you use analytics tools to pull information from internal systems ranging from call center logs to CRM databases. In both cases, you must accurately match customer records to survey respondents. Otherwise you won't be able to create a reliable chain of cause and effect. Making that match isn't hard if you know you who you're surveying, which you will if you're reaching out to specific customers by phone or through email.[9]

When you put all of these metrics together—the perception metrics, the descriptive metrics, and the outcome metrics—you'll know how the customer perceived an interaction, what actually happened during the interaction, and the business impact of the interaction. That will let you identify problems to fix or opportunities to exploit, build detailed business cases that win organizational support, and drive continuous improvement over time. One company that does these things well is NetApp.

CASE STUDY: HOW NETAPP DRIVES CONTINUOUS IMPROVEMENT WITH METRICS

Connie Cassel is the director of customer advocacy at NetApp, a U.S.-based computer storage and data management company. She has worked in the high-tech industry her entire career, starting out in sales at Hewlett-Packard in the 1990s. Back then, HP was just beginning to measure customer satisfaction, a program that fascinated Connie. When she later moved to NetApp, she jumped at the chance to get involved with *its* first customer measurement program.

In the first year of the NetApp program, Connie hired Walker Information, a strategy consulting firm with expertise in measuring customer experience and tying it to business results. Together they launched a pilot program that surveyed the firm's largest accounts about their perceptions of major areas of the business including products, professional services, sales engagement, and technical support. The survey also asked questions designed to predict loyalty, like asking how committed clients were to their relationship with NetApp. That approach let Connie do a textbook job of tying perception metrics to outcome metrics.

Today Connie's survey findings feed a governance process that the business uses to prioritize improvement efforts and new projects. "As a company, we want to take action on those things that impact loyalty," Connie explains. "Our measurement program uncovers the drivers of loyalty, so we're able to recommend where to put the most emphasis. We know that products are by far most important, then overall quality, then being easy to do business with."

Here's how that process works: Within thirty days of receiving the results from their annual survey, Connie's team starts distributing summaries of their findings across the company, tailored to each recipient's needs. Then her team hosts workshops with each functional area to review the findings and create proposals for how to fix problems and take advantage of opportunities. Connie then rolls up all the initiatives proposed in the workshops and takes them to an executive team of vice presidents for decisions on which projects will get funded.

Connie's measurement program has become an integral part of how NetApp does business. The program succeeds because it systematically measures customer experience, identifies the drivers of customer experience quality, correlates customer experience quality with business results, and shares findings across the enterprise. That creates support not just for measuring customer experience, but for taking action to improve customer experience on an ongoing basis.

Connect the Dots Across Your Measurement Framework

All effective measurement programs model the relationships between customer experience quality, the factors that drive it, and business results. You need to do that with your program, too — and your customer experience measurement framework will help you do it. To evolve that framework over time, think about what you're measuring in the context of the customer experience pyramid from chapter 1: meets needs, easy, and enjoyable.

Meets Needs

Meeting needs is bedrock. It will make or break your business results — as Connie found out when she determined that the NetApp product experience is by far the most important driver of loyalty for its customers. That's why the first and most important question when measuring your customers' experience with your products, services, and channels is: Did we meet your needs?

The exact form of the question will vary based on the type of goal the customer was trying to achieve, and what touchpoint — like a product or communications channel—they were using to achieve it. For example, call center agents ask if the caller's issue or question was resolved completely, partially, or not at all. And it's become standard practice to give in-store shoppers a link to a web-based survey that, among other things, asks whether the shopper found everything she was looking for.[10]

Easy

Ease of doing business can also be critically important to your customers. To measure it, ask customers about the level of effort they expended to get their needs met. For example, some firms ask customers how many calls it took to resolve a problem and whether that was a reasonable number.[11]

Hardware and software giant Cisco Systems discovered that ease of doing business had become an increasingly important driver of loyalty for the company, right after core attributes like product stability. Kirby Drysen, senior director of customer listening at Cisco, dug into the underlying relationships. "We found a statistical correlation between ease of doing business and loyalty. That was easily supported by customer actions and verbatim statements—we were hearing from customers that ease of doing business with Cisco made a material difference."

If ease of doing business is this important to Cisco—whose no-nonsense IT customers use the vendor's hardware and software products to keep their companies running—then how important is it to *your* business? That's a question you need to answer through your own measurement program.

Enjoyable

Emotional engagement—how enjoyable something is—often gets ignored in measurement programs because it feels too squishy to drive business improvement. You might be tempted to shy away from it, too. But remember the feedback that Vanguard received when it streamlined its process for dealing with the families of clients who'd passed away, as described in chapter 3. Customers emphasized the compassion and concern they felt after the changes, not the fact that the process was easier because it took less time.[12]

If you still haven't bought into the importance of tracking customer emotion as a business metric, consider the story of the Southwest Airlines pilot who held a flight. He did it so a grandfather could make it to the hospital in time to be with his young grandson, who was about to be taken off life support after a tragic accident. The man's family had called ahead to the airline because they knew that the timing was tight for this unplanned, emergency trip. As the man ran from the security checkpoint in his socks, carrying the shoes that he didn't take the time to put back on, he was met at the jet bridge by the pilot, whom he thanked profusely. The pilot's response: "No problem. They can't leave without me anyway."[13]

We choke up whenever we think about that story. It makes us want to fly Southwest even though we don't expect a pilot to ever hold a flight for us. What we *do* expect is that we'll enjoy doing business with Southwest because they seem to care about their customers. And, in fact, their customers confirm our expectations: They gave Southwest the highest enjoyability score of any airline in our 2012 Customer Experience Index. That helped push Southwest to the top of our overall airline rankings, edging out even JetBlue and leaving all other competitors far behind in the dust.[14]

Let Measurement Power Your Customer Experience Efforts

Although the measurement discipline isn't as glamorous as strategy or design, it's like rocket fuel for all your customer experience initiatives. It drives interest in your programs by demonstrating results, and keeps people on track by connecting them to hard data about the effectiveness of what they're doing. You literally cannot afford to ignore the measurement discipline unless you want your efforts to run out of gas and die.

Customer experience metrics also provide a reality check for the other customer experience disciplines. By identifying the things that matter most from the perspective of your customers — and then measuring them systematically over time — you'll know whether your strategy is on track, whether your customer understanding is accurate, and how well the experience you designed is resonating with customers.

Measurement informs decisions. As you saw with NetApp, metrics are most valuable when you use them to identify and fix customer problems. But how can you make sure your company can act on those insights consistently? The solution to that problem is governance, the topic of the next chapter.

9

Governance

AFTER RETURNING HOME from a successful shopping trip to her local LEGO store in January 2012, Nancy Schaefer, an executive at a software company in southern California, sat down at her computer and typed the survey link that was printed at the bottom of her receipt. In her feedback, she gave specific praise to Xitlalic, a store employee who had been especially helpful during her visit. The next day, she received the following email:

> Dear Nancy Schaefer,
>
> Thank you for visiting our Anaheim LEGO® Store and for completing our store satisfaction survey. We are delighted that we were able to provide you with a great store experience during your January 30, 2012 visit.
>
> It is inspiring for us to share your enthusiasm for LEGO products and we want you to feel the same way about the experience you have in our stores. As manager of the Anaheim LEGO® Store, I am particularly pleased that you found our friendly staff to be exceptional.
>
> "Cece" is our nickname for Xitlalic, one of the supervisors here—I shared your feedback with her and she was very glad to

> hear that you had a great experience! Thanks from both of us for taking the time to recognize her in particular.
>
> I would like to personally invite you, at any time, to let me know how we are doing. You can contact me directly at _____@lego.com or by telephone at (714)991-_____.
>
> Sincerely,
> Tim Atwood
> Store Manager

Obviously this email wasn't an automatically generated reply. It was a personal letter that spoke directly to Nancy's comments about her in-store experience. And while this type of response may seem like common courtesy, it certainly wasn't what Nancy was expecting. Here's the message she sent back to Tim a few minutes later:

> Tim,
>
> Wow . . . your staff exceeded my expectations yesterday, and now . . . you did the same today! I almost deleted your email without reading it, assuming it was a form letter from your company's administration, acknowledging/thanking me for having taken the survey. But I was wrong. You — a real person and the RIGHT person in the organization — actually read it and responded to what I said. Again, wow.
>
> Continued success to you and your LEGO crew in Anaheim! See you again soon, I hope (I now have six great nieces & nephews . . . and they never have enough LEGOs . . . does anybody?).
>
> Thanks very much for the personal attention,
> Nancy

Make Customer Experience Governance Part of Basic Job Responsibilities

Tim's email to Nancy wasn't a random occurrence. As part of the responsibilities of his position, Tim is *required* to follow up with customer emails, and he does so every single time one arrives in his inbox. Tim hasn't been singled out for extra work or punishment. Key people in the LEGO customer experience ecosystem, from marketing managers to the company's external shipping partner, have specific customer experience responsibilities that are appropriate for their roles. These assigned responsibilities, combined with a robust process for making sure the tasks get done, enable the LEGO Company to manage its customer experience proactively. That's what the governance discipline is all about: intentional management and oversight.

The word *governance* may stir up images of executives in closed-door meetings talking about compliance. And yes, teams of senior decision makers are an important component of governance at many organizations. But governance isn't about a committee that hands out edicts from on high. And we're not suggesting that you form a police force to issue tickets for customer experience infractions.

In reality, governance models are as varied as the organizations they support. For example, Adobe and the Bank of Montreal both have centralized customer experience steering committees that include employees from multiple departments and functions. Avanza, Sweden's largest Internet-only bank, appointed Lisa Lindstrom, CEO of Stockholm-based service design firm Doberman, to sit on its board of directors and bring a customer experience focus to all of the board's decisions. And the customer experience at SEB, another Swedish bank, thrives with a decentralized approach and no single governing body.

No matter what kind of organizational model you choose to implement, the governance practices that we'll discuss in this chapter will help you drive accountability by assigning specific customer experience management tasks to specific people within your organization. These practices will also help you develop new business processes and establish oversight across your company's customer experience initiatives. We'll look first at how you can institute processes for monitoring customer experience quality and improving it on a continuous basis. Then we'll show you how to keep bad experiences from getting out the door in the first place.

Find and Fix Customer Experience Problems

In previous chapters, we described many different types of customer insights and the three flavors of customer experience metrics: descriptive, perception, and outcome. It's one thing to gather and process all of that valuable information, but it's quite another to put it to work. You need to use your insights and metrics to identify customer experience improvement opportunities and, as you put new programs into place, keep tabs on the progress of those initiatives. To illustrate what we mean, we'll show you how this works at Adobe, a company that's got governance down to a near science.

Review Customer Experience Insights and Metrics on an Ongoing Basis

As we mentioned in chapter 6, Lambert Walsh from Adobe aggregates ongoing customer feedback and metrics from sources like call center transcripts, social media posts, and customer satisfaction surveys. To make sure his efforts don't go to waste, the company has established a customer advocacy council with senior leaders from product development, customer support, finance, marketing, business process management, and its two largest business units. Every month, and on an ad hoc basis as needed, this group convenes to look at the latest data. They size, scope, and prioritize issues that they believe will make the biggest improvement to the customer experience *and* have the biggest financial impact, based on a combination of the severity of the problem and the number of customers affected.

On one recent report, the council highlighted problems with the company's software return, refund, and exchange processes that were impacting more than one hundred thousand customers each year. "We kept hearing from customers that they had to wait too long and contact us too often to get their money back," says Lambert. "In the meantime, they were losing productivity. But what's worse is that they were losing trust in us because they thought we weren't straightforward in how we were handling those transactions."

When the customer advocacy council looked at the related financial impact, they found that the company was spending millions of dollars each year to process returns. "That's *just* the expense of managing those conversations," says Lambert. "Then there's the lost revenue. We knew from the feedback that many customers bought the wrong product online, realized it right away, and wanted to spend more money on the right product, but couldn't because it often took weeks to get their money back."

You, too, need a group that's dedicated to reviewing customer insights and metrics on a regular basis. It's the only way to know when it's time to adapt your customer experience to customers' ever-evolving needs and changes within your own business.

Maintain a Dedicated Queue of Customer Experience Improvement Projects

It's important to talk about customer feedback and the financial impact of customer problems. But talk is cheap. That's why your next step is actually committing to a continuous pipeline of initiatives that will fix customers' top issues.

At Adobe, this is the role of the business process improvement council, another cross-functional group of senior leaders working under the charge of the company's CFO. Based on the input provided by the customer advocacy council, this group regularly agrees on several customer experience improvement projects to sponsor. For each approved project, they define the desired end state and measures of success. Then, in monthly meetings, the group reviews all open projects and monitors progress toward the stated objectives, making necessary adjustments to resources and staffing as needed.

"Because the business process improvement council includes people from across the entire organization," Lambert explains, "we get a holistic view of how we should prioritize our corporate resources."

Hold People Accountable for Their Role in Improving the Customer Experience

Once you've got a queue filled with customer experience improvement initiatives, it's time to think about how you're actually going to drive them to completion. That's no easy task. Most customer issues have complex root causes that span multiple departments and functions.

Rounding up all the required contributors can be like herding cats, and getting any one of them to take ownership for a given problem can seem next to impossible.

The returns process at Adobe is a great example of this. The company's product management, logistics, finance, legal, credit, and e-commerce teams all owned a piece of it. "There's no single group in Adobe who could have fixed this problem," says Lambert. Getting all of these departments to pitch in was essential.

To ensure accountability, the executives on the business process improvement council allocate people from their own departments to work on each approved initiative, and jointly appoint an executive sponsor, an operational sponsor, a program manager to guide day-to-day decision making, and a project manager to keep things on schedule. "This drives shared accountability across the organization," says Lambert.

The program manager and project manager must provide weekly status updates to the business process improvement council — and if they meet with any roadblocks, they turn to their project sponsors for help. "Often these roadblocks show up as competing objectives," explains Lambert. "Our legal team was really concerned with software piracy and protecting Adobe's intellectual property. That's incredibly important, of course. But the project sponsors helped them look at the potential piracy risk within the context of other factors, like the millions of dollars it took to service returns every year."

Part of Adobe's governance process also includes rolling new projects out to a control group before moving on to broader adoption. "We're just in phase one, and already we've gone from eight painful steps to three less painful steps," says Lambert. One victim of their handiwork: the "letter of destruction," a legal affidavit that customers used to have to sign to attest that they'd destroyed the software they'd originally purchased. "We've completely taken that responsibility off of customers by deactivating the serial number on the back end. Once that's done, no one else can install the software."

Not surprisingly, the reduction in steps has also reduced the average return time from fourteen days to six — and Lambert expects to shave off even more time as they roll the program out more broadly. "We're continually improving. We got a comment recently from a customer that it took seven minutes for him to get his refund for Photoshop Elements," Lambert recalls. "That felt great."

Adobe isn't the only company with a strong governance practice. Barclaycard US also employs a governance process to systematically find and fix customer experience problems. In its approach, one executive has ultimate oversight over each part of the customer journey.

CASE STUDY: BARCLAYCARD US ASSIGNS ACCOUNTABILITY FOR KEY PARTS OF THE CUSTOMER JOURNEY

Since 2004, Barclaycard US has grown from a virtual startup to one of the country's top-ten bankcard issuers.[1] Ed Macchi, who oversees operations strategy and analysis, won't deny that the company's trajectory has been fantastic. But meteoric growth has brought with it a bumpy customer experience. "We had way too many mistakes, complaints from customers, inefficient processes, and 'whose job is it?' issues," Ed says. "We can't continue to give customers an easy reason to do business with someone else."

To get Barclaycard on the right track for its continued growth agenda, Ed took a cue from the world of business process management and rolled out an initiative called Level 0.[2] The program centers on nine high-level processes that constitute a major part of the customer journey, like acquiring a customer, servicing customer issues, and collecting on delinquent accounts. One senior executive is responsible for each Level 0 process.

For example, Paul Wilmore, Barclaycard's senior director of consumer markets, owns the process of acquiring new accounts. "I'm responsible for every step of that chain," Paul explains. As a Level 0 owner, Paul works with eight Level 1 owners, each one in turn responsible for the eight subprocesses that support the end-to-end acquisition process. "It starts with building the right credit-card products in our systems and sending out the right marketing messages to the right target market," Paul says. "Then, when someone applies for the card, I look at how we're handling the inbound call, online application, or direct mail response and how underwriting is working. And at the end of the process, I look at how the applicant gets an approval answer and I make sure that the applicant is assigned to the right product on the back end."

"Paul doesn't have direct control over all of the pieces," says Ed, pointing out that the people responsible for all of these functional areas—like marketing, underwriting, systems development, e-business, and the call center—don't report up into Paul's consumer markets organization. "But he's got ultimate accountability for all customer-facing issues in that Level 0 acquisition process."

"So many different groups touch the consumer along that acquisition chain," says Paul. "In the past, we had accountability orphans. Siloed groups pointed at each other: 'You didn't explain the offer clearly' or 'You didn't build the offer the way I asked.' Rather than jumping in to fix problems, people shuttled them back and forth. By putting ownership and accountability across all those touchpoints, I can now say, 'I don't care where it broke or what function you're in, I'm assigning you responsibility for fixing this.'"

The Barclaycard US CEO has given Paul and the other Level 0 owners complete authority to stop any initiative—from a marketing campaign to an IT rollout—if it looks as though it's going to create a problem for customers. They also have access to a separate capital investment pool that's earmarked for customer experience improvements. Ed worked with the nine Level 0 owners to rank the group's top twenty investment ideas based on customer impact instead of Barclaycard's typical criterion of net present value. "Companies typically make investment tradeoffs between increasing revenue and improving the customer experience," Ed says. "In that world, fixing the basics gets deprioritized. We've made the Level 0 owners accountable and so we're also empowering them to make investment decisions."

The Level 0 owners report their progress and any new issues to the CEO during "pretty intense" monthly meetings that typically last from three to six hours. "Before, we didn't have a good process for communicating problems across the business," says Ed. "Sometimes we'd find out about major customer problems three months after the fact. These meetings have driven broad awareness of the issues that affect customers."

"It's been a breakthrough," Paul says of the Level 0 program. "It's enabled us to come together as a team to make sure we provide a better customer experience." Ed and Paul give credit to Level 0 for faster response times to customer issues, a reduction of the impact of internal problems on customers, and significantly fewer customer complaints.

Barclaycard's Level 0 program isn't focused solely on finding and fixing customer issues as they arise. Level 0 owners are also in charge of developing processes and systems that prevent new customer issues from arising in the first place. And that's what the next set of governance practices will help you do, too.

Keep Customer Experience Problems from Happening in the First Place

At Adobe, at Barclaycard US, and at your company, there exists a complex ecosystem of corporate policies, processes, technologies, and communications that span multiple business lines and functions. And every day, a lineup of brand-new initiatives is just waiting to add to this complexity. As you work to understand and tame your customer experience ecosystem, you need to avoid taking two steps back for every step forward. The easiest (and cheapest) way to do this is to add an extra layer of scrutiny to all new project proposals and business decisions.

Specifically, you need to ask two questions about new proposals: Does this change align with our overall customer experience strategy? And if so, what kind of impact will this have on the customer experience?

Your customer experience strategy should enable you to green-light the right initiatives quickly and veto the wrong ones without endless hours of debate. Consider a hypothetical proposal for Zipcar, the online/on-demand car rental company, to place personal concierges at each and every vehicle pickup spot. Zipcar's strategy focuses on self-service optimization, so a suggestion like that should be dead on arrival. Or imagine a proposal for Box Home Loans, the hand-holding mortgage company we mentioned in chapter 5, to develop an online help community that would enable customers to get answers from their peers and avoid calling the company. Its high-touch strategy makes this a terrible idea. Keep in mind that neither of these initiatives would result in bad customer experiences per se. As we discussed in chapter 5,they're just not the *right* experiences for these two companies.

For proposals that do align with your customer experience strategy, the next step is to assess the proposal's impact on customers. Because of the complexity of the customer experience ecosystem and the ripple effects that any new project or decision can have, this second evaluation step typically requires more time and discussion than the first.

For example, when the Bank of Montreal (BMO) acquired Milwaukee-based M&I Bank, the organizations' execs wanted to make sure that the integration with BMO's Harris Bank in Chicago proceeded as smoothly as possible for existing customers. For that to happen, the customer experience needed to be front and center for all integration decisions. "That wasn't going to happen by accident," says Kelly Harper, BMO's director of brand and customer experience. "Customer experience is based on every interaction that a customer has, so it *has* to be intentional. You *have* to think about what you're doing."

To get everyone from the three organizations to do just that, Kelly developed a customer experience assessment workbook that project leaders had to complete as part of every project plan. "It was part of the stage-gating process for funding," she explains.

The workbook contained four sections. The first assessed how employees, customers, and the broader community would be impacted by the proposed actions. The second examined more specifically how customers would be affected: Would they gain or lose functionality or access to information? Would they have to do something differently as a result of this change? The third part examined the project's alignment with BMO's three guiding brand principles: Is it *simplifying* something? Will it help us better *understand* our customers? Does it help us provide more *guidance* to customers? The fourth section got project leaders to think about project execution and rollout: What kind of training would be needed? What key messages or policy changes would customers need to receive?

"The workbooks really helped us think about issues that might otherwise have gotten lost in the short term," Kelly says. "To effectively inform the execution plan, we had to capture what was *really* going to happen to the customer. For example, if we were talking about moving from one statement platform to another, it helped us talk about what the new statements would look like, how they'd be different from the old statements, and what we'd need to do to guide customers through that change." Based on the proven success of the workbooks in the bank integration planning, Kelly's next step is to embed them into BMO's broader technology funding process.

Define a Consistent Set of Customer Experience Standards

Once you've green-lighted the right initiatives, you need to make sure they're implemented according to plan. You also need to make sure that employees don't lose sight of what's important during the day-to-day grind. This is where customer experience standards come in. Done wrong, customer experience standards can force your company into a de facto police state. Done right, they give your employees and partners helpful guardrails for making decisions.

Here's how Pamela Mead, the director of user experience at Telefónica Digital, the digital arm of the giant telecom operator, describes her approach to standards. "I'm a stickler for quality and I set high standards that my team needs to deliver to," she says. But she still keeps the guidelines for Telefónica's myriad websites, mobile apps, and tablet apps pretty light. "It's hard to make friends when you're policing things. Plus if guidelines become too heavy and cumbersome, then they get ignored. And we definitely want to allow room for innovation and out-of-the-box thinking."

How exactly does Pamela achieve this balance? "First, we try to minimize customization," she says. That's a lofty goal considering that Telefónica's digital products range from consumer-focused on-demand video services to cloud-computing applications for IT professionals to e-health products targeted at physicians. To tie such disparate products together, Pamela looks for basic elements that help Telefónica's developers and external partners create products that share a family resemblance.

For example, she's created an inventory of core functional elements that her team believes should become universal — things like search, login, and registration — that can usually behave the same way regardless of the product. Key to these "standards" are several different options for each element, which provide for the flexibility required for specific products and target customers. In addition, Pamela has just launched a user experience certification program that ties to metrics like task completion rates and customer satisfaction.[3] "We're creating an internal grading system in order to establish quality criteria that can then become a guide for people," she explains. "We want quality to be based on what we stand for as a company — Is it on brand? Is it easy to use? — and not just someone's opinion."

Customer experience standards aren't just for digital channels. The Bank of Montreal created a "Brilliant! At The Basics" card for employees to carry around that outlines the day-to-day activities that matter most, such as "Phone calls get returned . . . today" and "Sincere 'thank yous' every time."[4] As part of its "Gold Standards," the Ritz-Carlton Hotel Company provides twelve service values that guide employee actions, including "I own and immediately resolve guest problems" and "I am proud of my professional appearance, language, and behavior."[5]

Sören Lundgren, head of service management on the retail side of SEB, one of Sweden's largest banks, has taken a more distributed approach to standards. "In the past we had an extremely detailed service manual on things like how to open the branch and how to dress," he says. "But in 2009 we hid it so that no one can ever find it again. We're running a relationship bank, not a McDonald's. Our employees know that we need to open by ten a.m. and how to dress business casual. And if someone doesn't know those things, it's up to the local manager to say something to that person."

So instead of centrally mandated standards, Sören encourages each local branch to define what works for them — and to frequently test those standards by measuring customers' perceptions and business outcomes like additional sales. "Headquarters could tell the branches what to do, but that's an extremely risky strategy because the local differences are so huge. When I went to Latvia, they asked me, 'What are we going to do to improve our service quality and Net Promoter Scores?' I thought, 'Are you serious? Do you think that I, in the head office in Stockholm, know your business better than you do?'" Sören asked the Latvian branch managers what *they* wanted to do, something that no one at SEB had ever done before.

"The most important thing," says Sören, "is that you must really have the courage to believe that local managers and your staff want to create a good customer experience. It's about letting go of a bit of the control. That was the hardest part."

It may have been hard, but it's working. With his localized approach to standards, Sören has shown wild success — even turning around some poorly performing branches in as few as twelve weeks. "You can't change an organization by sending out slide decks or PDFs with service standards. You need to sit down and have coffee and debate about what you could do in your local market. When you release that creativity in local staff, it creates a lot of self-confidence — and you'll see it in the metrics the month after."

It's important to note that Sören didn't throw out the customer experience rulebook completely. Instead, he delegated governance responsibilities to each locality, which is now responsible for making and enforcing their own rules of the road.

What Will Be Your Customer Experience Rules of the Road?

From sole proprietors to multinational conglomerates, every company on the planet has some form of corporate governance. These guardrails help companies ensure that they adhere to sound business practices and, yes, stay out of trouble. The customer experience governance discipline is designed to help you do exactly the same thing: adhere to practices that will consistently deliver a great customer experience.

Governance doesn't have to be heavy-handed. Sure, every company could come up with a list of customer interactions that'll get an employee fired. But 99 percent of this is negotiable. Your job is to decide the rules of your own game — the right customer experience governance model and policies for *your* company.

To help reinforce the rationale behind your governance practices, and make sure that employees actually adopt them, you'll need to develop a customer-centric culture — as we'll discuss in our next chapter.

10

Culture

On a typical day, you might see twenty-four-year-old Carlos Gonzalez sporting large white-rimmed sunglasses, a plaid scarf, a lip ring, and a Mohawk. His appearance is important to him, but it doesn't matter to the U.S. Cellular customers who Carlos talks to every day on the phone. As a customer relations associate in the company's retention department, it's his job to try to hold on to customers who want to cancel their mobile service.

"It started out pretty normal," says Carlos, referring to the day in October 2011 when he got a call from Florence, a woman in her forties. She had called to cancel her service, just as thousands of customers had over his past four years on the job. But this call was different. A few minutes into the conversation, Florence explained that she was undergoing chemotherapy treatments and that her medical bills were piling up. She just couldn't afford her mobile phone anymore.

"She was crying, and she told me that she had never smoked a cigarette in her life and that this had come out of nowhere," recalls Carlos. "She was brave enough to tell me that she was losing her hair." Carlos, a smoker who had lost his own grandfather to cancer a few years earlier, could relate to the pain she was going through on multiple levels. "It bent my heart."

Carlos told Florence that he could help her out with U.S. Cellular's bill relief program, which gives customers in need a 30 percent bill reduction for six months. "She really did need the phone for calling her doctors and setting up appointments," he says. Florence was incredibly thankful for the assistance and, upon realizing that she'd get to keep her mobile phone, she starting crying more. Carlos started tearing up, too.

Then he did something that we're willing to bet no other customer service rep has ever done in the history of mobile operators. Carlos offered to shave his head. "I didn't want her to feel alone," he explains. "I told her that I'd do it in her honor and send her before and after pictures. She said that she was grateful and that it would mean a lot."

It would have been easy for Carlos to renege on his promise after he hung up the phone. After all, he'd spoken to Florence for fifteen minutes, tops. But he shaved off his Mohawk the very next morning. "I took the photo and sent it to Florence. It felt so good. It felt like something I needed to do for her."

Carlos's story is almost unbelievable. How, in the span of fifteen minutes, could he possibly have created a connection with a customer — a complete stranger — so powerful that he would shave off his impressive mane for her? Certainly, you can point to Carlos's personal character and kindheartedness. But he's quick to shift the focus to U.S. Cellular: "The culture here is very customer focused. I've gotten a lot of encouragement over the years to do good for our customers."

"U.S. Cellular is truly unlike any other client I've worked with," says Jeff Lewandowski, a partner at Andrew Reise, a customer experience transformation firm that's been working with the mobile carrier since 2004. "I've been through a lot of places where people put up signs that talk about taking care of customers. But the signs are just words on plastic. They don't really reflect how the companies operate. Carlos's story is a demonstration that these guys live it and breathe it every single day."

You Need to Build a Customer-centric Corporate Culture

We're not suggesting that head-shaving become the norm at your company. We're talking *culture* here, not *cult.* And Carlos's date with his razor is obviously an extreme example of customer empathy. But it's indicative of a set of values that U.S. Cellular has tightly woven into its standard operating procedures. Because those values have been institutionalized and continually reinforced, Carlos's supervisors can trust that he'll do the right thing for customers — and, clearly, he does. Not because he's told to, but because he really wouldn't consider doing anything else. Unfortunately, you can't clone Carlos. But you can help your own employees to think and act in customer-centric ways by actively working to shift your corporate culture.

How important is this? Over our past fourteen years of research on customer experience, we've asked hundreds of executives at some of the world's top companies about their organizational barriers and how best to overcome them. Year after year, they've dismissed the idea that organizational structure and reporting relationships can solve customer experience problems. Instead, they assert that culture has the single biggest potential to drive customer experience transformations.

"Culture is one of those squishy topics that people have a hard time getting their heads around in a business context," says Paul Hagen, Forrester's expert on customer-centric cultures. To make this discipline more concrete, think of it as creating a system of shared values and behaviors. Customer-centric values are the building blocks for reprogramming your corporate DNA. And behaviors are how you turn all of the practices from the other five disciplines — strategy, customer understanding, design, measurement, and governance — into habits that your company just can't kick.

So how exactly do you instill new corporate values and change employee behavior? First you need to overhaul your hiring practices so that you get customer-obsessed people (like Carlos) in the door. Second, you need to socialize the importance of customer-centricity through storytelling, rituals, and training. Third, you've got to reinforce new values and behaviors through informal and formal rewards. Tie it all together with a steady cadence of communication that never lets employees forget about why they're doing all of this in the first place.[1]

Hire for Customer Passion and Cultural Fit

Remember Kevin Peters from chapter 1? One of the key pieces of the transformation at Office Depot has been, in his words, "making sure that we have the right people in the stores." Several years ago Kevin asked all 22,500 store associates to take a personality assessment built around the Myers-Briggs Type Indicator test, designed to evaluate employees' skills, behaviors, and aptitudes as they related to serving customers. To his great dismay, a significant percentage responded affirmatively to statements like "If the job requires me to interface with customers, I'd rather not do the job."

"Over time, we had started to look for people who were most comfortable with their backs to the aisle, not with their bellies to the aisle," Kevin says, owning up to management's role in the situation. "As we went from being very customer-focused in the 1980s to being an engineering-driven organization in the 1990s and 2000s, the hiring profile of our associates began to change. We shopped for people whose skill sets were good for managing tasks. We hired the wrong people.

"That was the first crack in the concrete," Kevin continues. "Despite a plethora of incredible training materials, for some of our associates it just didn't matter." So as Office Depot rolls out its new strategy region by region, it's helping those associates who aren't a natural fit for its retail stores find other jobs. "We'll have turnover that will run higher than it did before," says Kevin. "That's disappointing and frustrating but we have to go through it."

Kevin has also rallied his human resources team to build new job descriptions and train store managers to do behavior-based interviewing. "In the past we asked questions that were largely binary. There were no probing questions, no open-ended questions to elicit info about candidates' background. You can ask, 'Are you comfortable helping a customer who wants to buy a laser printer?' Yes or no. But it's better to say, 'Tell me about an experience you had where a customer wanted to buy a tech product. What offers did you make? How did you qualify them? How did you close the sale?'"

As companies get serious about customer experience, some have started to follow the lead of Office Depot by either redeploying front-line employees that aren't committed to customers, or easing them out the door. But many firms still aren't prepared to take that kind of action. No matter your approach, screening candidates for customer-centric values as part of the hiring and selection process is one of the most effective ways to shift the overall makeup of your workforce. Why? Because finding people whose values and personalities match your target culture is often easier than changing the underlying beliefs of current employees.

In addition to probing for customer-centricity, you also need to screen potential candidates for the specific skills they'll need to deliver on the organization's customer experience strategy. For example, some Best Buy stores give applicants a *New York Times* crossword puzzle, an Internet connection, and an hour to see how far they can get. The goal is to test applicants' curiosity and facility to learn, key traits in helping customers who have a broad range of ever-changing questions. And trendy W Hotels Worldwide encourages employees to recruit staff from hip local bars and restaurants and to look for people who naturally exhibit actions in line with the hotel's Whatever/Whenever service obsession, which promises to provide guests with "whatever you want, whenever you want it."[2]

Socialize the Key Behaviors Required to Deliver a Great Experience

While the hiring process focuses on finding people with the right personality traits and values, socialization establishes new habits. Kevin Peters says, "You can't just wave a magic wand and change behaviors." That's true. But over time, you *can* embed new standards for employee behavior through a combination of storytelling, rituals, and training.

Storytelling

Scientific research shows that human brains are wired to tell stories.[3] Stories have been the primary vehicle for transmitting culture and community values for thousands of years. They'll be a key building block in reshaping your corporate culture, too.

Storytelling highlights real instances of customer-centric behavior and gives employees tangible examples of thinking from the customer's perspective. Zappos, the online retailer that's become famous for its customer-centric culture and service, has a "Wow Library" of praiseworthy recorded calls that its customer service reps can tap into at any time for inspiration on how to better open a conversation or explain a company policy. And Sage North America, a developer of accounting and human resources software for small and mid-sized businesses, invites customers to company meetings to share their experiences dealing with Sage.

Because storytelling gives the highlighted employees public kudos, it also encourages top performers to keep doing what they're doing. As Carlos told us the details of his head-shaving incident, it quickly became clear that he never expected to get any recognition for his actions. In fact, it wasn't until coworkers started inquiring about his missing locks that Carlos fessed up. But after that, it didn't take long for his story to spread across U.S. Cellular. His supervisor shared it with the call center's director, who posted it on the company's intranet site. "At first I didn't know. Then someone said, 'Hey, you're on the website!' They showed me the pictures and it was exciting. It was a good feeling."

Rituals

Rituals are activities that you integrate into employees' regular routines to reinforce what it takes to deliver a great experience. For example, the Ritz-Carlton Hotel Company has a daily fifteen-minute lineup used globally across all of its properties. This ritual includes a storytelling session, during which its employees, who are referred to as "Ladies and Gentlemen," share the great things they did for guests the day before. And Disney encourages its employees to take five minutes from their normal daily duties to do something special for guests. When an employee at one property heard that a guest wasn't feeling well, she brought chicken soup up to her room.

Rituals aren't just for frontline employees, and they don't have to happen every day. At online discount fashion retailer Gilt Groupe, customer-centric rituals extend to the behind-the-scenes teams responsible for developing Gilt's website and mobile and tablet apps. Michael Bryzek, Gilt's cofounder and chief technology officer, explains, "We celebrate technology that improves the customer experience, and we kill technologies that are no longer relevant." And when he says "kill," he means it. The company holds funerals for dead software applications.

Gilt's original content management system (CMS) — a complex program that helped the company cope with the onslaught of traffic it gets every day from 12 to 1 p.m. Eastern time — was the first to go.[4] When the engineering team rewrote a new CMS that made the site much faster for customers and deleted the old one from its code base, they celebrated. Gilt employees wrote poems and eulogies, erected tombstones, and deejayed a festive party in honor of the first CMS's demise.

When asked how the funerals help to build a customer-centric culture, Michael replies, "When things are useful for customers we invest in them, and when they're not, we invest to get them out of here." This sends a strong signal to Gilt's employees that they're expected to take ownership for projects and technologies that deliver a great experience. "It also strips away the ego," he says. "Just because you've created one great thing doesn't mean that you'll be better at creating the next. We want every single employee to express their creativity and feel empowered to create something that's great for customers."

Training

Training programs are an effective way to communicate your customer experience strategy and share customer insights. Training also helps employees develop the specific skills they need to participate in human-centered design projects, interpret customer experience metrics, or simply do their regular jobs in a more customer-centric way. Many companies think about training primarily as an activity for new employees — and certainly, onboarding is a fantastic time to indoctrinate employees into your customer-centric ways. But it's never too late to teach current employees new tricks.

Training programs often start at a grassroots level. However, to make a material impact on your corporate culture at large, you ultimately need to formalize your training initiatives. For decades, American Express had held formal customer service training sessions that focused primarily on industry- and company-specific technical skills and policies. But several years ago, a strategic shift ushered in by Jim Bush, executive vice president of world service, changed the nature of Amex's training programs dramatically. Jim explains the driver: "We started asking ourselves, do we want to be a transaction-based company where customers call in, we handle calls with scripted responses, and wish them well? Or do we want to be a relationship-based company that drives engagement with customers?" The company's leaders chose the latter, and the resulting training programs helped its Customer Care Professionals (what Amex now calls its phone agents) forge deeper emotional connections — not only with customers, but with the company as well.

In the first phase of the training program, senior leaders talk about the company's history, milestones, transitions, market opportunities, and public perceptions. Rick Bottner, vice president of global telephone servicing, explains, "We create an initial feeling for our employees that this is a high-quality company. We discuss our values: how we work, how we treat each other, and how we live in our communities. We make the connection that it's more than 'you come to work.' It's about living a role in your life and how this company can enrich that as well."

The second phase focuses on customer relationships, and starts with heart-wrenching stories of how Amex reps have helped its card members over the years. Care Professionals then learn skills such as actively listening to what the caller is saying and assessing the caller's mood, not just relying on the demographic information that's in the caller's customer profile. As we mentioned in chapter 2, they also learn how to help customers understand the value of their relationship with American Express by explaining relevant card benefits. Since implementing this new training program as part of its broader service reinvention, Amex has watched metrics like average card spend and willingness to recommend increase significantly.

To see how both grassroots and formalized training approaches can work together, let's take a look at John Deere Financial's Champions Program.

CASE STUDY: JOHN DEERE FINANCIAL'S TRAINING PROGRAM CREATES CUSTOMER CHAMPIONS

"Like many companies, we had a product and process focus for decades," says Erin Wallace, manager of customer experience at John Deere Financial, one of the largest providers of financial services to agricultural and construction customers in the United States. "Then in 2006, our senior leaders created a call to action to become more customer-focused. As part of that, we developed a new customer promise — only to realize that we didn't have the right culture in place to deliver on it."

John Deere Financial's senior vice presidents stepped in to sponsor the Working As One Champions Program, a curriculum intended to give employees customer insights and practical skills that they could take back to their departments. "The Champions Program is about driving a deeper understanding of customer and channel needs into the organization's cultural DNA," says Erin. "It was the start of a grassroots movement to instill the fundamentals of our John Deere Financial customer promises into our day-to-day actions."[5]

While the Champions Program embraces a strong grassroots philosophy, its two-year structure is planned and orchestrated at the corporate level. For the first year of the program, volunteer participants, who can be any employee in the company, regardless of position or grade, commit to monthly meetings that include deep dives into particular customer segments and training on topics like storyboarding (a process for sketching out customer interactions in comic-book style).

Many employees also opt to go through basic Six Sigma process improvement training so that they're better equipped to drive change. That's important, because in year two, the champions begin the grassroots portion of the program: They create and manage customer experience projects within their own teams.

One recent Champion developed his own customer immersion program, making it possible for any employee to spend a full day in a John Deere dealership. The participants in this program complete tasks that dealers typically must do to work with John Deere Financial, such as completing a credit application, navigating through finance options, working through a collections issue, or interacting with customer service. This immersion helps employees understand firsthand the challenges faced by dealers when interacting with the firm.

Another Champion from the collections department developed storyboards and a department-wide training to help employees understand customers' business challenges, such as agricultural production cycles and cash flow. Armed with this new knowledge, the early-stage collection teams can now ask better questions and get more relevant information, which helps them be more flexible when managing accounts. "After all, our objective is to retain customers so they can continue to buy equipment," says Erin. Ultimately, this program improved communications between early-stage, late-stage, recovery, and litigation collection teams. It also turned a typically dreadful activity into a positive experience for customers. Erin reports that the John Deere financing experience score for the collections touchpoint is one of the highest in the company.[6]

"The Champions Program is having a huge impact on our organization," Erin says. "It's allowed us to bring more conviction to our customer focus and feel more capable in executing it."

Reward Employees to Reinforce Customer-centric Behaviors

Unfortunately, many companies make huge investments in hiring and training only to inadvertently encourage employees to focus on the wrong things. How? They create operational targets for frontline employees instead of basing their incentives on the quality of the service they provide.[7] And they reward behind-the-scenes employees for plowing through lists of internal tasks and projects while providing zero recognition for work that improves the customer experience.

To keep employees focused on what's important, you need to back up your hiring and socialization practices with the right types of incentives. These include informal rewards that recognize personal achievement and formal rewards that compensate employees based on customer-centric metrics.

Informal Rewards

Informal rewards programs — like certificates, prizes, and perks — celebrate customer-centric behavior and don't typically take a lot of time or money to plan or execute. For example, the Starbucks Green Apron awards program encourages employees "to create a positive environment by aspiring to be welcoming, genuine, knowledgeable, considerate, and involved."[8] There's no nomination process for these awards — employees simply present them to each other at formal and informal plant, department, store, district, and regional meetings.

Circles, a concierge service for corporate employees, has an array of programs that reinforces the importance of going the extra mile for customers. For example, its Top Dog Award recognizes employees who help out with extreme requests. Recent winners include an agent who sent a caller night-vision goggles to help locate her lost cat and another who helped a family find a place to stay after their home was destroyed by a natural disaster. In addition to awards, Circles agents can accumulate points based on customer satisfaction surveys and redeem them for prizes, including additional time off.[9]

Informal rewards can also come in the simplest of forms: Titles that convey to employees their true importance to the organization. In addition to Ritz-Carlton's "Ladies and Gentlemen" and American Express's "Customer Care Professionals," firms with this approach include Starbucks, which calls its employees partners, and Disney, which refers to its employees as cast members. American Express also provides each agent with personalized business cards. Why do these things matter? They focus employees on their primary role—creating amazing customer experiences—and provide daily reinforcement of their value to the company.

Formal Rewards

Formal rewards programs structure raises, bonuses, and promotions around customer-focused metrics. Because they put hard cash in employees' pockets and can significantly boost their career paths, these initiatives take more rigor to implement.

At Enterprise Rent-A-Car, no one with below-average scores on the Enterprise Service Quality index can move up to senior management. On the flip side, Zappos realized that many of its call center agents were happiest in frontline jobs that provide direct customer contact. To ensure that these agents also have continued career development opportunities, Zappos created optional three-month to six-month rotations in areas such as online chat, email, and Twitter that let high performers learn new skills and earn a bump in pay.

On the financial front, companies ranging from Philips Electronics to Maersk Line, one of the world's largest container shipping companies, tie employee bonuses to Net Promoter Score targets. And insurance company Allstate ties its 401(k) match to a customer loyalty index for 80 percent of company staff, including all of its customer-facing employees.

While formal incentives can be incredibly powerful, you need to deploy them carefully. The processes, policies, and technologies that make it possible for employees to deliver a great experience should be in place before you tie compensation to customer-focused metrics. Dangling the carrot of additional pay and promotions prematurely just isn't fair and can lead to employee frustration.

Formal rewards are meant to reinforce customer-centric behavior, not be an end in themselves. Companies that jump straight to instituting formal rewards risk having employees focus on doing the bare minimum to get their payouts instead of working to develop customer-centric behaviors. Rick Bottner from American Express put it this way: "Incentives should be the cherry on top for providing superior service."

One company that successfully uses formal and informal rewards is Safelite AutoGlass, the largest vehicle-glass repair and replacement service in the United States. Its cultural transformation is a good illustration of just how powerful these levers can be.

CASE STUDY: SAFELITE AUTOGLASS USES INFORMAL AND FORMAL REWARDS TO DRIVE CHANGE

Tom Feeney, Safelite's president and CEO, admits that spending money with Safelite isn't exactly enjoyable. "We compare it to stepping in gum," he says. "It's a nuisance to get your car fixed." For years, the company's marketing materials touted customer satisfaction. "But it was just lip service. We were a cost-driven company at our core."

All that changed in 2008, when Tom took over and ignited a rapid growth strategy. "Prior to 2009, people didn't have any awareness that our business category even existed," says Tom. That's when the company launched a radio and TV ad campaign starring real Safelite technicians. Over the next several years, the company's ads began to focus less on category awareness, and more on how easy it was to work with the company and why customers would want to choose Safelite over its competitors.[10]

This was the big motivation for Tom. "Up until that point, research showed our Net Promoter Score was lower than that of our competitive set. If it stayed that way, then we would have spent all of this advertising money in vain. We needed a customer-focused culture in order to deliver on the brand promise."

Safelite's ten thousand technicians service 95 percent of the U.S. population — and four out of five of its jobs take place at customers' homes or offices. Many executives might have seen inherent challenges in uniting such a geographically distributed workforce under a common culture, but not Tom. He capitalized on Safelite's distributed structure by introducing competition.

Tom pitted market against market in a race to improve their Net

Promoter Scores. Each quarter, the company rewards the top-performing market with a celebratory dinner and a chance to hobnob with several of the company's execs, who in turn make a big fuss over the people who are wowing Safelite's customers. "Dave, a general manager in Boise, Idaho, is posting a 94 percent right now," Tom says. "He's done a fantastic job and takes it personally if they get a detractor."

It's unfortunate for the other markets, but Dave keeps winning the national contest. So to even out the playing field, Tom continually seeks out pockets of excellence and then, in his words, "We leverage the hell out of them!" When a team in Orlando, Florida, starting posting off-the-charts scores, several executives traveled there to find out what they were doing right—and brought a film crew to document what they saw. In the video (which, believe it or not, is, as of this writing, the top search result on YouTube if you search for "customer delight") General Manager Jon Laski proudly announces, "We've been number one for three months here in Florida."[11] He also shows off the office Hall of Fame, a wall filled with plaques and framed certificates that celebrate his employees' work.

In addition to competitions between markets, Safelite provides financial incentives for every employee to work toward higher scores. Customer service reps and technicians can earn additional money for their market's scores, while corporate staff members have part of their annual bonus tied to the company-wide score. "The reason we're all here is to service our customers or support the people who directly interface with customers. If someone's in accounts payable, we want them to make sure they're paying glass suppliers on time so that we have the glass to give to customers. The incentives get people to think about our overall mission as a company and help them to broaden their view of their own role."

In the five years since Safelite started this program, its Net Promoter Scores have risen from a respectable 73 percent to an excellent 85 percent. The company has also doubled its sales during that time period. "Our growth is pretty amazing when you consider that in today's economy people are much more likely to drive around with a cracked windshield," Tom says. "I believe with my whole being that creating a customer-centric culture has enabled us to do that."

Solidify Your Customer Experience Efforts with a Customer-centric Culture

No matter how solid your strategy is or how carefully you design your customer experience, it's simply impossible to plan for every single customer interaction at every last touchpoint. At some point, you need to put your trust in your company's most valuable resource, its employees, to do the right thing for customers. Similarly, sharing customer insights, measuring the results of your work, and introducing governance programs will only get you so far if your company's workforce — from your top execs down to entry-level staff members — isn't ready to embrace new ways of working.

That's why building a customer-centric culture is critical to your success.

You've now read about the six customer experience disciplines and the forty individual practices that will help you envision and implement a great customer experience. But how broadly does your company implement these practices across your organization? The answer to that question will help you gauge your company's customer experience maturity, and it's what we'll talk about next.

PART III

HOW CUSTOMER EXPERIENCE TRANSFORMS COMPANIES

11

The Natural Path to Customer Experience Maturity

TODAY, RADU CIOCAN has a much more sophisticated understanding of customer experience than he did in 2004. Unfortunately, he had to earn that understanding the hard way.

Radu is the head of customer service operations for Deutsche Telekom in Europe. Deutsche Telekom is a giant, diversified telecommunications company operating in both Europe and the Americas. It owns a number of brands, including the wireless carrier T-Mobile.

A big part of Radu's job involves transforming the company's call centers to run more effectively. In 2004, his marching orders were to bring T-Mobile's call centers in line with the overall Deutsche Telekom aspiration of becoming the "Most Highly Regarded Service Company." That may sound like an overly ambitious goal to you, but Deutsche Telekom was dead serious about it; they even started using the acronym MHRSC in company presentations.

One of the key strategies for accomplishing MHRSC was to delight customers. Not just satisfy them, but truly delight them so they'd renew their contracts when they expired and keep doing business with T-Mobile. Therefore, T-Mobile set out to delight customers. Radu got involved in a project called T-Moments, where the idea was to wow customers during interactions that were especially important to them. "For example, the first time a customer called the call center, we'd try to explain everything he didn't know, treat him special. Be so nice and impress him. We coached the agents to care about the customer and not care about the length of the call."

But there were two fatal flaws with the goal of delighting customers in the first place. Remember that T-Mobile was trying to delight customers *as a means of keeping them longer.* But as they later found out, delighted customers didn't stay with T-Mobile any longer than merely satisfied customers. That meant there was no business benefit in taking them from just happy to absolutely delighted. There was, however, extra expense: The time that call center agents put into delighting customers ran up costs for T-Mobile like crazy. "I listened to a lot of calls. Agents asked, 'How about the weather? How about that last game in Manchester?' The customer was happy, but the costs exploded." Ultimately, the combination of zero benefit and soaring costs made it clear that fighting churn by delighting customers was a dead-end approach.

Radu realized that he'd gotten off to a false start. He was determined to pick a better path, one that would improve customer retention *without* increasing costs. He analyzed the calls to his contact centers and noted that most came from customers with fundamental difficulties, such as getting the wrong bill. That led him to two important conclusions. The first was that he shouldn't try to delight customers, he should just try to fix their problems as quickly as possible. He stopped coaching agents to bond with customers, and started training them to resolve issues on the first call. When that worked, it made customers happier and also cut costs for T-Mobile because customers didn't need to phone back and try again.

Radu's second conclusion was even more important than his first. He realized that there was a limit to how much his contact centers could *ever* do to make customers happy. "Calls are generated by mistakes in other parts of the organization, from finance to IT to marketing or whatever," Radu explains. "If the customer calls about receiving the wrong bill, you can solve the problem and be very nice but that won't make the customer want to renew his contract. You should instead get him the right bill." He decided to attack the root causes of customer unhappiness: the problems that made them call in the first place. Only then would the business see a major, sustained improvement in customer satisfaction, and a corresponding drop in customer churn.

Radu began identifying the business owners responsible for irritants that caused customer contacts, and showing them the wasted costs and customer churn that resulted. His goal was to get them to stop creating problems for customers — and, subsequently, for Radu's customer service team. Today these conversations happen in a structured way. "Each month at the executive level we show the reasons for dissatisfaction and the owners of these issues. And we attach a dollar cost to the problems and show it to the responsible organizations, which take accountability for solving and reducing this kind of waste."

Ultimately, Radu made his contact centers the catalyst for an ongoing, systematic improvement process that now reaches into every part of the company's ecosystem. As one customer experience problem after another gets solved, these efforts have a huge business impact. Radu estimates that over the last two years, call center costs in Europe have gone down by 10 to 15 percent as a result of removing the root causes of dissatisfaction. That adds up to tens of millions of euros saved for a company the size of Deutsche Telekom.

Customer Experience Efforts Don't Have to Include Well-Intentioned Missteps

Why did T-Mobile's efforts to improve customer experience get off to the wrong start? T-Mobile's employees didn't understand that the way they conducted business *created* the customer experience problems that everyone expected the contact centers to solve. So unless they changed the way they operated, their company would continue to generate an endless stream of irritants for customers.

What could have helped T-Mobile reach this conclusion faster? Like every company, they needed to understand the situation they were in so they could make an informed decision about what to do next. They needed to figure out *what* steps to take in order to deliver a great customer experience, and *what order* to take them in. That would have helped Radu change his course years sooner, avoiding tens of millions of euros of cost in the process.

This lesson applies to your organization, too. It's not enough to be passionate about satisfying or delighting your customers. Your good intentions can just as easily send you down the wrong path as the right one. You need more than passion. You need a plan.

In the rest of this chapter, we're going to show you how to set the correct course—without the wasted effort. We'll do that by first describing the natural path companies follow on their way to customer experience maturity. Then we'll explain how you can determine your company's current maturity level by examining the extent to which you've adopted each of the practices from the last six chapters. We'll conclude by helping you set your priorities for moving forward so you can get started down the right path for you.

Where Are You on the Path to Customer Experience Maturity?

Based on our research over more than a decade, we have seen that organizations that pursue customer experience as a business strategy follow similar paths of evolution. That's despite the fact that these organizations span the gamut of business-to-consumer, business-to-business, nonprofit, and government. The path passes through three phases: Improve, Transform, and Sustain (see figure 11-1).

Phase One: Improve

In this first phase, organizations focus on finding and fixing customer experience problems. We've told you how Sprint, Charter Communications, Vanguard, Virgin Media, and FedEx, among others, have done this effectively on a large scale. Done right, the Improve phase is a great starting point because it produces steady, incremental advances to the experience over time. This progression creates economic benefits like cost savings and increased customer loyalty. And those benefits get the rest of the organization excited about customer experience, which helps build support for progressively larger efforts.

Figure 11-1: The Natural Path to Customer Experience Maturity

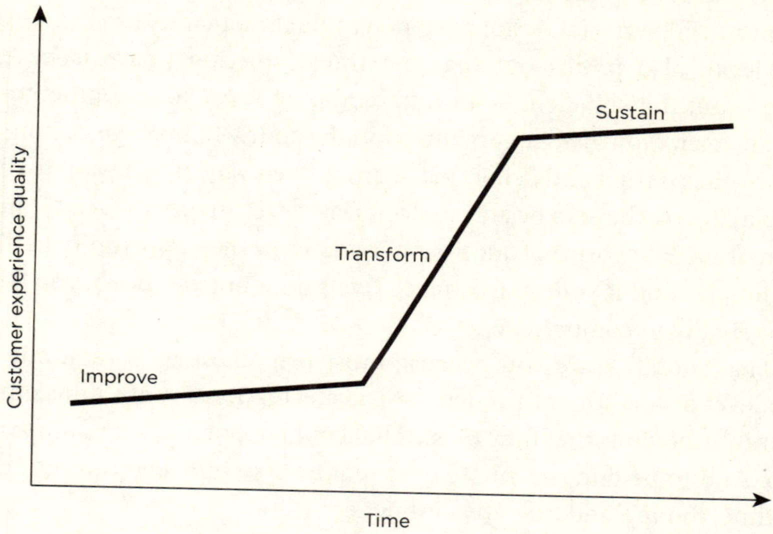

As effective as the Improve phase can be at producing results, companies can't fully profit from customer experience unless they move beyond this phase. That's because a find-and-fix approach attacks problems as they arise. Meanwhile, your organization will keep creating new problems by operating in the same ways that created the old problems.

Additionally, the find-and-fix approach will not differentiate your company over the long term. Sure, delivering service that doesn't suck can create short-term differentiation for companies in industries like health care and cable TV. But customers won't stay with you because you're less bad than you used to be. If you want a shot at winning their loyalty, you need to be consistently good. And to do that, you need to transform the way you do business.

Phase Two: Transform

In this phase, companies focus on adopting the six disciplines of customer experience. Their goal is to stamp out the root causes of customer experience problems by changing the way they operate. According to Megan Burns, Forrester's lead analyst on customer experience maturity, "The point of the Transform phase is to create an environment in which mistakes don't happen in the first place."

Megan also points out that the transformation phase is necessary—but not sufficient—for differentiating from your competitors. "Transformation gives an organization the ability to manage customer experience design and delivery in a disciplined way. If you want to differentiate, you have to be able to do at least that." In other words, transformation is the price of admission if you want the opportunity to differentiate. And if your marketplace rivals do it but you don't, you'll be perpetually *un*competitive.

That should scare you because most firms hesitate to commit to the level of investment needed for transformation—until it becomes painfully obvious that they must. That could happen at your company, too. And to be fair, this phase *does* require a significant commitment of time, money, and executive influence.

Virgin Media is one company that decided the commitment is worth it. Sean Risebrow, who you may remember from chapter 3, explains why: "At the start, our strategy was to fix things that annoy customers. We think it will take us between three and four years in total to switch from that phase to transformation. A lot of companies give up before they're finished because they're faced with making the big investments. It's not an easy transition, but our CEO is using customer experience as a reason why people will love us. It's a differentiator. It's black and white."

Phase Three: Sustain

When you routinely perform the practices in the six disciplines, you'll consistently deliver the customer experience that you want to deliver. Maintaining the practices will require the same level of effort as maintaining any sound business practices—not trivial, but significantly less than what you'll go through adopting them in the first place.

The obvious benefits of the Sustain phase will help you retain support for customer experience efforts regardless of how business conditions change. Your customer service costs will be lower because customers will have fewer problems to resolve. You'll keep your current customers longer because, as we showed in chapter 2, better customer experience correlates strongly to future purchases and reduced customer defection. And you'll add more customers over time due to more positive word of mouth. That's a great place to be.

We hope this vision of customer experience maturity excites you. To help you get there, we'll next explain an essential concept you need to know: the four levels of adoption for customer experience practices.

The Four Adoption Levels of Customer Experience Practices

To proceed up the levels of maturity without missteps, you need to understand your starting point. Specifically, you need a realistic assessment of your current adoption level for each of the customer experience practices we've described in chapters 5 through 10.

You can think of adoption levels this way: The phases of maturity (Improve, Transform, Sustain) are like grade levels in school (freshman, sophomore, junior). Customer experience practices are like the courses you have to master in order to advance to the next grade, and adoption levels are like the marks you get for each of those courses. It's a rough analogy because your adoption level is a measure of how *consistently* you perform each practice, not necessarily how *well* you perform it. But don't worry about that. We've observed that companies that consistently perform practices that are sound are way better off than companies that perform practices that *might* be better — but only do so on occasion.

To gauge how consistently your organization performs each practice on a continuum from not at all to all of the time, you'll need to determine whether each practice is Missing, Ad Hoc, Repeatable, or Systematic (see figure 11-2).

- **Missing:** Your organization doesn't perform this practice at all. For example, you may not measure customer experience at your company, or you may not have a customer experience strategy. If a practice is at this level, it's either because not enough people

Figure 11-2: The Four Adoption Levels of Customer Experience Practices (MARS)

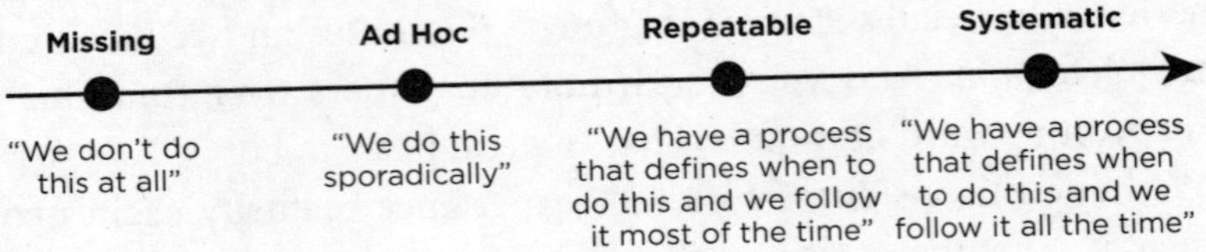

considered it important enough to do or no one thought of doing it in the first place. Regardless — it's just not happening.

- **Ad Hoc:** Your organization performs this practice sporadically. There is no defined process that specifies when it should be performed, how, or by whom. So when you see the practice performed, it's because some people realize that it's important enough to do at least some of the time. A few of them may even do it consistently. But it's all down to a matter of choice for a person or an isolated team. For example, you may find that your e-commerce division decided to use all or most of the design practices when overhauling your website, but typically makes incremental changes with little customer experience design discipline.
- **Repeatable:** Your organization has a defined process that specifies when this practice should be performed, how, and by whom. Your organization even follows the process most of the time. That means that people within your organization *could* perform the practice consistently all of the time — they just don't. When we see practices at this level it's often in one of two situations. In the first situation, some business units or departments follow the defined practices consistently and others don't. If you're a bank, for example, maybe your retail division conducts observational studies of its customers on a regular basis but your wealth management division prefers to just have informal phone conversations with its well-heeled clients. In the other situation, every part of the business will sometimes skip a practice like regular reviews of customer experience program status and metrics — it's not yet part of their DNA.

- **Systematic:** The organization has a defined process that specifies when this practice should be performed, how, and by whom. The organization follows that process all of the time. For example, you'll find that everyone in your organization who requests funding for a project checks their proposal for alignment with the customer experience strategy—*every* time they submit a request. And you'll find that everyone who measures customer experience quality uses the same measurement framework. Think this adoption level is unattainable? There are some things that organizations do the same way *every* time to produce consistently high-quality results, like paying people on time, filing their taxes, and performing generally accepted accounting practices. If you're a manufacturer, your production processes probably come up to this level, and if you're a software developer who sells to the U.S. government you need *certification* that your development process is at this level.[1] So yes, you can get to this level with your customer experience practices—you just have to want it badly enough.

Establish Your Baseline Level of Adoption

Now you need to figure out which adoption level your company is at today for each practice. And yes, just in case you've been in denial about what we've said so far, you do have to make this judgment call *practice by practice.* That's because no company we've seen is at the same level of adoption for every practice—yet. We expect to see that change over the next few years. But for now, even USAA, a leader in customer experience overall, is far more advanced in the practices of the culture discipline than it is in most of the other practices.

You've got two options for determining your adoption levels. You can take a top-down approach by conducting interviews and fact-finding workshops with the people who should be performing the practices. Or you can take a bottom-up approach by surveying your organization and asking their opinions on adoption levels.

The top-down approach will give you more actionable results. It will also cost you more in terms of both time and money (assuming you use outside help, which you probably should).[2] But even with the extra costs factored in, this is the approach we prefer *unless* you work in an organization that fixates on quantitative data. In that case, you'll need to go with the bottom-up approach by surveying your organization and asking your employees' opinions on how consistently they've adopted the forty practices we listed in chapter 4. If that *is* your situation, the good news in that your data-addicted organization almost certainly has a research department that can help you out by fielding the survey.

Ultimately you want the entire company to perform the same practices, the same way, every time. But when you first grade your adoption level you should do it business unit by business unit or function by function — and when you get your results, expect to find that different parts of your organization will be at different levels of maturity. If you want to keep things simple, start with just your own business unit. You're still almost certain to find inconsistency between departments and individuals, even at that scale.

You're also likely to see some common patterns emerge. If your company shows signs of being systematic in any disciplines, those disciplines will probably be customer understanding and measurement. Why? All types of organizations typically see the need to conduct some research about their customers and collect some type of data about key transactions. Extending these efforts into practices that are explicitly related to customer experience is a logical progression. As we'll discuss in chapter 12, that's what happened at the Washington Post, where research led directly to the creation of an enterprise-level customer experience practice.

In contrast, your company is probably weak in customer experience strategy, design, and governance. Why? For companies that haven't been thinking about customer experience as a business discipline (and few have), adopting the practices in these disciplines is not a natural progression but a major leap. When we see this kind of leap happen it's usually because someone brought a more sophisticated point of view on customer experience into the organization. That's what happened when Fred Leichter brought design thinking into Fidelity, as we talked about in chapter 7.

Whatever you find when you determine your baseline levels of adoption, you'll be able to set your priorities for moving forward. Next we'll give you guidance on how to do just that.

Set Your Transformation Priorities

Hopefully we've been clear that you need to embed all of the customer experience practices into your organization. Your next round of decisions will therefore be about what to tackle first, second, third, and so on — *not* what to do or not to do.

We're not going to give you a one-size-fits-all formula. Business transformation isn't that simple. Setting your course will call for sound business judgment based on your particular situation.

What we can do is inform your judgment by describing two overarching approaches for setting priorities, ones that we've seen work well. The first is to build out one or more disciplines where you're already strong, and the second is to shore up the disciplines where you're weakest. Let's take them in order.

Build on Strengths

When deciding whether to build on your strengths, you need to recognize that "strengths" is a relative term. Because each discipline consists of multiple practices, it's unlikely that you're systematic or even repeatable at *every* practice in any discipline. But if you do see that you're systematic — or close to it — for *most* of the practices in a discipline, you have an opportunity: Double down and master that discipline, then use it as a lever to move your organization toward adoption of the other disciplines.

For example, Discover has been building and refining its customer understanding practice, which you may remember from chapter 6, for many years. The ethnographic research it conducts and the personas and journey maps it creates help focus its many other customer experience efforts.

Shore Up Weaknesses

Instead of capitalizing on one or two relatively mature disciplines, you can choose to develop one or more exceptionally weak disciplines that hold back your other efforts.

Even a single weak discipline can hold you back because there are natural dependencies among the disciplines. For example, customer experience strategy sets the overall direction for everything else you do. If you're at the missing or ad hoc levels for the four practices in the strategy discipline, you're rudderless — you're wasting effort everywhere else. Similarly, the customer understanding discipline informs the strategy discipline by telling you what your customers really want and will respond to. So if you are weak at strategy, customer understanding, or both, you'd do well to build them up before you wander off in the wrong direction.

Example: Making the Choice

Let's take a look at how your decision either to lead with a strong discipline or to shore up weak disciplines might work. We'll do it by constructing a hypothetical example that's based on real experiences at some of the companies we've studied.

Acme Corporation, our hypothetical company, is a business-to-consumer financial services company. Carl Erickson is in charge of customer experience for the company. He recently got the assignment to put together a transformation road map as part of the annual planning process.

By doing a survey, Carl has determined that Acme is relatively strong in the customer understanding and measurement disciplines and relatively weak in all other disciplines. However, even customer understanding and measurement are poorly integrated into some parts of the business. Why? Analysis of verbatim employee comments from quarterly surveys indicates that some employees don't understand the concept of customer experience as a business strategy. That makes them apathetic toward the practices they've been exposed to so far. They just don't see the point.

Now Carl and the management at Acme have a decision to make. On the one hand, they could focus on getting all the practices in the customer understanding and measurement disciplines — where they're strong — all the way to the systematic level across the organization. That would connect employees to the real wants and needs of customers, which would help guide their efforts to improve the experience as well as measure the results of those efforts. Over time, that approach would help more people grasp the fact that customer experience is, in fact, a discipline, which would make them more receptive to the other disciplines.

Alternatively, Acme's management could develop its weak disciplines. Building up the strategy discipline would keep other efforts from wandering aimlessly by providing a clear plan. And because they're strong in the customer understanding discipline, there's a great chance that the strategy would be realistic and actionable. Additionally, the fact that cultural change has a very long lead time might lead Acme's leadership to decide to jump into the culture discipline as another priority. Over time, cultural change would solve the problem of employees not understanding customer experience as a business discipline because rituals, storytelling, and training would bring them around.

Okay, now that you've seen Acme's two options — which should Carl follow?

Either could work. Both will result in customer experience practices getting implemented *in a natural order*. Therefore, taking either path will avoid the missteps we described at the beginning of this chapter. In fact, the one option we *know* to be wrong at this point in the process would be for Acme to become paralyzed by the desire to find the perfect answer and do nothing. We've seen this happen. An organization we worked with spent so much time analyzing the deep details of all the ways their customer experience was broken that they missed the overall point: They needed to pick any natural starting point and begin making improvements.

This Is a Journey, Not a Project

Transforming your company from the outside in by adopting the six customer experience disciplines is a major undertaking. It will take years to follow the path from wherever you are today to the Sustain phase. And even when you reach that phase, you won't be finished working to improve your customer experience, you'll just be vastly better at improving it.

Kevin Peters of Office Depot put it eloquently when we spoke to him. From the beginning, he told his people: "'This is a journey, not a project. It has a beginning but it doesn't have an end.' That helped people reset their expectations that this was not a 'check the box' exercise. That this was about redefining who Office Depot is in the marketplace and how we compete."

Some companies are taking this journey faster and farther than their competitors because they have a distinct advantage: They have a new type of executive leading their customer experience transformations — the chief customer officer. We'll describe this new member of the "C" suite in our next chapter.

12

The Rise of the Chief Customer Officer

DR. JIM MERLINO WAS completing his fellowship training at Cleveland Clinic when his father entered the hospital for treatment of his bladder cancer. The medical procedure his father needed went well but there was a complication, which Jim describes as "nobody's fault." His father ended up staying in the hospital for five days after the procedure, and at the end of that time he passed away.

Jim believes that the medical treatment his father received was first-rate, but he was disappointed by his dad's experience as a patient during those last five days. Nurses didn't respond when he called, he asked for things that never arrived, and his doctor didn't look in on him regularly when he was making his rounds. "My father's experience defined the way I practiced medicine," Jim remembers. "We should pay attention to patient's perceptions of the care we deliver. They don't care what medications we prescribe so much — their only measure of quality is how we treat them."

Ultimately, the lack of patient-centered focus and poor employee engagement at the clinic were critical reasons Dr. Merlino decided not to practice there when he finished his training.

That was in 2004. Things began to change for the better at Cleveland Clinic almost immediately afterward. The clinic got a new CEO, Dr. Delos (Toby) Cosgrove, who placed a high priority on patient satisfaction.[1] To help make that new priority a reality, he appointed the clinic's first chief experience officer.[2] Soon the efforts of Dr. Cosgrove and other clinic leaders moved the organization toward more patient-centered care. Things improved to the point where Jim felt comfortable accepting a position as a staff surgeon at the clinic when a former mentor recruited him in 2009.

Nine months later, an intriguing opportunity opened up for Jim. The original chief experience officer had decided to move on, leaving the position open. Jim was encouraged to apply for the job based on his track record of high patient satisfaction. He became one of three finalists for the position, earning an interview with the CEO. When asked why he wanted the position, Jim told Toby the story about his father and how that shaped his thinking about the practice of medicine. Shortly after he left the interview, Jim got a call from the clinic's chief of staff. He had gotten the job.

Since taking the job of chief experience officer, Jim Merlino has helped accelerate the pace of change at Cleveland Clinic. He helped lead an initiative to put all forty-two thousand employees through a half-day exercise designed to help caregivers to have empathy for the patient as an individual and to care about the patient's family as well as the patient. His team crafted a service excellence program called "Communicate with HEART," which trains employees in customer-centric behaviors like listening to patients, responding to their needs, and empathizing with them. The program also teaches managers and others to be coaches, so that the result is a "self-monitoring workforce" — a culture of caregivers who encourage each other to deliver a great experience.

These efforts and others like them are working. Jim knows this because the clinic also runs a customer experience measurement program that tracks customer satisfaction at a unit level, a department level, an institute level, a hospital level, and an enterprise level — as well as at an individual level for physicians.

The clinic's results are borne out by more than just numbers. During a debrief after a recent inspection by a health-care accreditation team, the lead surveyor told the clinic's executives, "You have beautiful buildings, high-tech equipment, and intensely complicated patients . . . but it is your people who are your greatest asset. They are engaged, passionate, and compassionate. Congratulations."[3]

A New Type of Executive Emerges: The Chief Customer Officer

Jim Merlino helps bring customer experience discipline to Cleveland Clinic. His position allows him to be a powerful catalyst for organization-wide change.

Jim is also part of a trend: a rapidly growing number of C-level executives with a mandate to improve customer experience. You might not have spotted this trend because even though the ranks of these executives is swelling, they're still few in number — we've identified hundreds of them, compared to the thousands of marketing and IT execs in the world. But as you'll see, they're already a force to be reckoned with in many organizations. We call these senior leaders by their most commonly held title: chief customer officer (see table 12-1).

A chief customer officer, or CCO, is in charge of customer experience for more than a single channel, such as a website or call center, and more than a single department, such as sales or marketing. A chief customer officer is an executive tasked with leading customer experience efforts *across an entire company or division.* To qualify as a CCO, these senior leaders need to sit on the executive management team of their organization. They also need to report directly to a top decision maker like the CEO, COO, or a division president.[4]

Here's why you need to know about these people: they're showing up at companies in many industries, and they create a strategic advantage for the firms that appoint them. That means that in the near future you'll be facing off against a competitor that has a CCO. You may *already* be in that situation. And if that makes you squirm, it's because your company is going to have to make a choice between two potentially scary options: Try to deliver a competitive customer experience without a chief customer officer, or ask your board of directors to appoint a new C-level executive.

Table 12-1: Titles Held by Executives in the Chief Customer Officer Role

TITLES BY POPULARITY	
Chief customer officer	30%
Chief client officer	15%
Chief experience officer	10%
Other	45%

OTHER TITLE EXAMPLES
Chief customer experience officer
Executive vice president, member experience
Chief global customer and marketing officer
Chief customer advocate
Chief customer process officer
Chief strategy and client officer
Chief customer process officer
COO and chief customer officer
Chief client officer and president of sales and marketing
Chief customer success officer

Base: 165 randomly selected people from the 550 people identified through interviews, news announcements, Google searches, and Hoover's searches

Source: Forrester Research interviews, news announcements, Google searches, and Hoover's searches

Will your organization need its own chief customer officer? The answer is probably yes. The more interesting question for most companies is: When? We don't say this lightly. We know that CEOs and boards of directors rarely create new C-level positions. Probably the last time they did that at your organization was when they appointed your first CIO, or maybe your first CMO (if you have one, which over 60 percent of Fortune 500 companies do).[5]

In this chapter we'll help you make a decision about which course your company should take: appoint a CCO or go it alone. We'll do that by answering the tough questions about CCOs: Why do companies need a chief customer officer? Where do CCOs fit in an organization? Which companies already have them? Is your organization ready for one? And if you think the CCO job sounds intriguing, would *you* make a good one?

Why Do Companies Need a Chief Customer Officer?

Let's start with the fact that merely appointing a chief customer officer sends a signal to employees and shareholders. By appointing a CCO, your business announces that it is elevating customer experience to the same level of importance as the other disciplines that have chief officers — disciplines like information technology (CIO), marketing (CMO), and finance (CFO).

The timing is right for making this move. Remember that CIOs showed up in large numbers when information technology became important to the way companies compete.[6] As we enter the age of the customer — when empowered buyers force yet another shift in the way companies compete — appointing a CCO tells the world that you're in touch with market forces.

More importantly, a chief customer officer is a catalyst, one that most organizations need if they're ever going to implement customer experience practices at a company-wide level. Without a CCO, most firms will *never* see disciplines like customer experience strategy, governance, and measurement take hold.

To understand why that is, think about the main reason companies appoint a chief *marketing* officer. Companies have CMOs because they believe that marketing is critical to the success of their business. Therefore they want it done with consistently high quality across the entire organization. That's good management practice: Try imagining what would happen if you axed your head of marketing and scattered your marketing department around the company to work in an uncoordinated fashion. You'd still have marketing, but it wouldn't be as good as it was and it sure wouldn't be consistent.

CCOs serve a similar function to CMOs. They also provide a central point of focus for efforts that would otherwise be scattered across lines of business and departments. And they also implement a set of consistent, high-quality practices.

Think of Wayne Peacock at USAA, who we described in chapter 4. Once he took on the CCO role, he immediately launched a number of company-wide changes. For example, USAA broke down organizational barriers by structuring the company around how members shop for financial products. They took that a step further by bringing everyone in the ecosystem who talks to members — like marketers, contact center employees, and the team that runs digital channels — onto one team to ensure a consistent message across channels. And USAA even made fundamental improvements to how it interfaces with members. One of its programs added secure video-conference links in USAA retail offices so members can have "face-to-face" conversations with financial experts at the company's San Antonio headquarters.

Wayne also started to embed customer experience practices as a competence across the organization, bringing increased business rigor to the activities we described in the previous chapters. For example, he coordinated the disparate customer understanding programs around the company so that all insight goes into a central repository, where it can be analyzed to deliver a 360-degree view of each member. He also launched a program to train his workforce — which was highly motivated but focused on transaction skills — in relationship-building skills.

So far the new organizational model is bearing fruit. USAA had another record growth year in 2011 despite a down economy, continued its exceptional member retention rates, and entered 2012 as the top performing brand across all industries in our Customer Experience Index.[7]

You may be thinking that before Wayne became CCO, USAA *already* stood for great customer experience; he just kicked it up to the next level. Can a chief customer officer catalyze business transformation at a company that's starting its customer experience journey from scratch? The answer is yes, as Rosetta Stone discovered.

CASE STUDY: ROSETTA STONE TRANSFORMS ITS BUSINESS

In 2008, Jay Topper was the CIO at Rosetta Stone, a U.S.-based language learning company. It was a nerve-racking time: The company was about to begin a major business transformation.

From its inception, the company's business model had revolved around selling software CDs that taught new languages. But to continue growing, company leaders knew they had to add online companion activities like coaching by experts and peer-to-peer interactions between learners. As Jay puts it, "If you're going to learn French, you can study it all day on your computer, but sooner or later you want to go face-to-face with a French person."

However, there was a problem. To succeed in its transformation, Rosetta Stone needed its customers to engage with the new online offerings: to take sessions with coaches, and participate in peer-to-peer game nights with other foreign-language speakers. Jay and the other company leaders knew that engaging customers would be key to success, but they had no idea *how* to engage customers.

To understand how the company got into this situation, you have to realize that they'd never known much about how customers used their products. That's because their sources of customer understanding and measurement were fragmented. Each department reported its raw data (which was mostly about sales) to a different executive, not to a centralized analytics function. Therefore, no one assembled the data into a coherent picture of what mattered to customers, or reported their findings back to the business as actionable insights.

What's worse, even when the data did surface a customer experience problem or opportunity, it was often unclear who was supposed to do anything about it. "The only thing we cared about was abandonment on customer service calls," Jay explains. That's an important problem, but it's one that occurs very late in the game as a result of more important problems that happened earlier when customers were finding, buying, or using Rosetta Stone's products.

It became clear to Jay that the company needed to centralize all post-sales customer contact. That way the company could consolidate its customer data into a coherent source of insight, and assign responsibilities for dealing with customer experience problems and opportunities as they arose. He put together a proposal to do just that and, in a case of be-careful-what-you-wish-for, the proposal was approved and he was put in charge of the new organization.

As of this writing, it's been a little over a year since Jay took the job as senior vice president of customer success. Since then, many things have changed. Rosetta Stone successfully launched its online product extensions like the chat sessions and games. Now Jay monitors and manages thirteen different customer conversion points, most of them tied to engagement but not directly to sales. "I'll trade everything for engagement. Whether that's with us, another learner, a coach, or a Facebook page. Because I know the customer will be more successful if they engage."

Jay is able to say this with confidence because he knows a lot more about his customers. He knows that 91 percent of the ones who participate in a webinar — like a coaching session — say they're satisfied. What's more, they're twice as likely to use the product they bought and five times as likely to renew if they're using the online, subscription-based version of the product. In short, Jay knows that better customer experience translates into better business results for Rosetta Stone.

More things will change for customers at Rosetta Stone in the future. Jay currently has a prioritized list of sixteen projects for optimizing the customer experience while helping the firm financially *and* building its brand. The projects get considered on an equal footing with all other business proposals because they're based on the same business case fundamentals as those other proposals, including their impact to revenue, cost of acquisition, and Net Promoter Score.

Sometimes customer experience projects at Rosetta Stone win out on their merits and sometimes they don't; but for all projects, the impact to customer experience is a consideration. "If something is going to net $20 million a year without detracting from the customer experience," Jay says, "that's going to be heard loudly. But nothing gets approved without considering the impact to the customer experience."

Where Do Chief Customer Officers Fit in an Organization?

Jay Topper brought customer experience discipline to an organization that hadn't had it before, and by doing so made the customer-centric transformation at Rosetta Stone possible. He accomplished these things by taking direct charge of the customer-facing part of the organization. This is similar to the way Wayne Peacock is transforming USAA, where he oversees all nine thousand customer-facing employees. We classify this approach to the CCO position as an "operational" reporting structure.

However, there is another model that's more common and can be equally effective: CCO as matrix manager and orchestrator. That's the situation for Jim Merlino at Cleveland Clinic, John Birrer at Charter Communications, and Fred Leichter at Fidelity Investments. These senior leaders create change by influencing business decisions, as opposed to directly controlling them. Their teams tend to be smaller than those of CCOs with an operational reporting structure, at least relative to the size of their respective companies. Their impact, however, is large.

Take Laura Evans, for example. In 2011, she was appointed the chief experience officer at the Washington Post, reporting to the president of the company on business matters and the CEO and publisher on anything that has to do with content. She's part of a group of roughly a dozen executives who meet each week and review what they've learned about their customers and what they're doing with that knowledge. "The end goal is to be customer-centric in the way we operate the business, so that it underlies every one of the company's priorities," Laura explains. "My role is to embed process and build customer voice into the entire structure and planning of the company."

Laura had been at the Post for nine years prior to becoming its first chief experience officer, most recently as chief researcher. In her previous role she observed a critically important trend that was problematic. "People use more than one of our products every day. They use our mobile site in the morning and our website in the afternoon and our iPad app and the print version of our paper later in the day."

The problem that trend created for the Post was not easily solved. Some of its products had been around for over one hundred years and some had been around for just a few months. The people who designed, built, and managed those products on a daily basis operated in disconnected silos. "We weren't set up to have the larger vision of what users are like across our product lines. Of course we need specialists to optimize products, but we also need people who look across products and groups." Without those people in place, the customer experience was disjointed and the brand suffered.

To solve this problem, the Post created Laura's new position. Now she runs an organization that seeks to understand how use of one product by a customer influences the perceptions and usage of other products. She also has a formal role helping guide product development in the context of that larger vision. For example, future Post products will have greater personalization across platforms. "We want a greater understanding of your exposure prior to coming to a particular product, to see you on our website and understand that you are a news junkie and that on the way to work you already checked your phone for mobile news, so we can take that into account."

Although Laura is one of the first CCOs to appear at a major media company, she's confident that the need for chief customer officers will become clear to more companies in the near future. "They're needed at companies that are diverse in their products but not in their brand. That's happening to every media company."

What Companies Have Chief Customer Officers?

It's clear that CCOs can have a huge positive impact on customer experience regardless of their organizational model (operational or matrix). So why haven't more companies realized this and taken the step of appointing a chief customer officer? The answer is that it's early days for CCOs, a position that didn't even exist until a few years ago.

To get a handle on what types of companies have appointed chief customer officers so far, we looked at a random sample of executives who fit the CCO profile. We found that company size doesn't matter much. In 2012, we identified CCOs at firms ranging in size from very large (more than $20 billion in annual revenue) to relatively small (less than $250 million in revenue) (see table 12-2).

Table 12-2: Chief Customer Officers by Company Revenue

CCOS BY COMPANY REVENUE	
$20 billion or more	14%
$5 billion to less than $20 billion	21%
$1 billion to less than $5 billion	21%
$250 million to less than $1 billion	16%
Less than $250 million	29%

(percentages do not total 100 because of rounding)

Base: 111 people at firms with publicly available revenue data; drawn from 550 people identified through interviews, news announcements, Google searches, and Hoover's searches

What industries do CCOs work in? Overall we found chief customer officers in twenty major industries (see figure 12-1). Despite the fact that most people identify customer experience with consumer-oriented businesses, more than half of the CCOs we found work at business-to-business companies. These B2B firms range from professional services firms — as diverse as advertising agencies and network-management companies — to computer software vendors and product manufacturers.

There are two reasons for the large number of chief customer officers at business-to-business companies. First, B2B firms have a lot fewer customers than B2C companies. Losing even a single customer, especially a large client, can be *very* painful. This led many B2B firms to devote executive-level attention to customer experience sooner than their business-to-consumer peers. Secondly, a B2B company's success

Figure 12-1: Chief Customer Officers by Industry

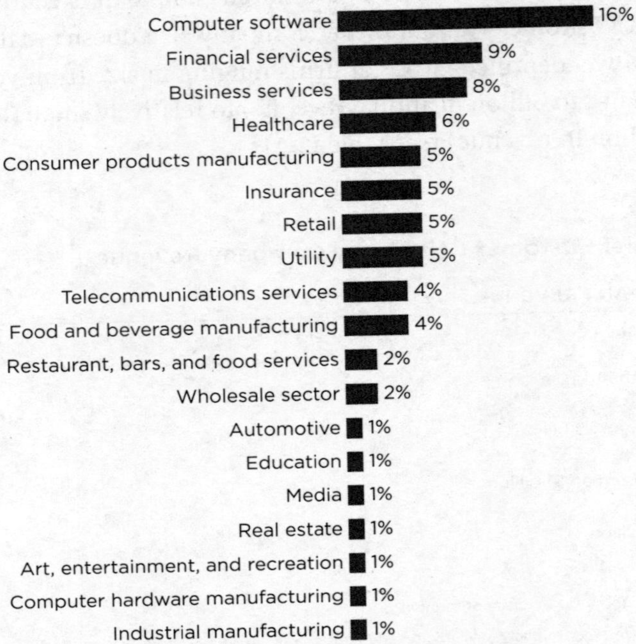

Base: 157 randomly selected people from the 550 people identified through interviews, news announcements, Google searches, and Hoover's searches (percentages do not total 100 because of rounding)

often depends on the success of *their customer's customers.* This can turn them into de facto customer experience consultants out of necessity. Think back to Debbie Newport at FedEx, who spends time making sure that FedEx customers—retailers and manufacturers—get their products to consumers when promised.

Which is not to say that business-to-consumer industries don't have CCOs. We found many across the spectrum of financial services companies, from investment firms to banks to insurance companies. We also found them in smaller numbers at retailers, utility companies, media companies, and even sports teams—like the Colorado Rockies.

Here's the bottom line: Chief customer officers are popping up at almost every type of company, and they're starting to gain serious traction in some industries. To quote science-fiction author William Gibson: "The future is already here; it's just not very evenly distributed."

Would your organization benefit from appointing a chief customer officer? To help answer that question, let's look at a company with a hundred-year track record of success that decided it would: Walgreens.

CASE STUDY: WHY WALGREENS WAS READY FOR A CHIEF CUSTOMER OFFICER

If you've shopped at a Walgreens drugstore, it might be because there's one near you. At the end of 2011, the company had 7,818 drugstore locations.[8] This is an enviable situation: Nearly two-thirds of all Americans live within three miles of a Walgreens, and six million customers walk into their stores daily.[9]

Walgreens is a trusted brand. That, together with the convenience of its many locations, differentiated the company for many years. But even though trust and convenience are still important assets, the company now competes in a marketplace that includes large competitors with their own strong value propositions and almost as many locations.[10] What's more, customers can go online for many of their pharmacy needs, making physical storefronts less important in general.

These facts were not lost on Walgreens president and CEO Gregory D. Wasson. He told his store managers that "location, location, location" would not be enough to win in the future: The company needed to move to "experience, experience, experience." His vision includes turning his stores into a staple for everyday shopping by creating a more upscale shopping experience, with prestige cosmetics and healthier food choices. He also envisions reinventing the pharmacy by letting customers do things like order prescriptions online, then pick them up at in-store kiosks. That change will free up pharmacists to get out from behind their counters and spend time counseling customers.[11]

Of course, radically transforming everything from the products you offer to how your people interact with customers is hard. That's why Greg Wasson personally recruited a chief customer officer to help make it happen.

"He did a one-man selling job on me," remembers Graham Atkinson, who had previously worked at United Airlines in a number of roles, including chief customer officer.[12] "My one condition for taking the job was to report to the CEO so I'd have a top-down mandate." Wasson agreed; putting his weight behind a customer experience transformation was exactly what he had in mind. Graham took the job, which he began in January 2011.

Graham does a number of things for Walgreens in his role as CCO. For one, he organizes facts about what customers actually want through customer understanding programs. Based on that understanding and the company's strategy, he leads change-management efforts aimed at improving the customer experience. And he measures results to make sure that transformation efforts are actually getting done and producing positive results.

Graham is optimistic about his ultimate chances for success. That's because he has broad organizational support. "It starts at the top: your CEO and your senior team talking with one voice. It has to be owned by everybody: It can't be Graham's little project." For example, a cross-functional employee and customer experience council composed of senior executives meets monthly to review progress and provide support for next steps.

Frontline employees support these efforts, too. Graham positions changes to store managers by explaining how they'll help them seamlessly handle problems — many of which they surfaced — and look like heroes to customers. That's going over well with customer-facing employees like cashiers, who've started using a new checkout system. "It's such a pleasure to hear from frontline employees," Graham says. "They are so excited about this new technology we've given them."

There's a lot riding on Walgreens' commitment to customer experience. It's how the company plans to differentiate itself and beat out its competitors. Graham believes that's a winning plan. "If you put the combined assets of location and trust together and can deliver an experience against that, it's a pretty tough bar for our competitors to jump over."

Is Your Organization Ready for a Chief Customer Officer?

Walgreens is a textbook example of a company whose executives were ready to benefit from appointing a chief customer officer. "Textbook" because they were able to answer "yes" to three important questions: Is there a clear business purpose for having a CCO? Is the culture ready to accept a CCO? Is the business willing to create a CCO job position with the power to create change?

First and most important, Walgreens had a clear business purpose for hiring Graham. He was brought in to help implement the company's new strategy, which involved significant change across all the channels and business units of the organization. Therefore his position wasn't a "nice to have," it was mission critical. That meant he arrived on day one with a strategic mandate to help transform the business and everybody knew it.

Second, the company had a culture that was ready to accept a CCO. The executive team wasn't starting from square one; they had already launched successful projects aimed at improving the customer experience. At the same time, frontline employees were eager for change. That's because they were both customer-centric and frustrated by things that got in the way of serving customers.

Third, CEO Greg Wasson made the CCO position one of his direct reports. That move gave Graham immediate credibility and the opportunity to exercise real influence over strategic decisions, including funding.

If these same success factors are in place at your company, then you're ready to appoint a chief customer officer. In fact, you probably need one. But don't just guess at whether you're ready. Instead, assess your readiness with a self-test (see table 12-3).

Table 12-3: Self-Test: Is Your Organization Ready for a Chief Customer Officer?

Please rate your level of agreement with each statement. Apply weightings to calculate total points. (Responses on a scale of 1 [strongly disagree] to 5 [strongly agree])

Strategic Mandate		SCORE
A clearly defined purpose	Our company has a clear purpose for appointing a CCO.	
Part of company strategy	Our executive management team has made customer experience an actionable part of the company's strategy.	
Aligns with business performance	Our company has identified key customer experience metrics that correlate with key business performance metrics for the firm.	
Cultural Majority		
Project portfolio	Our company has a portfolio of successful customer experience projects that demonstrate real business value.	
Engaged employees	Our company regularly engages front- and back-office staff to develop new processes that improve customer experiences.	
HR involvement	Our company has engaged HR to hire, socialize, and reward employees for delivering great customer experiences.	
Viable Position		
Power	The CCO will sit on the executive management team and will have credibility among peers.	
Operational linkage	The CCO will have the ability to influence operations company-wide that affect customer experience.	
Budget influence	The company has designated a budget for the CCO and gives the CCO influence over other budgets.	
	TOTAL	

Scores of more than 36 indicate high readiness.

Scores of less than 36 and more than 27 indicate medium readiness. These firms should work with customer experience teams to improve readiness.

Scores of less than 27 indicate low readiness. These firms risk wasting time, money, and effort by appointing a CCO.

Figure 12-2: Backgrounds of Chief Customer Officers

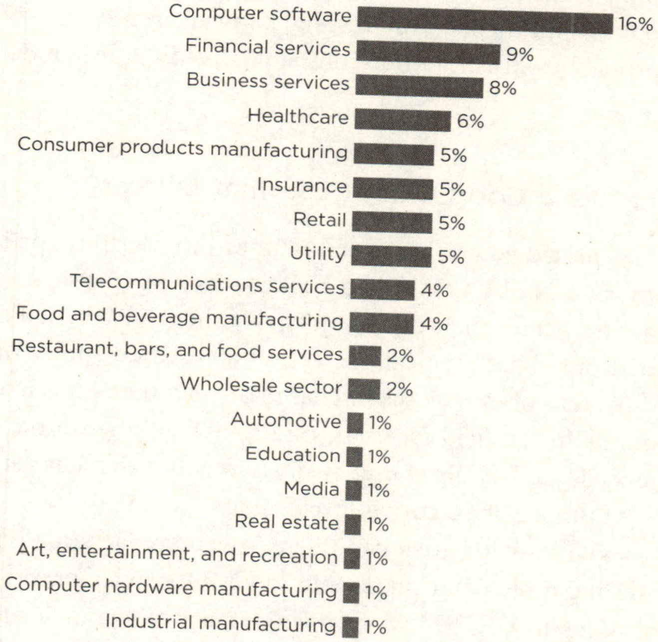

Base: 157 randomly selected people from the 550 people identified through interviews, news announcements, Google searches, and Hoover's searches (percentages do not total 100 because of rounding)

If these critical dependencies aren't in place at your company, *please* don't jump on the CCO bandwagon. You won't be doing your company or the new CCO any favors. In early 2009, we interviewed a recently appointed head of customer experience for a business unit of a giant U.S. corporation. He was a seasoned business leader who had managed hundreds of people in his previous role, and he was worried. "My job description was to improve customer experience for my line of business. That was it. No other specifics. The people that run my company look at my job as discretionary. It looks strategic, but if I wasn't here tomorrow, would it matter to them?"

That's the situation you want to avoid. But if your organization *is* ready for a CCO — if there's a business need, and a culture that's prepared for change, and executive support — then where should you look for someone to fill the job? Interestingly, the answer is that your future CCO probably works for your company already. It might even be you.

Would You Make a Good Chief Customer Officer?

It might have surprised you to learn that neither Jim Merlino nor Jay Topper — both successful CCOs — had backgrounds in customer experience before they took their current jobs. Neither did Wayne Peacock, as it turns out. That's typical, in fact: Our research shows that fewer than 10 percent of executives in charge of customer experience have backgrounds in the field (see figure 12-2).[13] That's because customer experience is a relatively young business practice that has yet to produce a large number of executive-level leaders.

So where do you look for great candidates given the lack of a typical career path like director of marketing to CMO, or vice president of network services to CIO? Most companies turn to senior leaders in other parts of their organizations to step into the CCO role. That works out well when they pick candidates who have two defining characteristics.

The first characteristic is a strong personal brand. One third of the chief customer officers whose backgrounds we examined had experience as division presidents or general managers. Almost as many had résumés that included senior leadership roles in marketing, operations, sales, or service. That gives them the ability to speak with authority to the people they're trying to influence. Jim Merlino said it best: "Being a practicing physician gives me credibility. It's a hurdle for doctors to hear advice from nondoctors."

The second defining characteristic is their unwavering belief that focusing on customers yields positive business results. That gives them the passion to keep customer experience front and center as a business practice on par with sales, marketing, or technology — something that's essential in these early days. Jay Topper put it this way: "Nothing is better than a convert. I had managed product support for a year and hated it. But then I flipped and became maniacal about the customers. This job is about taking my new passion and instilling it throughout the organization."

When you find a senior leader with a strong personal brand who believes in the business value of customer experience, then you know you've got a CCO candidate. If you have these characteristics now, you may be that candidate. If you don't have these characteristics but still think you'd like to become a chief customer officer someday, you now know what to work on when it comes to personal development.

What happens when companies don't find the right person already inside the organization? Typically they go look for someone who fits the profile at a company with similar business dynamics, like selling products or services to the consumer mass market. That's how Walgreens recruited Graham Atkinson from United Airlines.

The Future of Chief Customer Officers

Here is what you can count on happening with chief customer officers. When it will happen for you depends on the level of customer experience maturity for your company, as well as for your industry. In other words, although the future will continue to be unevenly distributed, you can influence its spread within your organization.

The first thing you can count on is that the number of chief customer officers will continue to grow, and that the growth rate will accelerate. Some of this growth will result from people doing what we just advised you *not* to do and appointing a CCO just because it's fashionable. That's a mistake you can help avoid at your firm, and it's important that you do. Companies that do make this mistake will create high-profile chief customer officer failures. Those failures will cause a temporary backlash against the CCO role. The backlash will pass in a year or two at most for businesses in general, but will set back customer experience efforts by several years at companies where a chief customer officer imploded.

Most of the growth in the number of CCOs, however, will come in response to the shift in market forces as we enter the age of the customer: commoditization, new types of competitors, and empowered customers. To compete in that world, companies will need to step up their customer experience game. The smart firms will realize that appointing a CCO—with the right preconditions for success—will be like pouring jet fuel into their car's gas tank in the race for competitive advantage (only safer).

Here's how these two dynamics—hype CCO appointments and rational COO appointments—will net out. The growth curve in the number of CCOs will look like a hockey stick with a bad dent in it. The dent is the backlash we talked about, and it will appear shortly after the curve starts shooting up. That will be remembered as the brief period of time when CCO naysayers got away with saying, "I told you so." Remember not to buy the backlash any more than you buy the hype—unless, of course, you think that customers will ever become unimportant to the success of your business.

As to where the growth will occur, industries will appoint CCOs when competitive disruption hits them so hard that it hurts. For example, The Washington Post appointed Laura Evans chief experience officer in October 2011, making her one of the few CCOs in the media industry. Her appointment makes utmost sense given the threats to the business model of traditional newspapers, which struggle to charge for their online content or to counter the proliferation of nontraditional competitors like bloggers. Similarly, you'll see cable companies appointing CCOs when Verizon lays fiber-optic cable down the streets of more and more of their franchise towns, and health-insurance providers appointing CCOs as more competition comes to health-insurance markets.

One consequence of these trends is that we'll start to see more professional chief customer officers—executives who go from one CCO job to another. Although there aren't many of them yet, we're already seeing a few career CCOs out there, like Karyn Furstman, vice president and customer experience executive at Safeco Insurance, who had been senior vice president and customer experience executive in retail banking at Washington Mutual.[14] At the point at which chief customer officers start to go mainstream, people like Karyn will be highly sought after—especially by extremely large, conservative companies who want the safety of an executive with a proven track record as CCO (ideally combined with industry expertise).

Where will this end? Not every company has a chief marketing officer, and not every company will have a chief customer officer, either. But just as you'd be hard pressed to find many companies without a head of marketing today, you'll be hard pressed to find a company without a head of customer experience in the future. That will mean a much bigger talent pool and a lot more competition among top customer experience professionals for CCO jobs, especially within industries. It will also mean that a lot more people will be attracted to customer experience as a profession, and that more executives who don't have customer experience backgrounds will want to take a tour of duty as a CCO to improve their own marketability. In short, customer experience will come into its own as a profession.

13

The Customer Experience Race Is On

WHY DON'T MORE executives prioritize their investment in customer experience? Don't they believe it will pay off? These are the questions Jon Picoult wanted to answer. Jon runs Watermark Consulting, a management consulting firm with a focus on customer experience, so this wasn't an idle exercise for him.[1]

Jon decided to examine the impact of customer experience on a company's stock. To determine that impact he compared two stock portfolios, one holding stocks in companies that are customer experience leaders, and one holding stocks in companies that are customer experience laggards.

Here's how Jon's calculations worked. For each of the first five years that Forrester published its Customer Experience Index, he compared the total return of a portfolio that held the *top* ten publicly traded companies in the CXi to the total return of a portfolio that held the *bottom* ten publicly traded companies in the CXi.

To visualize that, imagine that at the beginning of the first year you'd invested ten thousand dollars equally among the stocks of the top ten companies in the CXi for that year. Meanwhile, your buddy next door split ten thousand dollars equally among the bottom ten.[2] At the end of the year, you and your buddy both sold your portfolios. You reinvested your returns—including any dividends—in the next year's leaders, and your buddy reinvested in the next year's laggards. You both kept doing that until you got to the end of five years.

The results of Jon's analysis were striking. Over the course of the five-year period, the customer experience leaders spanked the laggards in stock performance. The leader portfolio had a cumulative total return of +22.5 percent, compared to a -1.3 percent decline for the S&P 500 market index. The laggard portfolio trailed even farther behind, posting a decline of -46.3 percent for the five-year period (see figure 13-1). For four of the five individual years, this performance pecking order held, with the leader portfolio outperforming the market index, which in turn outperformed the laggard portfolio.

"This five-year period spanned both up and down markets, and even included the depths of the Great Recession," Jon notes. "While the leader portfolio declined like the rest of the market during the

Figure 13-1: The Watermark Consulting Analysis of CXi and Stock Performance

5-year stock performance of Customer Experience Index (CXi) Leaders vs. Laggards vs. S&P 500 (2007-2011)

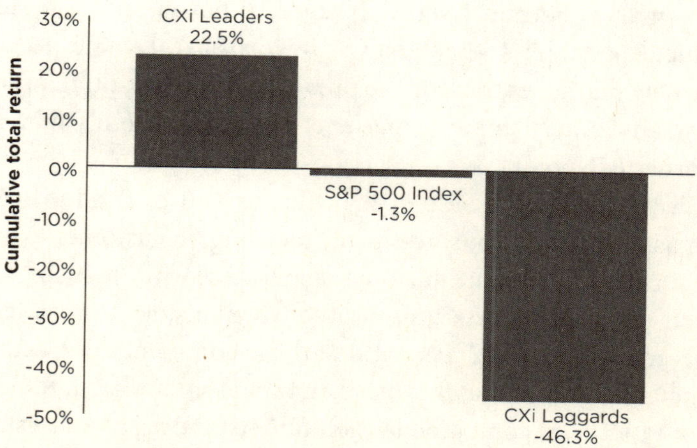

Source: Watermark Consulting

financial crisis, the impact on those firms' stocks was not as severe. In addition, they bounced back stronger when the economy began to recover. What this illustrates is that companies that deliver a great customer experience are often the last place consumers will cut back when times get tough, and among the first places to which they return when times improve."

Here's what Jon concludes: "For five years running now, we see that companies that bring great customer experiences to the marketplace are being rewarded — by consumers *and* investors alike." He attributes that to the same factors we've been telling you about since the beginning of this book: higher revenues resulting from better customer retention, greater share of wallet, and positive word of mouth, plus lower expenses due to happier customers who don't run up your service costs.[3] So what's the new news here? It's that the markets *notice,* and award higher valuations to companies that deliver a truly great customer experience.

Winners and Losers

Is customer experience a silver bullet that will kill off all your company's problems and make your stock price soar? No. If there is such a bullet, we haven't seen it. The fact is, regardless of your customer experience, you can still get clobbered by a big, strategic threat, like a new market entrant (Netflix if you're Blockbuster) or a substitute product (digital photography if you're Polaroid). That's especially true if the new market entrant or the provider of the substitute product offers an amazing customer experience (Amazon.com if you're Borders or Barnes & Noble).

Now here's the flip side of that: Just as you can't afford to ignore other aspects of your business while focusing on customer experience, you can't afford to ignore customer experience while focusing on other aspects of your business. And it's the latter mistake that's a far bigger risk at most companies. It's not that those companies don't care about their customers, it's that they have an immature understanding of customer experience compared to their understanding of well-established disciplines like marketing and logistics. Meanwhile, a growing number of their competitors not only get customer experience, they're racing to improve it.

This situation reminds us of one of our friends, an avid sailor who races competitively. Even when she's just out sailing for fun she'll often pick another boat at random, put on speed, and leave it in the dust. As she passes the other craft she likes to tell this joke: How many boats does it take to make a race? Answer: Two. How many captains need to know they're in a race? Answer: One.

Just like a clueless captain, the CEOs of companies that ignore customer experience are in a race that they won't win because they don't even know they're in it. They're not dumb — far from it — but they're not attuned to the outside-in perspective of their customers, and how critically important that's become in the age of the customer. That dichotomy between the tuned in and the tuned out sets the context for the coming years, in which some companies are already ahead in a race that their competitors are already losing.

In the rest of this chapter we'll look at some of the most important races that are already underway, and tell you the likely winners and losers.

Big Banks Will Lose the Retail Banking Race

The business models of U.S. banks have been under virtual assault by federal legislators, who have placed limits on how much banks can earn from credit cards, overdraft protection, and debit-card merchant fees. That's not surprising in an environment where many voters — the banks' customers — are furious with the banks for their part in creating the credit crisis that resulted in the Great Recession.

The combination of these new restrictions and a weak economy has cost banks billions in revenue. The big banks have responded by looking for new ways to get revenue out of their retail customers (consumers), such as charging them for using a debit card, getting paper statements, seeing a teller, and even closing an account.[4] From the outside-in perspective of a customer, that last one seems truly unbelievable: Normally companies charge for providing services, not for *ceasing* to provide services.

It's unsurprising that Bank of America had a very low score in our 2012 Customer Experience Index. Other banking giants — including Citibank, Wells Fargo, and Chase — also scored poorly. In contrast, credit unions scored higher than any bank except USAA, and far higher than the biggest banks. Those high scores correlate with record growth in the credit-union business from customers who fled banks; during the four-week period in the fall of 2011 when Bank of America and other large competitors were announcing new fees, credit unions added about 650,000 new customers and $4.5 billion in new savings accounts.[5]

Banks that keep on operating as they did ten years ago will continue to lose customers as they ignore customer experience while playing a game of cat and mouse with legislators and consumers over new fees. It's not just the change in the regulatory environment. It's the fact that news about proposed fees now reaches consumers through Internet-fueled media in a virtual heartbeat. That sparks consumer activism like Bank Transfer Day, an initiative calling for consumers to switch from commercial banks to credit unions that was organized over Facebook.[6]

Who will win if nothing changes? USAA Bank and credit unions, obviously. But other winners will include many small regional and local banks, plus online banks like Ally, which offers a checking account that pays interest and lists "We do right by our customers" as one of its three guiding principles.[7] We see banks like Ally thriving outside of the United States, as well. First Direct, a telephone and Internet-based retail bank in the U.K., successfully cherry-picks profitable customers from the other banks in the U.K. through its superior customer experience.

Will things change at the big banks? Not anytime soon — business as usual has been too damn profitable for too long. That's why they'll continue pursuing their familiar strategy of growing profits by trying to extract more revenue from each customer, despite the negative impact to customer experience. In fact, banks are now looking to charge consumers new fees for basic products like checking accounts.[8] That means their customers will see an experience that spirals downward even as they're wooed by credit unions, local banks, and digital banks.

Meanwhile, big banks can expect waves of higher service costs from questions and complaints after they enact each new round of fees, immediately followed by waves of lost customers.

Health Insurance Carriers with Mixed Business Models Will Surge Ahead

The health insurance industry has anchored the bottom of our Customer Experience Index since it began five years ago. That shouldn't come as a surprise. The CXi is a consumer survey, and most consumers in the United States don't get to pick their own health insurance. Instead, they get locked into whatever health insurance options their employers offer, like them or not. Sure, consumers *could* buy health insurance on their own, but their employer-sponsored options are highly subsidized, so they rarely opt out. That's a good deal in terms of money, but often results in a poor customer experience because the insurance carriers focus on serving the *buyers* of their product—employers—and put relatively little effort into serving the *users* of their product, the consumers.

Even though insurers run up costs by providing a bad experience to consumers, their virtual monopoly lets them raise prices to compensate.[9] And that's exactly what they've done: Premiums for workers rose 131 percent between 2001 and 2011.[10]

But now the competitive environment is changing due to new legislation. As a result of new health-care reform laws, a greater percentage of insurers' business will come *directly* from consumers starting in 2014. That means health insurers need to understand consumers *as customers* for the first time in order to attract and retain them—especially the healthiest ones who are most profitable. What's more, to keep costs down for themselves and their customers, insurers need to encourage consumers to change their behavior in ways ranging from taking better care of themselves to opting for generic drugs and medical treatment within their plan's preferred network of medical providers. That's not something insurers can do unless they've built a trusted relationship with consumers by providing a much, much better experience than they have had to date.

Transforming to become more consumer-centric will be hard — this is a major shift in how this industry thinks. It will much less difficult, though, for insurers with a mixed business model that integrates health *insurance* and health *care*, like Kaiser Permanente in Northern California, Geisinger Health Plan in Pennsylvania, and Group Health in Washington state and Idaho. That's because these organizations have medical professionals working directly for them to provide and arrange for medical care for insurance plan members. They already understand that consumers are customers, and that engaging with customers produces better outcomes for all parties. As a result, these integrated systems will transform soonest and lure customers from competitors.

A few other insurers have a good shot at turning the corner into the transformation phase before bleeding out. Companies like Humana, Regence, United Healthcare, Blue Cross Blue Shield of Michigan, and Cigna have already begun adopting the six customer experience disciplines. For them it's a matter of increasing the priority and scope of their initiatives as opposed to having an epiphany and starting from scratch.

Auto Insurers Will Get Stuck in the Improve Phase

Auto insurers in the United States received their first jolt from customer experience disruption back in the 1990s. That's when GEICO and Progressive came out of relative obscurity to challenge the market leaders with lower-cost insurance that customers could buy directly over the phone or online, without going through an agent.[11] By meeting consumer needs with a cheaper product that was easier to purchase, those two companies successfully challenged the industry leaders, State Farm and Allstate.[12] GEICO, in particular, did such an impressive job that Warren Buffet's Berkshire Hathaway bought them in 1996.[13]

Today the industry feels a new sense of urgency around customer experience. Digital disruption makes it easy for customers to find the lowest price from among a wide range of companies online, and then switch providers in minutes — which they do. The situation has gotten so bad that one in five U.S. auto- and home-insurance buyers could change insurers during 2012.[14] The result: Good-bye customer loyalty, hello downward pressure on profits.

In response, the four largest private passenger-auto insurers — State Farm, Allstate, GEICO, and Progressive — have all started emphasizing the quality of their customer experience as much as their prices. For example, GEICO greets visitors to its website with the tagline, "Real Service. Real Savings," while Allstate touts its unique "Claim Satisfaction Guarantee."

All four companies are sincere about wanting to deliver a superior customer experience. Allstate even appointed a chief customer officer. But they haven't yet committed to the level of change required to deliver a differentiated experience, as evidenced by their uniformly mediocre scores in our Customer Experience Index.[15]

Here's how this situation will shake out: In the near term, none of the four biggest auto insurers will likely adopt the customer experience disciplines to a level that would kick them into the Transform phase. They're all too busy wrestling with market changes that have them taking a hard look at which states they even want to compete in. In particular, State Farm and Allstate are too large and too steeped in legacy to pivot quickly. That means all four will be stuck in the Improve phase, making incremental gains but not breaking through to differentiation.

If one does break out of the pack within the next three to five years, it will be Progressive. They've already implemented a standout voice of the customer program, and they've invested heavily in monitoring customer feedback in social media, as well as responding to it transparently.[16] The company also has a history of customer experience innovations that continues today. For example, Progressive's "Pay As You Drive" service — Snapshot — tracks customer driving habits with a small device that plugs into their vehicles, then rewards them with personalized discounts for driving less and driving in safer ways.[17] Ironically, this innovation increases the importance of customer experience by increasing the frequency of customer interaction; Snapshot users must log in to their accounts online to view their projected discounts.

Wireless Service Providers Will Make Steady Improvements While Seeking Innovations

The wireless industry's customer experience has been on a roller-coaster ride since 2007. Back then, AT&T set a new, game-changing high bar by offering the iPhone in an exclusive deal with Apple. That set it apart from its two biggest competitors, Verizon and Sprint—*especially* Sprint, which had the lowest Customer Experience Index score by far of any wireless carrier due to dropped calls, confusion about their plans, and the other problems we described in chapter 2.

Now things have changed. Devices alone can't differentiate a carrier anymore; every major carrier, Verizon and Sprint included, now offers a wide variety of smartphones, including the iPhone.[18] What's more, Sprint has now improved its customer experience to the point where its CXi score is slightly above that of AT&T. The result is that all three players are within a few points of each other.

How will the players compete? Sprint continues to make customer experience its top priority. In the near term, Sprint's customer experience strategy centers on improving its network. That's the right thing for Sprint to do because a reliable high-speed network is a critical dependency for meeting customer needs. Unfortunately, it's not differentiating—*every* carrier needs a reliable high-speed network just to be in the game. What's more, this approach is expensive, which unavoidably limits Sprint's other options for the near term.

In 2012, AT&T *also* made customer experience its top priority. With its currently superior network and better financials, AT&T will be able to do more about that than Sprint. Expect it to overhaul its customer service experience while also innovating around multidevice ease of use, leveraging its control of wireless and landline networks. Those options could include cross-channel identity management, improved cross-carrier video experience for telepresence, and the convergence of mobile and landline communications. In that last scenario, imagine taking a video call on your phone at home, then walking out to your car and having the video stream transfer seamlessly to a display on your dashboard.

Ultimately, customer experience will become a major focus of all three players — it has to now that device differentiation will be increasingly difficult. The unappealing alternatives: build out a significantly bigger network footprint, which would be staggeringly expensive, or compete based on price, which would kill margins.

Enterprise Software Vendors Will Feel the Competitive Impact of Customer Experience

The software-as-a-service model (SaaS) for buying and using enterprise software is a game changer. It's more closely aligned with software buyers' needs and risk tolerance than the traditional software ownership model, which forces corporate customers to buy software licenses before deploying and using the software. Typically the traditional model also tacks on a hefty annual "maintenance and support" fee for each license purchased. It doesn't matter if the company isn't using the software licenses, or if the solution doesn't work well — you can't return the licenses, and the buyer's still stuck with the maintenance fee.

But under the SaaS model, there are no up-front costs — customers pay as they go under a subscription-based pricing arrangement. This lets buyers test out a solution without making a huge commitment. If the customers like the product, they can add more users at a predictable cost. This situation naturally forces SaaS vendors to pay more attention to customer experience, keeping customers happy as a way of protecting their subscription-based revenue stream.

One vendor, Salesforce.com, decided to double its bet on customer experience, as you can see by taking a look at their leadership team, which includes a chief customer officer, a chief adoption officer, and an executive vice president of customers for life. This added focus on customer experience helped Salesforce become the premium-priced customer relationship-management (CRM) SaaS application, and they seem to be holding on to this price advantage.

But now the dominos have started to fall. RightNow, a Salesforce competitor, has been winning sales by claiming that their customer experience is *even better* than that of Salesforce. Our surveys of their reference customers show that the claim is true, so it isn't surprising to note that RightNow also commands a premium price.

Traditional software vendors like Oracle and SAP are responding to this situation. Oracle bought RightNow, and SAP has become much more flexible in their licensing-fee structure, making it easier for customers to do business with them by tailoring commercial terms to their needs.

This new focus on customer experience will gather steam in the enterprise software market. The buy-as-you-go business models will force SaaS vendors to focus on experience, and the continued success of SaaS vendors will force traditional vendors to try to catch up. The real winners in this situation won't be the vendors. It won't even be the vendors' direct customers, the business technology professionals who make the purchase decision. It will be the employees of the companies that buy these products, the end users of the software, who'll get their needs met with less effort.

Customer Experience Innovations Will Provide a Competitive Edge

Our predictions aren't foregone conclusions — you can still turn things around even if you look like a loser in the race *as it's being run today.* If your organization has the commitment needed to adopt the customer experience disciplines we've described, you can move up and be among the winners in your industry — whatever industry that is.

To win the race, though, you'll need an edge. What kinds of changes to customer experience will give you that edge and allow you to pull ahead of the competition? Where should you look for your future advantage? As we look ahead we see a number of areas where leaders will tap into relatively unexploited — but mission critical — opportunities.

Digital Channels Will Continue to Change Everything

When we started working in the field of customer experience, business websites were the only important digital channel, and they were experiments. Now a variety of digital channels including websites, extranets, mobile apps, and tablet apps are so tightly integrated into the way most companies do business that simply having them won't differentiate you at all. What *will* differentiate you is what you do with them.

Companies that improve basic usability in a big way will seize a huge opportunity. Out of twenty major consumer websites we tested with our website review methodology at the end of 2011, only one — Orbitz.com — received a passing score, and even that site had some serious shortcomings.[19] To make matters worse, those test results only reflect the problems that customers and prospects encounter with a web browser on a PC. When we tested sites on the increasingly popular tablet devices we found even more problems, like video that can't be played and rollover menus that can't be opened.[20] Companies that do nothing more than require their agencies or digital design teams to follow sound, human-centered design practices will set themselves apart by making it easier for customers to do business with them. That will lead to more sales and more loyal customers — regardless of the devices customers use.

Moving beyond the basics, firms can find opportunities to differentiate through data visualization. As the sheer volume of data about personal finances, travel options, social media connections, and other areas of your customers' lives grows exponentially, they'll gravitate toward companies that make it easy to cope with all that information. For example, travel search site Hipmunk came out of nowhere to gain popularity by making it easy to compare large arrays of flight and hotel options at a glance. Any business that offers complex options to its customers can jump on a similar opportunity to differentiate by adopting tools from vendors such as Tableau Software and Visually, or by working with an interactive agency with data-visualization expertise, such as R/GA.

Human-to-Human Interaction Will Become the Oldest Newest Experience

Many of today's customer experience practices have their origins in the science of human-computer interaction. Because of that legacy, there's a natural tendency to think first of improving interactions between people and things like people and websites, or people and Interactive Voice Response (IVR) systems. But there's another opportunity that's easy to overlook as firms rush to embrace the next big thing: reinventing the human-to-human experience.

This will *only* be an opportunity for companies that do the hard work of adopting the practices in the culture discipline. Once they've done that work, they'll naturally gravitate toward this approach. Their competitors will be unable to follow suit until they overhaul their hiring, onboarding, and rewards systems, and add new rituals and storytelling to the mix.

We see instances of this today among companies with customer-centric cultures. For example, Blue Smoke restaurants in New York — owned by customer experience icon Danny Meyer's Union Square Hospitality Group — spends seven days training waiters. Each day includes an area of focus and a quiz on topics like reading the body language of everyone at a table, and learning how to adjust interaction style to meet the specific needs of that table, such as setting them at ease if they're having a tense business meeting.[21]

Reinvented human-to-human interactions will occur over the phone, as well. American Express is an early example. As we mentioned in earlier chapters, it spends 70 percent of its call center training time on skills like active listening that are needed to "read" a caller and then tailor a conversation. Companies that invest similarly will gain an edge on rivals who keep teaching agents to parrot back robotic-sounding scripts.[22]

Multichannel Orchestration Will Improve Every Channel It Touches

Companies naturally organize into silos, and often those silos are channels — like websites, phone, and retail. But as we've seen throughout this book, customers pass through multiple channels in pursuit of their goals.

Firms that adopt the customer understanding practices and the design practices we've described will see customers' end-to-end journeys clearly, then create a consistent, continuous experience at every touchpoint along the way. That's a clear opportunity for companies that take a disciplined approach to customer experience; it's impossible for companies that don't.

Multichannel orchestration around customer journeys will allow companies to do more than just synchronize channels. Firms will also create new types of experiences that cross channels. For example, we've described how Walgreens will let customers renew prescriptions online and pick them up from an in-store kiosk. That saves time for the customer and frees up the pharmacist to deliver one-on-one advice to customers.

Customer Experience Will Matter in Emerging Markets

Western companies aggressively study emerging markets to determine what consumers there need. That's the right start: Meeting needs is the base of the customer experience pyramid. But customer experience leaders will seize the opportunity to move up the pyramid by also making themselves easy and enjoyable to do business with in these new cultural contexts.

Firms that want to succeed in the BRICs — Brazil, Russia, India, China — and beyond will jump on this opportunity. A few have begun the process already. Aviva, a global insurance company headquartered in the U.K., maps customer journeys in China. Nokia, the Finnish multinational communications company, conducts extensive ethnographic research in emerging markets like India, where few customers can afford an iPhone but many bank online using SMS text messaging. These kinds of insights about what customers find acceptably easy are critical for Western companies to generate — something they'll only be able to do through the practice of the customer experience disciplines. If they don't adopt those disciplines, they'll lose out to local incumbents who can more easily understand what it's like to be customers in their own countries.

Right now, most Western firms are just beginning to think about systematically immersing themselves in the customer experience of emerging markets. Meanwhile, some firms in emerging markets have already committed to immersing themselves in the customer experience of established markets. In early 2012, Haier Group, the multinational Chinese manufacturer, announced plans to move its Asian headquarters to Osaka, Japan. Why? According to its press release, "What is most important for us is to better understand Japanese consumers, and provide high-quality appliances to meet the demands of their lives through our localized operations."[23]

What You Should Do Next

We're going to end where we started by taking you back to chapter 1. Kevin Peters, the president of Office Depot, had just realized that the employee he wanted his store manager to discipline for not helping customers was, in fact, the store manager himself.

When we asked Kevin what happened to that store manager — who we'll call Mark — his answer surprised us. "That day I was ready to fire him," Kevin recalls. "But there was something in his eyes that made me feel like he deserved another chance. I talked to his district manager and regional vice president. We decided to reinvest in Mark. My commitment to Mark was that I was going to give him a second chance but stay close to his performance.

"That was a year ago. I visited Mark's store three times since that first visit and each time it was a delightful experience. Eventually his store became one of our top-ten stores in the nation in customer service scores. And his comparable store sales were positive for a twelve-month period. Mark tried focusing on customers, ended up liking it, and it worked."

It encouraged us that Mark, who was once our poster boy for bad customer experience, turned things around at his store this drastically. We hope it encourages you, too, no matter how insurmountable the barriers to improving customer experience at your organization might look at the moment. Because, like Mark, you have an important choice to make. Are you going to commit to transforming the customer experience at your organization, or go back to business as usual and hope for the best?

For those of you who choose the path of customer experience, we'd like to leave you with some of our very best advice on how to start the transformation — not just within your organization but within yourself, as well.

First, internalize the fact that you need your customers more than they need you. Go ahead and write that down — "I need my customers more than they need me" — and post it where you'll see it and be reminded of it every day. You might think that you don't need this reinforcement, or that posting something that's so simple and obvious isn't worthwhile. Maybe it even seems a little embarrassing. But keep in mind that companies around the world *lose sight of this fact every day.* And when they do, it leads them to make choices that drive customers away.

Second, examine the reason why your company exists in the first place. Do that by reviewing your organization's mission statement. Virtually every company has one, either posted on their website for everyone to see or tucked away on an intranet. If you haven't looked at yours in a while, it's time. Because whether your firm exists to "bring inspiration and innovation to every athlete in the world," like Nike, or "to facilitate the financial security of . . . members, associates, and their families," like USAA, there are implied customers at the center of what you do. Understanding who those customers are and what you're supposed to do to meet their needs will focus you. It might even give you a sense that there's more to your job than just earning a paycheck.

Third, spend time learning what it feels like to be your customer. Go to one of your retail locations, if you have one, and buy one of your products or services. Or go to your website and try to find the answer to an important question. If you encounter a problem, call your call center and see what it takes to resolve that problem. We've walked people through this exercise countless times with their own companies. Something about the way their firm does business *always* surprises them, whether it's product descriptions that leave out essential information or call center agents who each give a different answer to the same important question. If *you* perform this exercise regularly, you'll always have a deep-rooted sense of why customer experience is important, as well as a personal queue of specific customer experience problems to fix.

Fourth, talk to your customers. Make it a part of your everyday life. When you're in that retail location, tell a fellow customer that you're an employee — as well as a customer — and that you'd love to know whether they found what they needed on that visit, and how easy or hard that was. Asking might feel awkward at first and some customers will refuse. But many will welcome the opportunity to provide feedback. When we tell people that we do research on customer experience, they often spontaneously describe a really great experience they had or, more often, a really bad one. If your company doesn't have a physical presence, visit social media sites where people talk about you on Facebook, Twitter, and consumer blogs. Hearing the authentic voice of your customers will connect you viscerally to their real thoughts and feelings.

Fifth, talk to your frontline employees. Customer-facing employees — like people in sales or service — talk to your customers every day. They hear the questions customers ask, their problems, and their frustrations, as well as what ultimately satisfies their needs. They pick up on problems, they see patterns, and they get ideas for solutions, ideas that they're dying to share *if only someone would ask.* So ask. Befriend a few people in sales or in your contact center or, better yet, both. Check in with each of them every couple of weeks and ask what they're hearing from customers, what they think is going on, and what they would do about it. For the cost of a few hours of time and an occasional cup of coffee or lunch, you'll buy broad insight into your firm's customer experience and a portfolio of ideas about how to improve it.

Sixth, try mapping a customer experience ecosystem for one of your company's most important customer journeys. We told you how to do that in chapter 3 — now set aside some time and take a stab at it. It doesn't matter whether you get it exactly right on your first attempt. In fact, you probably won't. Don't worry about that; the simple act of making the attempt will help you look at everything your organization does from the outside-in perspective of your customers. It will get you in the habit of looking for root causes, and seeing yourself and all your coworkers as part of the broader customer experience ecosystem. And that, as we've shown you, is the key to finding the real solutions to your customer experience problems.

Seventh, try connecting the dots by building a simple business case for a customer experience improvement project. You may have built business cases for projects before, but you probably haven't built one in support of this kind of project. When you do, you'll get in the habit of thinking and talking about customer experience as a way of doing business. That will give you more certainty that you're doing the right thing as you move forward, and make you more convincing when you work to bring others in your company along on your journey.

When you follow this advice, you'll begin to change the way you think. Over time you will change your perspective about your organization, your job, and your coworkers. That change will happen naturally — it will come as an inevitable result of putting your customers at the center of your business.

And if you now believe, as we do, that nothing is more important to your success in the age of the customer than putting customers at the center of your business, our hope for you is simply this: that you will learn to adopt an outside-in perspective, and use that perspective to drive positive change for your customers, for your company, and for yourself.

What Next?

If you liked the ideas in this book and want to act on them, here are some resources you can use to go further.

The website for the book is http://outsidein.forrester.com. The site includes resources and data that go beyond the content in the book, as well as links to additional information.

You can read a blog by the authors and other Forrester customer experience analysts at http://blogs.forrester.com/customer_experience or http://forr.com/CXblog.

You can follow the authors on Twitter. Harley is @hmanning and Kerry is @kerrybodine. Forrester Research is @forrester.

Want help with your company's customer experience strategy and execution? We and our fellow customer experience analysts would love to work with you. You can follow up at http://www.forrester.com/CXhelp. We can help with sessions or workshops on assessing your customer experience maturity, crafting your customer experience strategy, improving your digital channel experience, mapping your ecosystem, co-creating a breakthrough experience with your customers, and developing customer experience metrics.

To hire the authors for speeches, or if you would like us to participate in your event, email speakersbureau@forrester.com.

For bulk book orders, see the information on our book site at http://outsidein.forrester.com.

What Next?

[illegible]

Acknowledgments

Forrester Research is an amazing place to incubate an idea. That's just what we were doing for many years when the opportunity to create *The 6 Disciplines of Customer Experience* appeared. Helping clients with customer experience is a fantastic job. The chance to take what we learned while doing that and pull it all together into a book is even better. We are both deeply grateful for the opportunity to do that. And we're doubly grateful to our clients and their agency partners, many of whom bravely allowed us to tell their stories here.

It took quite a team to make this book possible.

The first person we'd like to thank is Josh Bernoff, Forrester's author-in-residence and the coauthor of the company's previous two books, *Groundswell* and *Empowered.* We'd both done many different types of writing before, but never an entire book. It's safe to say that without Josh's enthusiastic support and expert guidance, *The 6 Disciplines of Customer Experience* would not have been written.

If you found this book valuable, know that Forrester's management gave us the support we needed to create it. The CEO of Forrester Research, George F. Colony, and the COO, Charles Rutstein, created an environment where we could serve customer experience professionals with the best research possible. Dennis van Lingen, managing director of Forrester's Marketing & Strategy client group, believed in the project enough to allow us to spend a big chunk of research time on it. And Dwight Griesman, who was Forrester's CMO for the bulk of this project, bought into our vision and contributed the resources to boost its visibility, inside and outside the company.

We reserve our highest praise for the members of Forrester's customer experience research team. Moira Dorsey, who leads the practice, made it possible for us to spend the time needed to write the book by literally doing three more-than-full-time jobs (really well!) for six months. Victoria Bough, Moira's predecessor, deserves credit for getting the project started. We are also grateful to the analysts on our team, whose research serves as the foundation for this book: Jonathan Browne, Paul Hagen, Ron Rogowski, and Adele Sage, and former analysts Liz Boehm, Vidya Drego, and Andrew McInnes. We're especially grateful to Megan "Fifth Beatle" Burns, the analyst who created the maturity framework we explored in chapters 4 through 11; and our research associate, Allison Stone, whose attention to detail kept us on track throughout this long and painstaking process.

We'd be remiss if we didn't also thank the other members of the customer experience team, who not only put up with our lack of availability but pitched in when we needed help: Customer Experience Council advisors Sam Stern, Allie Viglianti, Ali Hellberg, and Amelia Sizemore, and former advisor Tracy Shouldice; consultants Jeremy Sweeney and Katie Thompson; and our other research associates, Belle Bocal and Jennifer Peterson.

We'd like to recognize the rest of the Forrester staff who contributed selflessly to our little project. These include Amy Lewis on the website, Jens Kueter on graphics, and Katie Petroff on our events. The Forrester marketing and publicity team worked tirelessly to create visibility for our work. Gail Mann (our hero) deserves two gold stars for resolving our legal issues. Thanks to Merlina McGovern for saving us from hyper-hyphenation.

Our agents, Ike Williams and Katherine Flynn, shepherded the proposal to completion and helped us to make the bold decision to choose Amazon Publishing as our publisher. And David Moldawer, our editor at Amazon, had the confidence to make us Amazon's first business book and edited our manuscript even as he navigated the rapids of helping launch a new publisher. Thanks, David. Now get some sleep.

Harley would like to thank his wife, Kit—a darn good writer herself, from a family of writers—for her unwavering encouragement and support, and his son, Alex, who upon hearing an early draft of our opening story read aloud, said "I'd be interested in reading this book even though I'm only ten years old." Kerry would like to thank her husband, Haven, for bringing love, humor, and serious design mojo to many late-night conversations about the ideas in this book.

And to all the customers out there: Always remember that the companies you do business with need you more than you need them. We hope that in some small way we're helping you to get what you deserve in return for your hard-earned money—a great customer experience.

—Harley Manning and Kerry Bodine
Cambridge, Massachusetts, and San Francisco, California
May 2012

Notes

Much of the information in this book comes from direct in-person, telephone, and email interviews by the authors with the people and representatives of the companies described in the book. Facts and quotes that do not have a note come from these personal interviews.

In these notes, when citing a long web address, we typically use an equivalent address of the form http://forr.com/outinX-Y. We created these site references for the convenience of the reader. Enter the web address into your browser and you will be redirected to the appropriate site online.

Please note that, as in all cases with web addresses, people sometimes change or remove content that we have cited. Web content cited was visible at the time the book was written.

Many of these citations are Forrester reports. If you are a Forrester client with appropriate access, the cited address will take you to the report page online where you can read or download the full report. If you are not a client or your relationship with Forrester does not include access to the report, you'll see a short excerpt of the report. If you're still interested in the full report, you can sign up to become a client or purchase the report.

1. You Need Your Customers More Than They Need You

1 Kevin A. Peters, "Improving the In-Store Customer Experience" (speech delivered at Forrester's Customer Experience Forum, 2011, New York, NY, June 21, 2011). Supple-

mental information from interviews conducted for the April 18, 2011, Forrester Report, "How Companies Raised Their Customer Experience Index Scores, 2011," available at http://forr.com/outin1-1.

2 Interview conducted with Steve McCallion of Ziba for the December 2003 Forrester Report, "The Power of Design Personas." Report no longer available online.

3 Elizabeth B. N. Sanders, Ph.D., "Converging Perspectives: Product Development Research for the 1990s," *Design Management Journal* Vol. 3 No. 4 (1992): 49–54. Sanders described the three-level hierarchy as useful, usable, and desirable, terms drawn from the field of product design. As we broadened the concept of the pyramid beyond just products, we found it helpful to also broaden the terminology used in the pyramid. See http://forr.com/outin1-3.

4 Harley switched from Comcast to Verizon FiOS in December of 2008. During that time period, Comcast's Internet service provider offering ranked No. 105 out of 113 brands in Forrester's Customer Experience Index. During the same time period, Comcast's TV service provider offering ranked No. 109.

5 These changes in the competitive environment will cause companies to shift spending to real-time customer intelligence and enhanced customer experiences, and shift their sales and marketing mind-set from push to pull. See the June 6, 2011, Forrester Report, "Competitive Strategy in the Age of the Customer," available at http://forr.com/outin1-5.

6 Don't just take our word for it. As strategy guru Michael Porter has said, "Where the buyer has full information about demand, actual market prices, and even supplier costs, this usually yields the buyer greater bargaining leverage." Michael E. Porter, *Competitive Strategy* (New York: Free Press, 1998) .

2. Customer Experience Means Billions to Business

1 Fidelity, like many of the companies highlighted in this book, uses Net Promoter Score as one of the tools for managing its customer experience. In Net Promoter terms, a detractor is anyone who rates their likelihood to recommend the product or service to a friend at a 6 or lower on a scale ranging from 0 to 10. For more information about Net Promoter score, see http://forr.com/outin2-1.

2 Sprint was dead last in J. D. Power rankings and was also the lowest-rated company in Forrester's Customer Experience Index.

3 Released in May of 2011, the ACSI survey also shows that Sprint is the number-one most-improved company in customer satisfaction, across all industries, over the last three years. See http://forr.com/outin2-3.

4 Technically a Crown corporation is owned and operated by the monarch of the commonwealth. For more information about Crown corporations, see http://forr.com/outin2-4.

5 Assuming you're not a math wonk, here's the nonwonk way to think about these findings. Correlations at or above 0.5 are typically considered high. But correlations above 0.8 are often suspect — sometimes they mean that you actually measured the same thing two different ways. These results of 0.71 for purchase intent and 0.65 for likelihood to recommend fall into a sweet spot of the range: impressively large while still quite believable. For more information about these correlations and how they connect customer

experience to loyalty, see the March 26, 2012, Forrester Report, "The Business Impact of Customer Experience, 2012," available at http://forr.com/outin2-5.

6 Technically it's an inverse correlation, sometimes called a negative correlation. This means that the higher the score, the less likely the customer is to switch to a competitor.

7 Given that there are only three companies in the CXi data set for parcel shipping and delivery firms, we opted not to model that industry this year. We also did not model the PC manufacturer industry this year. That's because our analysis of the data suggests that factors other than customer experience may be bigger drivers of likelihood to buy another PC from the same manufacturer. See the March 26, 2012, Forrester Report, "The Business Impact of Customer Experience, 2012," available at http://forr.com/outin2-7.

8 For each of the eleven industries on our model, we segmented companies into two groups: those with CXi scores at or above the industry average and those with scores below the industry average. We then calculated the average loyalty scores for each group and compared the two. Our findings show that the average loyalty scores for leaders were better than the average loyalty scores for laggards in every industry. Note that this does not include PC manufacturers because purchase intent does not correlate with CXi for several of them. We don't know why, but suspect it's because people intend to switch to Apple even though they're not unhappy with their Sony and Dell PCs. It also does not include package shippers because there were only three so we couldn't calculate an "above average" or a "below average."

9 You can see the National Retail Federation's list of the top one hundred retailers by sales at http://forr.com/outin2-9.

10 Or at least the customer didn't know that her other cards offered the same benefits. These results were described in a speech by Jim Bush, executive vice president, world service, American Express, delivered at Forrester's Customer Experience Forum, 2011.

11 As reported in the August 12, 2010, Forrester Report, "Lessons Learned from Three Award-Winning Voices of the Customer Programs," available at http://forr.com/outin2-11.

3. The Customer Experience Ecosystem

1 T-Mobile is a holding company for Deutsche Telekom AG. It operates mobile communications subsidiaries in ten European countries, the United States, Puerto Rico, and the U.S. Virgin Islands.

2 If you think this kind of behavior is unusual — it's not. In a 1961 experiment, Yale University professor Stanley Milgram asked volunteers to deliver increasingly strong electric shocks to people (who were supposed to be test subjects but who were really actors) if they answered certain questions incorrectly. Four out of five volunteers continued to "shock" the actors after they heard them cry out in pain. In a more recent version of the study, seven out of ten people delivered the fake shocks. See http://forr.com/outin3-2.

3 For details about what happened in Zion National Park, see William J. Ripple and Robert L. Beschta, "Linking a Cougar Decline, Trophic Cascade, and Catastrophic Regime Shift in Zion National Park," *Biological Conservation* 133, 2006: 397–408. Available at http://forr.com/outin3-3a. If you just want the highlights, see Betsie Blumberg, "Impact of a Cougar Decline on Zion Canyon, Zion National Park," *ParkScience* 26:2, available at http://forr.com/outin3-3b.

4 Assets of February, 2011. See http://forr.com/outin3-4.

5 For details on the Bank of America fiasco, see Tara Siegel Bernard, "In Retreat, Bank of America Cancels Debit Card Fee," *The New York Times,* November 1, 2011, available at http://forr.com/outin3-5a. For the credit union perspective, see this opinion piece by the president and CEO of the National Association of Federal Credit Unions: Fred R. Becker, Jr., "Commentary: Credit Unions Reported a Surge in Membership After Bank Transfer Day. Now What?" *The Washington Post,* November 13, 2011, available at http://forr.com/outin3-5b.

6 The 5 Whys is part of the Six Sigma methodology. For a good, brief explanation, see the April 3, 2012, blog post "Determine the Root Cause: 5 Whys" on the blog *iSixSigma* at http://forr.com/outin3-6a. There is also an interesting blog post about the 5 Whys on the HBR site by guest blogger and noted author Eric Ries. See the April 30, 2010, blog post "The Five Whys for Start-Ups" by Eric Ries on the blog *HBR Blog Network* at http://forr.com/outin3-6b.

7 For insight into Virgin Media's brand transformation, see http://forr.com/outin3-7.

4. From Bumper Sticker to Business Discipline

1 For 2008, when most financial services companies posted record losses and the S&P 500 Index total return dropped by 37 percent, USAA reported earning $423 million in net income. See http://forr.com/outin4-1.

2 In our Customer Experience Index data for 2008, USAA's credit card business had come in second *among all industries in the study.* Its insurance business was almost as highly rated. As incredible as it seems, both lines of business scored better than customer experience icons in other industries, including Southwest Airlines and Apple. However, we did not get a statistically significant sample for its banking business in that year. In subsequent years USAA was a customer experience leader in banking as well. See the December 12, 2008, Forrester Report, "The Customer Experience Index, 2008," available at http://forr.com/outin4-2.

3 For more about USAA and its mission, see http://forr.com/outin4-3.

4 In case you're tempted to think that just focusing on building a customer-centric culture will get you to the head of your industry like it has for USAA, Southwest Airlines, and Zappos.com, good luck with that. All three of those companies, as well as a handful of others like them, *started out* with customer-centric cultures that they've evolved over time. Although we'll show you how to transform your culture to be more customer-centric in chapter 10, do keep in mind that you're not going to match USAA's culture, so you will need to adopt the other disciplines we'll tell you about, as well.

5 If you want to learn more about maturity frameworks, see the People CMM (Version 2), from the Software Engineering Institute at http://forr.com/outin4-5.

6 For a brief discussion of Geek Squad personas, see Lisa Sanders, "Major Marketers Get Wise to the Power of Assigning Personas," *Advertising Age,* April 9, 2007, available at http://forr.com/outin4-6.

7 This comes from the report in which we first laid out the maturity framework for customer experience. See the September 12, 2011, Forrester Report, "Customer Experience Maturity Defined," available at http://forr.com/outin4-7.

8 This parallels what Amazon's Jeff Bezos said about brand: "Brand is what people say about you when you leave the room." See Dean Crutchfield, "A Brand by Any Other

Name," *Adweek*, January 25, 2010, available at http://forr.com/outin4-8.

9 Starbucks incorporates a variety of informal (i.e., nonmonetary) awards into its culture. You can learn more about them at http://forr.com/outin4-9.

5. Strategy

1 Consider customers' expectations of U.S. retailer Costco Wholesale versus Apple. Costco customers expect bare-bones service in return for low prices, while Apple customers expect innovative products at relatively high prices. These firms deliver radically different experiences, yet they both delight customers. Should your company be like Costco or like Apple — or something else entirely? Your customer experience strategy should answer that question and focus the activities that turn your vision into reality. See the September 28, 2010, Forrester Report, "What Is the Right Customer Experience Strategy?" available at http://forr.com/outin5-1.

2 "Citi Rolls Out Its Version of the Apple Store," TheFinancialBrand.com, January 25, 2011, at http://forr.com/outin5-2.

6. Customer Understanding

1 What *is* the Virgin experience? "It's a cheeky sense of fun, it's challenging the status quo, it's finding spaces where we can make a difference — then making it. It's giving our Members amazing value and a smile." See http://forr.com/outin6-1.

2 Net Promoter is a concept developed by Bain, Fred Reichheld, and Satmetrix Systems to help organizations measure and improve customer loyalty. Net Promoter Score (NPS) is a metric designed to serve as a proxy for how customers feel about an organization based on their responses to the question, "How likely is it that you would recommend [company name] to a friend or colleague?" Respondents rate their likelihood to recommend on an eleven-point scale ranging from 0 (not at all likely) to 10 (extremely likely). Based on their answers, respondents are classified as Promoters (those who answered 9 or 10), Passives (those who answered 7 or 8), or Detractors (those who answered 6 or less). NPS is calculated by subtracting the percentage of respondents who were Detractors from the percentage of respondents who were Promoters — hence the Net aspect of the score. See the November 21, 2011, Forrester Report, "Executive Q&A: Net Promoter for Customer Experience Professionals," available at http://forr.com/outin6-2.

3 For this study, Virgin Mobile used the online diary 7DaysInMyLife.com, developed by Zilver Innovation.

4 A voice of the customer program is a systematic approach for collecting customer insights and incorporating them into business decisions. See the April 11, 2011, Forester Report, "Executive Q&A: Voice of the Customer Programs," available at http://forr.com/outin6-4.

5 According to Forrester's Consumer Technographics data, 40 percent of U.S. consumers took a survey to provide feedback about an unsatisfactory experience with a company. However, nearly as many called (37 percent) or sent an email (29 percent) to the company. In addition, 24 percent provided feedback through a social channel such as a review on the company's website or a comment in a customer forum. See the June 20, 2011, Forrester Report, "Updated 2011: How Consumers Complain About Poor Service," available at http://forr.com/outin6-5.

6 Approximately two-thirds of the enterprise feedback management vendors that Forrester recently surveyed said that they can tap unsolicited feedback from social media and social networking sites. Only IBM, MarketTools, OpinionLab, RightNow, and Service Management Group said that they can collect unsolicited feedback from all of the sources we asked about, including social sites, employee notes, chat sessions, and emails. See the March 1, 2011, Forrester Report, "Customer Experience Professionals' Introduction to Enterprise Feedback Management Vendors," available at http://forr.com/outin6-6.

7 Chloe Rigby, "Best Buy Learns from the Voice of the Customer," *Internet Retailing,* May 31, 2011, available at http://forr.com/outin6-7.

8 Accor won a 2011 Forrester Groundswell Award in the Consumer International division for its work with Synthesio. In addition to making customer experience improvements, Accor has improved training and employee rewards based on this listening program. See Josh Bernoff, "Winners of the 2011 Forrester Groundswell Awards: Consumer International," *Empowered,* available at http://forr.com/outin6-8.

9 Panelists at Forrester's 2011 Customer Experience Forum explained that ethnographic research is a critical input for designing engaging and differentiated experiences because it reveals what customers actually do, what motivates them, and what opportunities exist to better meet their needs. See the August 22, 2011, Forrester Report, "What Three Companies Learned from Conducting Ethnographic Research," available at http://forr.com/outin6-9.

10 Employees have a wealth of insight about both customers and internal operations. Many also have the influence to quickly improve customer experience at the ground level through frontline interactions and behind-the-scenes decisions. Customer experience professionals should draw on employees' insight and influence to feed two key activities: improving customer experiences and building a customer-centric culture. See the January 28, 2011, Forrester Report, "How the Voice of the Employee Empowers Customer Experience Efforts," available at http://forr.com/outin6-10.

11 Intuit won a 2010 Forrester Groundswell Award in the Management division for its Brainstorm collaboration platform. Brainstorm increased ideas from employees by a factor of ten and the number of employees actively contributing ideas by a factor of five. New ideas at Intuit now get to market in an average of five months, as compared to thirteen months previously. This application generated 154 ideas the company has decided to pursue or implement, including the products "ViewMyPaycheck" (75,000 users) and TimeCatcher for Android. See "Winners of the 2010 Forrester Groundswell Awards (Management)," *Empowered,* October 29, 2010, available at http://forr.com/outin6-11.

12 For this exercise, Dann built a seemingly real profile of a high-value member: a California resident in her mid-forties with two kids, who had auto insurance, home insurance, and membership through AAA.

13 Design personas (first introduced in Alan Cooper's book *The Inmates Are Running the Asylum*) and customer journey maps are valuable tools that support companies' strategic customer experience initiatives and tactical design decisions. To get the most out of these tools, customer experience professionals should build design personas before customer journey maps, kick off research initiatives with workshops to gather stakeholder assumptions, craft tools to fit their purposes, and plan a calendar of ongoing engagement activities to keep personas and journey maps in the top of stakeholders' minds. See

the January 10, 2011, Forrester Report, "Executive Q&A: Design Personas and Customer Journey Maps," available at http://forr.com/outin6-13.

14 Joel Flom, "Boeing Partnership Takes UX Research to the International Level," *EffectiveUI Blog* January 31, 2011, available at http://forr.com/outin6-14.

15 Adobe won a 2011 Forrester Voice of the Customer Award. See the August 18, 2011, Forrester Report, "Lessons Learned from the 2011 Voice of the Customer Award Winners," available at http://forr.com/outin6-15.

7. Design

1 "South East England is a water stressed area. It has less water available per person than Sudan and Syria." See http://forr.com/outin7-1.

2 In addition to IDEO and Design Council U.K., Southern Water worked with: research firm STBY, which conducted ethnographic research in customer homes and created personas that outlined customers' attitudes toward using, saving, and paying for water; Radarstation, which explored the existing meter installation process from Southern Water's perspective and mapped out internal processes like taking customer calls, picking up parts, and informing customers about completed installations; and Boag Associates, which redesigned the water bill with graphs that show normal water usage for families of different sizes, descriptions of water amounts in common terms (like pots of tea instead of cubic meters), and water-saving tips.

3 The front side of the conversation guide illustrates three types of calls and the types of things that agents might say at various points during each. The back of the guide explains the value of each type of call for the customer (e.g., having their calls handled quickly), the employee (e.g., avoiding unnecessary inbound calls), and the company (e.g., finding upsell opportunities). See the April 6, 2011, Forrester Report, "Why Your Call Center Needs User-Centered Design," available at http://forr.com/outin7-3.

4 Design Council U.K. developed the original double diamond process model in 2005. Since then it has been widely adopted by the service design community. Service designers broadly define what they do as a collaborative process of researching, envisioning, and then orchestrating experiences that happen over time and across multiple touchpoints. See the December 20, 2010, Forrester Report, "Service Design Creates Breakthrough Customer Experiences," available at http://forr.com/outin7-4.

5 Following on from the success of its peer-to-peer public online communities, Verizon's e-commerce and product strategy teams recognized that social technologies and co-creation opportunities were a match made in heaven. See the June 13, 2011, Forrester Report, "Case Study: Verizon's Idea Exchange Connects Product Teams with Consumers," available at http://forr.com/outin7-5a. The *My Starbucks Idea* site allows anyone to comment on and potentially influence the company's product strategy. See the September 22, 2010, Forrester Report, "Case Study: Starbucks Uses Social Co-Creation to Drive Green Product Strategy," available at http://forr.com/outin7-5b. In 2010, Ford launched a social co-creation site called *Your Ideas,* where customers are encouraged to share their new ideas and concepts about how to improve Ford products and experiences. See the September 24, 2010, Forrester Report, "Case Study: Ford Pursues Co-Creation with an Ideation Site," available at http://forr.com/outin7-5c.

6 PayPal has also taken this type of approach. It recently worked with consulting firm

AnswerLab to retrofit its usability lab to look like the inside of a coffee shop to test a new mobile payment process. Researchers tested different scenarios, varying some part of the payment process, like allowing users to pay in advance via their mobile phone for an item or asking subjects to imagine that they were running late and trying out the new payment experience. This allowed them not only to understand whether someone would say that she would use some functionality but also to model *how* she might use it. For example, one user forgot that he had paid in advance and stood patiently in line. When he was reminded that he could skip ahead because he had already paid, he felt badly about jumping ahead of others in line and recommended creating a separate line for people who had paid ahead so that customers wouldn't have to make the perceived social faux pas of cutting ahead in line. See the January 25, 2012, Forrester Report, "How PayPal Uses Exploratory Research to Drive a Culture of Customer-Focused Innovation," available at http://forr.com/outin7-6.

8. Measurement

1 To learn more about Bonny, see her LinkedIn profile at http://forr.com/outin8-1.

2 JetBlue began flying in early 2000. See http://forr.com/outin8-2.

3 To understand which metrics they're using today, Forrester interviewed top customer experience professionals at companies in the travel, health-care, banking, and insurance industries. Our research shows that firms use a mix of metrics that captures what actually happened during customer interactions, how customers perceived those interactions, and what they will do as a result of the interactions. See the January 22, 2010, Forrester Report, "How Four Firms Measure Customer Experience Across the Enterprise," available at http://forr.com/outin8-3.

4 Even if you try to make ethnographic observations precise by including some form of survey as part of your study, your sample size will be too small to project to a larger population. There are other problems with using ethnography for measurement, but you get the overarching point, which is that it's the wrong tool for this job.

5 The American Customer Satisfaction Index (ACSI) scores on a 0–100 scale. It produces indexes for 10 economic sectors, 47 industries (including e-commerce and e-business), more than 225 companies, and over 200 U.S. federal or local government services. See http://forr.com/outin8-5.

6 We get asked about Net Promoter all the time. We put together a report to answer several of the most common questions, including "Why is Net Promoter so popular?" and "Is the Net Promoter Score (NPS) a good customer experience metric?" See the November 21, 2011, Forrester Report, "Executive Q&A: Net Promoter For Customer Experience Professionals," available at http://forr.com/outin8-6.

7 Forrester analyzed the correlation between how consumers rated their experience with companies on our Customer Experience Index and their answer to the NPS question for two industries: banks and retailers. The correlation coefficient for CXi and NPS for banks was 0.679, and for retailers, it was 0.618. For practical purposes, that's about as good as it gets. See the July 14, 2011, Forrester Report, "Better Customer Experience Correlates to Higher Net Promoter Scores for Banks and Retailers," available at http://forr.com/outin8-7.

8 Overall we really like NPS as part of a customer experience measurement program

when it's used correctly. The concept is easy for employees to understand and relate to, and asking just one question can greatly increase sample sizes.

9 It's less easy to identify customers when trying to match customer records with unsolicited customer feedback that you get through a comment form or social media. In that case, you'll need to either look up or ask for personally identifiable information. For example, after a recent flight, our Forrester editor Josh Bernoff tweeted that he'd had a bad experience with the Gogo Inflight Internet service. A representative from Gogo figured out Josh's email address from his Twitter account and sent him an email that apologized and offered free service on the flight back.

10 Collecting customer feedback across channels and tailoring reports for diverse internal audiences can present complex operational challenges. Enterprise feedback management vendors simplify these processes by giving companies a central system for feedback collection, analysis, and reporting. See the March 1, 2011, Forrester Report, "Customer Experience Professionals' Introduction to Enterprise Feedback Management Vendors," available at http://forr.com/outin8-10.

11 Customers don't always know whether their problem was resolved at the time they're surveyed by your call center agent. As a result, your survey data may show a high first-call resolution rate due to some number of customers hanging up with the belief that their problem is resolved when, in fact, it's not. For more information on customer experience metrics for the call center, see the February 23, 2011, Forrester Report, "Reinvent Your Call Center Culture to Create Amazing Customer Experiences," available at http://forr.com/outin8-11.

12 To measure enjoyability for our Customer Experience Index (CXi). Forrester asks consumers, "Thinking about your recent interaction with [firm X], how enjoyable were the interactions?" Respondents answer on a five-point scale from 0 (not at all enjoyable) to 5 (very enjoyable).

13 Natalie Avon, "Pilot Holds Flight for Man Going to See Dying Grandson," CNN.com, January 14, 2011, available at http://forr.com/outin8-12.

14 In the CXi, Southwest Airlines earned an overall score of 79, while JetBlue received a 74. The next most highly rated airlines (a tie between AirTran and American) came in a full ten points lower at 64.

9. Governance

1 According to the Barclaycard US's website, "In an effort to develop a U.S. consumer presence, Barclays bought Juniper Financial Corporation in 2004. Juniper's model — partnering with leading U.S. companies to deliver a cobranded credit card — was a great fit with our culture of customer-centric innovations." See http://forr.com/outin9-1a. A top-ten listing of credit cards based on purchase volume is available at http://forr.com/outin9-1b.

2 Barclaycard US worked with consulting firms West Monroe Partners and BearingPoint on a business process reengineering project that sparked the Level 0 initiative and greatly enabled its implementation. Note that many different modeling techniques mix activity sequence flow with functional decomposition — as opposed to business capability decomposition, which is about decomposing the organizational purpose, not its structure. It's quite common to hear business process pros talk in terms of process

levels, referring to Level 0 through Level 3 or even Level 4. Each of these levels represents a further refinement in the business area. Indeed, most industry reference models—such as those from the Supply Chain Council and the American Productivity & Quality Council—are organized around a decomposition approach. See the October 13, 2011, Forrester Report, "The Strategic Language of Transformation Unlocks the Power of BPM, Part 2," available at http://forr.com/outin9-2.

3 The term *user experience* is often used when referring to a customer experience that only involves digital touchpoints.

4 For the full list of Bank of Montreal's brilliant basics, please see the October 25, 2011, Forrester Report, "Customer Experience Strategy Best Practices," available at http://forr.com/outin9-4.

5 The Ritz-Carlton Gold Standards also include the hotel's credo, motto, three steps of service, and employee promise. See http://forr.com/outin9-5.

10. Culture

1 Leaders should apply hiring, socialization, rewards, and communication in a way that's consistent with their organization's customer experience strategy. See the November 19, 2010, Forrester Report, "How to Build a Customer-Centric Culture," available at http://forr.com/outin10-1.

2 The website for the W Retreat & Spa—Maldives even makes some suggestions: "A luxury speedboat ride to a private beach with a sunset dinner for two? An elegant commitment ceremony on your very own island? Lessons in Dhivehi? Our Whatever/Whenever team will deliver whatever you want, whenever you want it." See http://forr.com/outin10-2.

3 For more on storytelling and the brain, see John Bickle and Sean Keating, "Storytelling 2.0: When New Narratives Meet Old Brains," *NewScientist,* at http://forr.com/outin10-3.

4 Gilt.com launches daily sales at noon Eastern Time every day. Since shortly after the site's launch, its daily noon traffic has spiked to that of half of Amazon.com's estimated daily traffic.

5 John Deere channels include merchants, insurance agents, and John Deere dealers.

6 The John Deere financing experience score is based on the Net Promoter methodology.

7 Employees often do whatever it takes to meet internal numbers and avoid management scrutiny—even if that's to the detriment of the customer experience or larger corporate goals. To learn how to move away from employee targets that encourage bad behavior, see the February 23, 2011, Forrester Report, "Reinvent Your Call Center Culture to Create Amazing Customer Experiences," available at http://forr.com/outin10-7.

8 See the Starbucks Recognition site at http://forr.com/outin10-8.

9 Another company we spoke with recently awards points to staff members based on employee nominations. In this program, the nominator gets a portion of the points if the employee wins. This model encourages employees to take time to recognize their peers for customer-centric behavior instead of just getting on with their day.

10 Some Safelite commercials show customers reaching for their wallets and technicians waving their hands as an indication that their insurance company has taken care of the payment for them. See http://forr.com/outin10-10.

11 If the search results change, you can see the Orlando, Florida, Safelite video at http://forr.com/outin10-11.

11. The Natural Path to Customer Experience Maturity

1 For more insight into the CMM framework, see http://forr.com/outin11-1.

2 Forrester scanned the market for companies offering enterprise customer experience transformation services and found two types of providers: management consultants and boutiques. All of the fifteen vendors we interviewed help clients build an initial customer experience transformation road map. See the October 21, 2010, Forrester Report, "Enterprise: Customer Experience Transformation Consultants," available at http://forr.com/outin11-2a.

12. The Rise of the Chief Customer Officer

1 In the annual report for 2005, CEO Delos "Toby" Cosgrove praises the results of their World Class Service initiative and says, "We must never forget the most important figure at the entire Cleveland Clinic — the patient. As long as we keep ourselves focused on the patient, I am confident that we can be the leading academic medical center in America." See http://forr.com/outin12-1.

2 The Cleveland Clinic's first chief experience officer was M. Bridget Duffy, M.D., who is currently the Chief Executive Officer at ExperiaHealth.

3 For information about Joint Commission on Accreditation of Healthcare Organizations, see http://forr.com/outin12-3.

4 A relatively smaller number of CCOs report up to the chief marketing officer. That tends to happen in companies where marketing has a broad mandate, controlling more of the "Four Ps" of marketing: product, price, place, promotion.

5 Tom Seclow, Rick Routhier, and Art Brown, "Succeeding as an Organization's First Chief Marketing Officer," *SpencerStuart,* June 2011, available at http://forr.com/outin12-5.

6 Bank of America appointed perhaps the most prominent CIO of the modern era, Max D. Hopper, in 1982. See Richard Pastore, "CIO Hall of Fame: Max D. Hopper" *CIO,* September 15, 1997, at http://forr.com/outin12-6.

7 As a bank brand, USAA earned a CXi score of 89 out of 100, edging out three other companies in the Excellent category, Kohl's, Amazon, and Costco. As a credit-card provider it earned an 84, and as an insurance provider it earned an 83. See the January 23, 2012, Forrester Report, "The Customer Experience Index, 2012," available at http://forr.com/outin12-7.

8 For store statistics about Walgreens, see http://forr.com/outin12-8.

9 Presentation given by Sona Chawla, Walgreens president, e-commerce, at Forrester's Consumer Forum, June 2011.

10 For example, at year-end 2010, Walgreens competitor CVS Caremark operated 7,182 retail drugstores plus the CVS.com and Caremark.com websites. See http://forr.com/outin12-10.

11 As of this writing, the Walgreens stores with the new configuration are being tested in Chicago and Indianapolis.

12 Graham Atkinson's previous job had been president of United's MileagePlus program. See http://forr.com/outin12-12.

13 Chief customer officers' diverse backgrounds are actually a plus: Their broad business experience gives them the credibility they need to get customer experience taken seriously. See the January 20, 2012, Forrester Report, "The Chief Customer Officer (CCO), 2012," available at http://forr.com/outin12-13a.

14 See the LinkedIn profile for Karyn Furstman at http://forr.com/outin12-14.

13. The Customer Experience Race Is On

1 We can't disclose Jon Picoult's client list because he considers it confidential. However, we have seen it and it includes some very large companies in the financial services and telecommunications industries. For more about Watermark Consulting, see http://forr.com/outin13-1.

2 You couldn't actually do this exercise as described because you'd have to know the leaders at the beginning of the year, whereas we publish the leaders from the previous year at the beginning of the new year. Remember that this is an exercise to determine the companies whose stock performed well in the same year that their customers thought they were great at customer experience — and not an exercise in personal investment.

3 Jon Picoult, "The ROI of a Great Customer Experience," *WaterRemarks,* February 1, 2012, available at http://forr.com/outin13-3.

4 "Watch for New Bank Fees," *Consumer Reports,* November 9, 2011, available at http://forr.com/outin13-4.

5 For more details about banks, credit unions, and fees, see Ed Roberts, "Bank Customers Flee to CUs," *American Banker,* November 3, 2011, available at http://forr.com/outin13-5.

6 Bank Transfer Day was November 5, 2011 (which also happens to be Guy Fawkes Day). See the Facebook page at http://forr.com/outin13-6.

7 Ally Bank's two other principles are "We talk straight" and "We strive to be obviously better." See http://forr.com/outin13-7.

8 Dan Fitzpatrick and David Enrich, "Big Bank Weighs Fee Revamp," *The Wall Street Journal,* March 1, 2012, available at http://forr.com/outin13-8.

9 Bad customer experience runs up costs for insurers two ways. First, insurers do a poor job of helping consumers choose cost-effective care, which contributes to a rise in medical costs. Secondly, as we've seen in other industries, bad experience leads to more calls to customer service.

10 See the Kaiser Family Foundation and Health Research & Educational Trust report, "Employer Health Benefits, Annual survey 2011," available at http://forr.com/outin13-10.

11 Both Progressive and GEICO had been around for a while but weren't serious national players up until the mid-'90s when they began using the web aggressively. Progressive was founded as Progressive Mutual Insurance Company in 1937, and has a legacy of "nonstandard" insurance for people who were risky to insure (that's still a big part of their business). See http://forr.com/outin13-11a. GEICO was founded in 1936 by a former employee of USAA. See http://forr.com/outin13-11b.

12 For market-share information about car-insurance companies, see http://forr.com/outin13-12.

13 For more facts about GEICO, see http://forr.com/outin13-13.

14 In September 2011, Forrester surveyed 8,266 online consumers about how likely they

were to switch their auto- or home-insurance providers in the coming year. Five percent said they were likely or highly likely to switch, and another 15 percent were on the fence. That means one in five insurance customers are in play. The top reason given for why they'd consider switching was a lower price for comparable coverage, which dwarfed all other reasons. Interestingly, the second biggest reason for switching was "if they didn't treat me fairly when I field a claim." See the February 23, 2012, Forrester Report, "Gone Shopping: US Auto and Home Insurance Buyers Will Test Business Strategies in 2012," available at http://forr.com/outin13-14.

15 State Farm holds a slight advantage in CXi over the other three, but even its Okay score of 74 out of 100 isn't strong enough to keep customers in the face of other factors, such as lower price or changing needs over time.

16 For more about Progressive's voice of the customer program, see http://forr.com/outin13-16a. For a description of its agent experience after an accident, see Adam Richards, "Touchpoints Bring the Customer Experience to Life," *HBR Blog Network*, available at http://forr.com/outin13-16b.

17 Drivers have to go online with Progressive to check the status of the discount that their driving habits earned them. See http://forr.com/outin13-17.

18 Smartphone choice is critical because the consumer market and the business market are merging: About half of U.S. information workers already buy whatever phone they want for the office without regard for IT support, and they're choosing whatever experience they prefer. See the December 2, 2011, Forrester Report, "Consumerization Drives Smartphone Proliferation," available at http://forr.com/outin13-18.

19 Forrester's website user experience review methodology is a form of heuristic evaluation. We regularly use it to evaluate sites in four dimensions: value, navigation, presentation, and trust. See the November 18, 2011, Forrester Report, "Best and Worst of Website User Experience, 2011," available at http://forr.com/outin13-19.

20 Most sites are difficult to use when accessed from a tablet. Forrester has identified five quick fixes firms can make that can immediately improve the web-browsing experience from tablets. See the June 30, 2011, Forrester Report, "How to Make Your Website More Tablet-Friendly," available at http://forr.com/outin13-20.

21 Sarah Nassauer, "How Waiters Read Your Table" *The Wall Street Journal*, February 22, 2012, available at http://forr.com/outin13-21a. You can learn more about Danny Meyer in his book *Setting the Table: The Transformative Power of Hospitality in Business* at http://forr.com/outin13-21b.

22 For more details about how American Express reinvented its over-the-phone interactions, see the August 12, 2010, Forrester Report, "Lessons Learned from Three Award-Winning Voices of the Customer Programs," available at http://forr.com/outin13-22.

23 "Haier to Establish Asian Headquarters in Japan," *Want China Times*, February 23, 2012, available at http://forr.com/outin13-23.

Case Index

Case Studies and Examples by Industry

Numbers indicate chapters.
Italics indicates full case study.

Case Studies and Examples by Country

Index

About the Authors

Harley Manning

Harley founded Forrester's customer experience research practice when he joined the firm in 1998. Today he leads a team of analysts that cover customer experience topics ranging from strategy to design to metrics.

At Forrester, Harley has authored many top-read reports and created a number of widely used methodologies. The methodologies include the firm's Website User Experience Review, which the team has now used to evaluate more than 1,500 sites, as well as techniques for evaluating website brand experience and for modeling the ROI of customer experience improvement projects.

A highly rated speaker with a love of the stage, Harley is the founder of Forrester's annual Marketing Forum as well as its Customer Experience Forum, which he hosts and moderates. In 2011, the Customer Experience Forum became the firm's largest event, attracting over 1,300 leaders from the financial services, technology, retail, travel, and professional services industries.

Prior to joining Forrester, Harley spent eighteen years designing and building interactive services for companies including Dow Jones, AT&T, the pioneering online service Prodigy, and Sears. He developed his love of research while he was at AT&T Bell Labs, where he was brought in to design user-friendly interfaces for inventions in the field of applied artificial intelligence—work that resulted in two patents. He holds an M.S. in Advertising from the University of Illinois, Urbana.

Harley lives in Winchester, Massachusetts, with his wife and son.

Kerry Bodine

Kerry is CEO of the customer experience consulting firm Kerry Bodine & Co. She was formerly vice president and principal analyst in Forrester's customer experience research practice and the creative force behind the customer experience ecosystem, a framework that helps companies diagnose and fix customer problems at their roots.

Kerry leads Forrester's research on customer experience design. She taps into her past work as both a design practitioner and leader to help Forrester clients develop empathy for customer needs and co-create experiences that make their customers happy. In previous roles, Kerry has led consumer research teams; guided the design of websites, mobile apps, and branded social networks; designed interfaces for robots and wearable devices; and, in 1995, developed a social shopping prototype for AT&T Bell Labs. She's also completed stints as both a management consultant and an advertising executive.

Kerry's research, analysis, and opinions appear frequently on sites like *Harvard Business Review, Forbes,* and *Advertising Age,* and she blogs for Forrester and 1to1 Media. She contributes a regular column and sits on the advisory board for *Touchpoint,* the journal published by the Service Design Network. An accomplished and frequently requested speaker, Kerry has keynoted major conferences on customer experience, design, and marketing around the globe. She holds a master's degree in human-computer interaction from Carnegie Mellon University.

Kerry lives in San Francisco, California, with her husband.

JAICO PUBLISHING HOUSE

Elevate Your Life. Transform Your World.

ESTABLISHED IN 1946, Jaico Publishing House is home to world-transforming authors such as Sri Sri Paramahansa Yogananda, Osho, The Dalai Lama, Sri Sri Ravi Shankar, Sadhguru, Robin Sharma, Deepak Chopra, Jack Canfield, Eknath Easwaran, Devdutt Pattanaik, Khushwant Singh, John Maxwell, Brian Tracy and Stephen Hawking.

Our late founder Mr. Jaman Shah first established Jaico as a book distribution company. Sensing that independence was around the corner, he aptly named his company Jaico ('Jai' means victory in Hindi). In order to service the significant demand for affordable books in a developing nation, Mr. Shah initiated Jaico's own publications. Jaico was India's first publisher of paperback books in the English language.

While self-help, religion and philosophy, mind/body/spirit, and business titles form the cornerstone of our non-fiction list, we publish an exciting range of travel, current affairs, biography, and popular science books as well. Our renewed focus on popular fiction is evident in our new titles by a host of fresh young talent from India and abroad. Jaico's recently established Translations Division translates selected English content into nine regional languages.

Jaico's Higher Education Division (HED) is recognized for its student-friendly textbooks in Business Management and Engineering which are in use countrywide.

In addition to being a publisher and distributor of its own titles, Jaico is a major national distributor of books of leading international and Indian publishers. With its headquarters in Mumbai, Jaico has branches and sales offices in Ahmedabad, Bangalore, Bhopal, Bhubaneswar, Chennai, Delhi, Hyderabad, Kolkata and Lucknow.

SINCE 1946